I0221274

IN SEARCH OF LIFE'S METAPHYSICAL DIMENSION

Five Notebooks of a Spiritual Seeker

Richard Schain

Copyright © 2021 Richard Schain

All rights reserved.

ISBN: 978-0-578-92937-8

ΓΠ

Garric Press

Glen Ellen, CA

IN SEARCH OF LIFE'S METAPHYSICAL DIMENSION

Five Notebooks of a Spiritual Seeker

Traveling on every path, you will not find the boundaries of the soul; so deep is its measure.

Heraclitus, *Fragments*

Some of these notebooks that I began late in life were published for my private use. I wish now to put all the notebooks in collected form out in public view. I am an avid reader of the Judeo-Christian scriptures, which will be evident to anyone dipping into the entries (although I am no mindless follower of them). Jesus says no one should hide their lamp under a bushel basket; they put it on a lampstand so the light can be seen (Mt. 5:15). I have followed his advice. If they are noticed, I will be pleased, if not, I will not be overly disturbed. The preface for the first notebook is applicable to all of them; a revised version of it serves as an Introduction. Each notebook builds on the former ones leading to repetitiveness, but also to new thought. For me, repetitiveness is necessary; it solidifies my insights. Persons for whom reading all the notebooks is too demanding a task might turn directly to Notebook 5, since it contains my final published reflections on metaphysical matters

I have indulged myself by adding my essay entitled *Yeshua ben Yosef: Prophet and Teacher of Israel* as an addendum to this work. I could not find a religious journal willing to publish it.

Alamos, Sonora, 2021

Selected Books by Richard Schain

The Legend of Nietzsche's Syphilis, 2001

Reverence for the Soul, 2001

Interior Lights, 2012

Souls Exist, 2nd Ed., 2013

Toward an Existential Philosophy of the Soul, 2014

Landesman's Journal, 2016

Notebook of a Philosopher, 2017

Philosophical Artwork II, 2017

Landesman's Legacy, 2018

A New Radical Metaphysics, 2018

The Anarchist Banker by Fernando Pessoa, 2018

Philosophical Potpourri, 2020

TABLE OF CONTENTS

INTRODUCTION

"The noble soul has *reverence* for itself."
Friedrich Nietzsche, *Beyond Good and Evil*

This writing is a spiritual *notebook*, not a standard literary book. A book is directed to the needs of readers or scholars; a spiritual notebook expresses the soul of the writer. It is a personal affair of mine conducted over approximately five years. It could have lasted longer but I grew to feel its termination was necessary. There is no organization of subjects or development of themes. What it reveals, however, may be of interest to other seekers for a spiritual dimension in their lives.

My mind moves in unpredictable directions, giving rise to the unconnected, repetitive, and sometimes contradictory characteristics of the notebook. *The purpose of the writing became to express and clarify my feelings about myself, God, and the world in which I live*—a project that I consider to be essential for my own spiritual wellbeing. This thought is further developed in many of the entries.

Initially, this work started as a 'daybook' or conventional '*jour-nal*' that was more of a diary than a spiritual account. But then it became a 'nightbook' or nocturnal *notebook* in which I endeavored to note down my deepest thoughts and concealed feelings.

I never had the intention of publishing it in the sense of the Latin *publicare*, to commend it to a public. The writing is not scholarly, nor has it much 'literary' quality in my judgment. Its main virtue is honesty ("This is no book, Who touches it touches a man." said Walt Whitman about *Leaves of Grass* – I say the same). Still, there has appeared in me a strong undercurrent of feeling, in spite of my tendency to misanthropy, that I should make my writings available to whoever might be drawn to them. It is as if I feel it to be a commandment I must obey. I don't know where it comes from—certainly not from a desire for notoriety, which I have always avoided like the plague. My basic maxim regarding readers, taken from the *Journal* of Alfred de Vigny, is *attrape qui peut,* 'catch it who is able.' Hence its 'publication.'

As a sincere addendum, I advise any readers for whom this brief introduction does not resonate positively in some way to close this book and proceed elsewhere for their readings.

And as always with my writings, my wife Melanie Dreisbach has provided superior editorial attention to these notebooks and made possible their publication. I am forever grateful to her.

Alamos, Sonora, 2021

NOTEBOOK ENTRIES

Notebook 1

Someone once asked the Russian existential philosopher Nicholas Berdyaev how he knew all that he had written. His answer is not recorded. But if someone were to ask me the same question, I would answer in this way: I use the assertive forms of expression as a means of *developing* my own thoughts and not as dogmatic statements.

Richard Schain, *Toward an Existential Philosophy of the Soul*

June 30 2016

I envy Samuel Beckett who was able to switch writing from English to French. Conrad and Cioran both switched from their native tongues to English or French. I wish I could do the same to French, but I am afraid I am too old.

July 3 '16

Beckett is said to have received 42 rejections of his novel *Murphy* before a London publisher accepted it. Here is a model for me to attempt to surpass in the future. Why not? Perhaps I could reach 50.

July 4 '16

My ethnic and cultural ancestry is entirely Jewish. I am a New York Jew. There is no escaping it even if I entirely abandoned Jewish practices after the meaningless ritual of my Bar Mitzvah. I was not exposed to a Judaism that had any meaning for me. However, I have come to attend to Jewish literature that is significant to me. First and foremost, there are certain books of the Bible (including the Gospels of the New Testament, which I consider Jewish), then the writings of Abraham Joshua Heschel.

That's about it.

July 10 '16

My natural family, such as it is (family by blood), has limited meaning for me ever since I relinquished my role of paterfamilias. They are not really interested in me as an individual, only as a family member. Since at this time I am entirely oriented toward my *individuality*, my relationship with them is necessarily superficial. That is a reality.

My few friends are more significant to me than are my relatives. One real friend is usually worth an entire pack of relatives.

I must keep this fact in mind whenever I feel inadequate regarding my behavior toward the 'family.'

When I was a child, my parents knew nothing of the real me. The same is true for my offspring at the present time. It is better if I purge my mind of expectations of a relationship in depth with them. This may seem to be an unfeeling attitude but for me it is a necessary one.

July 11 '16

Enough of personal outbursts! It is time for me to pay attention to my own principles. Further creative writing seems unlikely for me— or desirable at my age. I would like to live out my remaining years in the most dignified manner possible.

I have done my deeds and said my piece. More additions would be self-defeating—even ridiculous.

July 12 '16

How to fill the empty hours? How did the forest seers of India manage in the wilderness? What did the Greek philosophers do in their eighties? Even nineties? These are questions rarely asked. No one talks about these issues. Voltaire advised tending one's garden—but I do not garden.

July 24 '16

My main interest now is displaying *Sententiae in Space.* I have over 400 boards. As is his wont, Jesus gets to the heart of the matter: "Men do not light a lamp and then put it under a bushel basket. They set it on a stand where it gives light to all in the house" (Mt 5:15). The trouble is that it is hard for me to find a stand.

The same applies to *Philosophical Artwork II.* It needs a stand.

I have to face the fact that all my writings will ultimately sink into oblivion in the near future. But is not this true of virtually all writings, even those that became famous icons in their times? It is merely a question of how long the process takes. But I can hope that my *thoughts*, not my books, will have their impact on a metaphysical reality, which I believe must exist.

July 28 '16

The ubiquitous metaphysical reality I intuit has carried the name of God. There is no reason to avoid the term. I aspire to fulfill for myself the great commandment of Dt. 6:5, "Thou shalt love the Lord thy God with all thy heart, all thy soul [mind] and all thy strength." Jesus quoted it as the greatest commandment (Mt. 22:37). These are enough authorities for me.

The temporary stand I have chosen for my books right now is the Frankfurt Book Fair. That will suffice; if no one notices them,

I have done my duty. I feel no requirement to engage in the odious tasks of marketing.

Aug 4 '16

Discovered Gnostic thought in Pagels and Jonas. Many of my ideas are repeats of theirs. The resemblance of Heidegger to them is striking to me. If I had lived in that era, I might have been a member of the Valentinian heresy!

Aug 5 '16

I've grown bored with Alamos. Have to get a new arrangement for my life with more time in Europe.

Reading Gauguin again. One must read his writings to appreciate his painting. He is the only artist I know who has combined literary and pictorial artwork in a meaningful manner.

Aug 11 '16

Hitting the agent trail again. It is most depressing to have these 'literary' agents judging my work. All they can judge is its market appeal—anathema to me. It is not easy finding a 'stand' upon which to place my writings.

Aug 12 '16

The great advantage of sending out queries is that I improve and refine what I think about my work. This is an inestimable benefit to me.

Aug 22 '16

My seeking approval from readers, critics, editors, agents, etc. is only setting up *surrogates* for what I really crave—divine approval. It is 'God' who must accept, approve, and assimilate my soul. I try to mirror my soul in my writings but they are not the real thing. There is no point taking judgments about them too seriously. All my writings are only *means* for developing my soul. It is my conviction that upon death, my soul will present itself for judgment. I use the terms 'divine' and 'judgment' loosely, having no real idea of the details of these expressions. I only believe something will happen to my soul upon death of the body and that some element of 'judgment' take place.

Aug 25 '16

Queries, queries, queries—all in an effort to publish. Ridiculous on my part. I must mend my ways.

Sept 2 '16

Landesman's Journal has finally appeared. It will need considerable marketing to become 'successful.' My publisher doesn't seem to be doing much in this respect. The burden will fall upon me. However, I hate marketing. My heart is not in it. What to do?

Sept 3 '16

My mood swings are increasing. I vacillate between calm serenity and restless agitation. Why am I not more stable in my feelings? Père Gratry would say because I lack faith. But I can't manufacture faith out of thin air. Perhaps God just doesn't like me and won't communicate with me. A disturbing thought.

Sept 16 '16

Some favorable comments about my writing have recently appeared. It's obvious to me how little they affect me. I really care nothing for the positive impressions of others. They give me no joy; in fact, they tend to depress.

So why do I labor to publish my writings? It seems I want them 'out there,' but that's the end of it. I don't care to read reviews or to listen to others' reactions to my work. It's as if I have a duty to perform to display what I write. Once that's done, then "*attrape qui peut*" as I never tire of repeating to myself.

My affair as a philosopher is with God; why should I shrink from saying it? I have something to contribute to Him. That is where my heart lies. We have a reciprocal relationship. Call it self-deception, arrogance, hubris—but that is how I feel during my best moments.

What a good feeling it is to write all this down in my notebook!

I am reading Henri-Frédérick Amiel who brings out the best in me. The echo of Emerson can be found in the young Amiel.

Sept 23 '16

I live in an absolute solitude as far as an intellectual life is concerned. There are a few email correspondents with whom I exchange views. I treasure these but it is not the same as direct personal contact. With an occasional exception (Fr. X.), the latter do not exist for me. I might as well be a hermit in the Syrian desert. However, I must admit this does not bother me. I think I am better off being an intellectual hermit. My library is a perfectly adequate substitute for personal contacts—probably a better one.

Sept 30 '16

It is quite clear that my writings have no impact on the American scene—or on any other scene. I have a few readers but these are just pebbles thrown into the ocean. It is for me to accept this situation, embrace it, and not allow it to affect me negatively. Intellectually, I have long since accomplished this goal, but there still remains some residue of pained feelings. These are gradually passing away.

My domain is metaphysics—a domain that has nothing to do with the sensation-seeking, information-minded, market-oriented, clique-ridden literary world. What can one expect from the decadent American culture? It gets what it deserves.

Oct 1 '16

Working on translating Fernando Pessoa's *The Anarchist Banker.* I am planning to write a commentary portraying it in a whole new light. It is not, in my opinion, a piece of absurd sophistic fiction as most literary critics have thought.

Pessoa has become the poster child of the Portuguese literati. His poems are admired for their innovative style and his *portuguesismo* gives them much pleasure. But his actual ideas are usually ignored. These are more clearly expressed in *The Anarchist Banker* than in many of his other writings. I take his thoughts about the 'social fictions' very seriously. I myself am free because I have subjugated the fiction of money. I have made enough to be free. It is too bad that Pessoa himself did not follow the advice of the banker to become financially independent. He would have had a better and longer life.

Oct 13 '16

My publisher seems not to have the slightest interest in the content of my writings—only in their marketability. This is a bit depressing but should not be, given my awareness of the state of culture in America. In publishing, sales are everything—substance is nothing, regardless of glib hypocrisies to the contrary. So be it. One must rise above a deteriorated culture and only be affected by one's own assessment of his writings.

Oct 14 '16

Years ago, I wrote that it was *exhilarating* to live and write in a deteriorating culture. I was never able to live up to that insight, but now I think I can. The insight was correct; it is I who has not been strong enough to live up to it.

Oct 15 '16

I think the goal of a society should be the production of an 'elite,' individuals who represent the highest form of humanity. Elites are always individuals, not rulers or members of cliques. Cliques are the death of elitism. Elite means a superior individual personality, never a member of any group.

Even worse for elitism is populism. The idolization of the populist aspect of Jesus Christ is one of the factors that have led to the ruin of western culture. Single individuals like Goethe, Max Stirner, Schopenhauer, and Nietzsche (All Germans!) have tried to rescue it but without success. American culture has descended to its low level in the name of democracy, which is the political manifestation of populism. There are also scholarly and intellectual cliques in America that have contributed to its decay.

The problem with Nietzsche's conception of an *Übermensch* was that he had populist leanings—reflecting his own needs. The best motto for an aspiring *Übermensch* is 'Atman=Brahman.' The Indian forest sages were not populists.

So is all this *exhilarating* for me? Yes!—if I do not allow myself to be intimidated by populist and clique-ridden propaganda.

The 'bend of the road' cannot be far off for me. Perhaps then a larger picture than the one I can currently see will be revealed. I hope so. I distrust all temporal revelations of 'the truth'—including mine.

Oct 18 '16

I am ready to retire from philosophy as a literary vocation. I need one more year to dispose of my manuscripts. Then what? We shall see...Some radical change in my life. All this assumes I will live for a few more years. If not, ...*non importa*. I will follow the bend in the road toward a different existence.

Oct 20 '16

When I am done with philosophy as a literary activity, I will turn to keeping a '*Journal Intime*' in a serious way. It will not be for the purpose of publication, rather it will promote my own inner development. I vow to do this. Richard Schain will finally become Leon Landesman, his alter ego. I am impatient to be done with 'Philosophy' with a capital P.

Oct 22 '16

A contact with the medical establishment in the USA reinforces my conviction of its corrupt nature based on greed and fear—greed of those providing medical care and fear of the general public of illness (wanting cures for all illnesses, real and imaginary.) The consequences are bankrupting the nation. To make matters worse, unscrupulous politicians support this situation.

Oct 27 '16

The literary milieu of America is composed of two main branches: a market-oriented commercial branch and an academic branch dominated by scholarly cliques. I fit into neither of these two branches; therefore, if I want to develop myself through writing, I must (like Fernando Pessoa) create my own literature. I don't feel the need for heteronyms; I am content with my own persona, which has enough facets for me to express what needs expression.

I can't wait a year to seriously involve myself with my *Journal Intime*; I must start now. Who knows how much time is left to me.

If there is no metaphysical meaning to my life, then it is truly a tale told by an idiot, full of sound and fury, but signifying nothing. Naturally I am biased against that possibility. But that doesn't mean it is not true. The possibility exists that all my mental activity is meaningless. An independent philosopher like myself must learn to live with this disconcerting possibility.

Oct 28 '16

The western world has adopted the philosophy of Epicurus with its glorification of prudent pleasures confined to this life—but I have not.

Oct 29 '16

Literary guilds deprecate "vanity presses" as if the traditional commercial presses do not equally depend on the "vanity" of their authors. The only difference is that the commercial publishers bear the expense of publishing a book themselves, betting that a skillful writing will make money for them. They 'market' a book, counting on the marketing to make money for them. Evaluation of the 'merit' of the book is entirely dependent on its salability to a public looking for artificial stimulation or utilitarian information.

Vanity is only one motive for publishing a book; the hope for fame and money are the main other motives. These latter two go together and usually are the principal reasons for an individual engaging in the arduous task of writing a book.

However, I have discovered an additional motive in myself for writing. It is the desire for self-development, I believe this is the underlying motive of 'existential' writing, writing derived from the soul of the writer and best exemplified in the literary life of Sören

Kierkegaard. Self-expression leads to metaphysical self-development. The writer enlarges the scope of his interior self, his soul. The 'intimate' journal is the main vehicle for this type of writing.

Enlarging the scope of the soul is a means of associating it with the greater metaphysical reality of which it should be a part. Just as traditional worship is supposed to be a method of connecting oneself with 'God,' so enlarging the scope of the soul is a similar, *but superior*, method of connecting to a greater metaphysical reality. Expression of self can be conceived as a type of worship. However, it requires the intelligence necessary to transmute vague sentiments into objective linguistic form. This ability distinguishes Homo sapiens from other life forms.

Attention "directed toward one's own soul is highly beneficial for an individual. It is rare in contemporary culture, thus accounting for the cultural decadence of modern times.

I have at last and most definitively come to the conclusion that my philosophical persona has no place in the society in which I live. My opinion is that it is a commercialized, pleasure-seeking, status-driven, *decadent* way of life, but that is only my opinion. The objective fact is that I have no place in it.

This is an exhilarating awareness for me! I feel freed, released, liberated from the necessity of adapting myself to it. I am free to expand the scope of my own self. I do not care any longer how others see me as a writer—I am my own man.

I will still print out my writings—at my own expense— because it is important to me to objectivize my thoughts in a stable form. I can turn to them at my leisure and place them on any stand that seems suitable to me.

Enough 'I's! Basically, the culture I live in is without a metaphysical sensibility. There are religious elements within it but these are constrained by idol-worshipping dogmas. America is Christianized if not overtly Christian. No place in it for me.

The essay *Yeshua ben Yosef: Prophet and Teacher of Israel* proposes that this historical figure who during his lifetime lived, learned, and taught as a Jew, should have a place within Judaism without the need to 'worship' him. He was an exceptionally spiritual individual as evidenced by the impact he had on his Jewish listeners. The circumstances of history led to his deification and worship as the central figure in Christianity to which many legends are attached, but none of this occurred during his lifetime. The paper points out that all the available evidence indicates that he always felt himself to be a teacher for the Jewish people. Today, most of his statements could easily fit into the writings of Jewish philosophers like Martin Buber or Abraham Joshua Heschel. The ascendency of Christianity as the established religion of the Roman Empire and later of all Europe made it impossible for Jewish religious thinkers, orthodox or otherwise, to evaluate Yeshua (anglicized as Jesus) without endangering their lives and the lives of other Jews. But now times have changed and an ecumenical spirit is prevalent throughout the world. It should be possible for the teachings of Yeshua of Nazareth, son of Yosef, the carpenter, to be considered as part of the religious history of Judaism without idolizing him. The exceptional metaphysical consciousness of Yeshua is emphasized and the intimate relationship of his ideas with those of traditional Hebrew Scriptures is documented, especially the books of the prophet(s) Isaiah. It asserts that it is unnecessary to 'worship' him in order to 'value' his teachings.

Oct 30 '16

The introductory *trecho* to Fernando Pessoa's unique prose writing, *Livro do Desassossego*, contains an acute insight into Pessoa's personality. His heteronym Bernardo Soares describes his conception of death as a 'diligence' taking an individual somewhere, although that 'where' is a great unknown. The individual waits passively at an inn (one's life) for the trip to occur. Nothing he does at the inn affects where he will go. He merely tries to amuse himself at the inn, while waiting for the diligence to arrive.

I differ greatly from the passive attitude of Soares-Pessoa. I am committed to the concept that how one develops his soul affects his afterlife. The details are obscure to me but the principle is there—not very different from the Hindu notion of Karma. Pessoa put all his literary energies into the destiny of Portugal; if he had concentrated more on his own destiny, his life might have turned out better.

Oct 31 '16 – Short Autobiography

I have devoted myself during my entire life to anything and everything except the wellbeing of my soul. During my adolescent years, it was the usual distractions of school, girls, and friends. Then in adult life, I threw myself into the self-serving hypocrisies of medical academic life. My 'career' was everything to me. By the time I reached forty years of age, I had come to realize the lack of fulfillment for me in that life. Instead, I entered into the life of a Don Juan, chasing women, one after another, in search of erotic fulfillment.

At fifty years of age, I gave up the evanescent pleasures of sexual conquests and turned back to my youthful interest in philosophy. I began writing down my thoughts about myself and the world in which I lived. But very quickly, the devil of public acclaim entered into my soul and I began to strive toward publication and reputation. This devil has maintained a hold on me to this day. I can see the similarities between my past academic life and that of a 'philosopher,' even though I have prided myself on being an independent philosopher, devoid of university constraints. The orientation toward public recognition is the same for both.

Now, however, I recognize that neither career development nor sexual pursuits are truly fulfilling to the soul, at least my soul. The experiences may be valuable but one must move beyond them. One must focus on enlarging and strengthening one's soul. It is not easy to accomplish this today since there is widespread disbelief in even the existence of souls, but the effort needs to be made. Reading, learning, and spiritual self-expression are essential. Significant experiences such as erotic love, societal accomplishments, and personal combat can foster spiritual development but cannot be ends in themselves.

November 1 '16

I need to forget about my age. My needs today are the same as when I was 21 years old. I need learning and self-expression as much now as sixty years ago. The main thing is to abolish society from my mind and to concentrate on what is important to me. I don't have much more time to prepare my soul for what is ahead.

Focusing on self instead of society is not easy at any age. All the forces of habit, tradition, and societal pressures operate against it. The Christian ethic opposes it. But if one wishes *metaphysical fulfillment*, it must be done. The soul is one's principal reality.

The herd instinct is still active in human beings. Like the instinct of sexual aggression or violence against others, it must be overcome. The ten commandments of Scripture are prohibitions against man's baser instincts. But overcoming the herd instinct is most difficult of all, especially since one's society generally supports it.

If an individual does not believe in the existence of his soul, it is very difficult to oppose the herd instinct. A metaphysical sensibility is essential for a genuinely successful life. It is a mystery of the human condition as to how this comes about.

I have written much on the subject of the soul, none of which has received any public notice, much less public acclaim. Either my perceptions of metaphysical reality are self-deceptions or my society is impervious to its existence. I will leave it at that since one cannot be creative and judge his creative activity simultaneously. Many writers have disavowed their earlier writings (Heine, Tolstoy, Van Wyck Brooks) but I do not think this will be my case since I have already reached an advanced age and am still convinced of the correctness of my views.

I plan to finish the publication of my completed manuscripts. After that, *adieu* to publication.

Nov 2 '16

Concentration on one's own soul does not mean obligations to society can be ignored. I owe much to my society in spite of my disparagement of it. I have made a modest contribution to it as a doctor, I pay my taxes dutifully, and I have published books that I think are a contribution to contemporary culture. My conscience is clear as far as my debt to society is concerned. Lately, it has done very little for me.

Nov 3 '16

Fernando Pessoa, whose prose I read daily at the present time, saw deeply into the human condition. He was a genial observer of human life. He may not have shined as a prophet but I always come away from him with some new insight into my own life.

The American presidential election is drawing to a close. It pits a narcissistic clown against a venal politician. A new *Ultimatum* of Alvaro de Campos is needed. "*Fora tu* Trump, *Fora tu* Hilary, *Fora! Fora!*" (Out!, Out!) The *Ultimatum* of 1917 was directed against a society that was killing millions of young men and causing untold suffering to millions of others. Yet twenty odd years later, the same insanity began again, caused by the same society but with a new crop of politicians. Robinson Jeffers fulminated against this war and was ostracized. No one listened to him.

Now the 'Great Powers' war dance is beginning again, with America leading the parade as it has ever since the founding fathers disappeared from sight. "Make America great again," or even worse, "America is great." It has become the self-appointed leader of the 'free world' as if that meaningless phrase meant anything other than interference in affairs all over the globe.

Russia, China, and the European Union are not far behind. France and the UK are the now Lilliputian figures bringing up the rear. In the background lurks Germany who has not recovered from the hangover of the Nazi era. *"Fora com isso. Tudo! Fora!"*

My position is one of internal emigration. I only hope the deluge will come after me since I see no possibility of the radical change in politics that is required. My metaphysical milieu is far more desirable than the physical one in which I live.

MERDA!

Unfortunately, Campos (Pessoa) added an inferior sequel to the *Ultimatum* that was composed years earlier—according to Richard Zenith, the noted Portuguese translator. It detracted from the full-throated work ending with "I am going to show the way." Pessoa left the promise unfulfilled.

Nov 4 '16

What is a soul? Does it exist as a reality or is it merely a mirage? What is its fate? These are the essential questions an individual must answer for himself.

It is difficult to bring into consciousness the concept of 'soul' as an entity since all our thinking of entities is oriented toward material objects. But the soul is not a material entity. This does not exclude its existence in time as I have shown in my book *Souls Exist.*

A description of a soul can only be of its qualities. A clear description of a soul is given by Socrates in his description of the famed philosopher Parmenides "I met him when I was young and he quite elderly, and I thought there was a sort of depth to him that was altogether noble" (Plato, *Theatetus*; Cornford, trans.). Depth and nobility; these are two qualities of the soul that resist deconstruction.

Nov 5 '16

"Live 'til you die." That is an appropriate guide for the elderly; I mean to continue preparing my soul for the next phase of its existence—whatever that may be. This means continuing to seek out the experiences that deepen it. The older one gets, the more difficult it is to accomplish this task, but it is the only justification for an aged person to occupy space and use up resources of the planet. It is not appropriate to just vegetate, waiting for a mortuary to take charge of your corpse.

A metaphysical consciousness is necessary to accomplish anything truly meaningful in one's life. Otherwise, an individual is just a laborer in the service of society. The activities of Homo sapiens ought to be conducted on a higher plane than simple mammalian existence. Our Judeo-Christian ethic has been thought to be an adequate metaphysics for a long time, but it has outlived whatever usefulness it may have had. Love and obedience are not the answer to the metaphysical need—whether they are directed toward God or one's fellow man.

The whole world has adopted the philosophy of Epicurus with its prudent pleasures confined to this life and denial of an afterlife—but I have not.

Nov 6 '16

For better or for worse, I have moved from a largely physical existence to a largely mental one. I have not chosen this path deliberately but it has come upon me without my wishing it. Nevertheless, I think it is the proper path for me. And I am tired of wearing masks.

I feel like a sailor marooned on a deserted island. There is no one on the island except me. Occasionally, I throw bottles with messages into the vastness of the sea but they always wash back onto the beaches of my island. My metaphysical being is slowly suffocating in the purely terrestrial environment of the island. But perhaps this is a kind of trial for me to endure. Someday I may be rescued into a new existence. This may be an optimistic viewpoint—it is the only one I can hold, however, and still survive. "Stay alive" was the admonition given to white prisoners of hostile Indians in early America.

I write this notebook knowing it may never be published. Why do so? It seems fulfilling to me to set forth my thoughts, to give them an objective existence. Beyond that, no reason of which I am aware.

Nov 7 '16

The task I have set is to create and express consciousness of the spiritual dimension of my existence. Whether anyone else feels this way, I cannot say. Few may do so. But for me, all the societal paths are secondary to this main end. I have committed myself to it. Family, profession, ethnicity, nationality, community are all secondary. This is all I know or need to know.

The technological society in which I live is very inhospitable toward my attitude. The existence of spirit is regarded as a vague superstition rather than a reality. Thoreau said he was born in Concord "in the nick of time," but this is certainly not true for me. I was born into a society that was already spiritually *decadent*.

Nov 9 '16

When I read works that Thoreau, Nietzsche, and Pessoa wrote in their early twenties, I realize I am a different type of human being. I have matured very late compared to them. They blossomed into consciousness early; when I was in my twenties, I was still a mental child. But I have lasted longer. Perhaps it is not good to mature philosophically too soon. However, the time for me to leave the banquet of life is approaching.

Nov 10 '16

I am looking forward to making dispositions of my recent writings. Then I will be free! I feel more important than my writings although they may be less superficial than I imagine. I don't regard them as 'straw' (as did Aquinas in his last days). What is significant is my soul. I have exercised it enough with writing books—now is the time to seek other paths for its development. 'Live 'til you die.' Henry David Thoreau at 24 years of age wrote in his journal, "Never for an instant forget that there are higher planes of life than this thou art now travelling on." At 86 years of age, I must not forget his admonition.

Nov 11 '16

The forest seers who created the Upanishads sat for years in their forest lairs meditating on the problem of existence. Ultimately, they came to the formulation, "Atman is Brahman," one of the profoundest products of the human mind. I should not be impatient in my self-imposed task of discovering the boundaries of my soul. Impatience is an American characteristic I must shed. The main thing is not to be distracted by the insect buzz around me.

The ever-changing panoramas of the evening skies in Sonoita are an inspiration to me. My soul must be as vast and multifaceted as the evening skies.

I am fortunate to have a life companion with whom I share my days and nights. Without Melanie, I fear I might freeze into a piece of ice.

Nov 12 '16

The election is over and Trump has won. For some, the American world has come to an end. California is talking of seceding if the new federal government interferes with its affairs. Shades of 1861! Methinks George Washington was our greatest president and we have been on a downward slope ever since. But perhaps Trump will surprise everyone and not be any worse than his predecessors.

Plato's *Theatetus* (Loeb bilingual) arrived in the mail today. I ordered it because of a single quotation from Socrates, "Parmenides seems to me to be, in Homer's words, one to be venerated and also mighty. For I met him when I was young and he was very old and he appeared to me to possess an altogether noble depth of mind." This is how I regard Henry David Thoreau—even though he was young and not old.

Nov 16 '16

Today I read that my friend D. R. Khashaba's writings are celebrated in the electronic journal *Pathways in Philosophy*. They are deserving of recognition. I am sure this recognition is gratifying to him. It would mean little to me.

I crave reality. My first philosophical book was entitled *Affirmation of Reality*. Reality for me is thinking, writing, seeing my thoughts miraculously be reflected in print. Reality for me is *meaningful* contact with flesh and blood individuals, with nature, with experiences that enlarge my purview. Reality is truth. As far as a remote 'public' is concerned, that idea is unreal, meaningless to me. 'Recognition' is just the sound of wind rustling the leaves in trees, to paraphrase HDT. Emphasis on it is the foremost sign of decadence in a society. What do I care for the opinion of fools or pedants. The cardinal quality of reality for Homo sapiens is *immediacy,* involvement of one's entire being. Everything else is 'unreal.'

Nov 17 '16

Finished reading Thoreau's entire Journal. How did he remember the names of all the flora and fauna he described? After his impassioned outbursts about the John Brown affair (1859), he avoided political or philosophical topics and confined himself to nature. The Journal ends in 1861, the year before his death at age 44 years.

Thoreau was a unique phenomenon in American life—his like will not be seen again. He represented the human condition in its highest possible form; his appearance in American life was like Christ's appearance in backward Galilee, a veritable miracle.

Saw the 'doctor' about my blood pressure. I told him it has been high as long as I can remember and I would only like to have about 4-5 more good years. Then 'que sera, sera.' He still wanted me to take more medications, but I refused. One day the curtain will be drawn on the hypertension scam of modern medicine.

The 'family' will descend on us for Thanksgiving. It has become an annual ritual with certain pleasant features. I will put on my best paterfamilias mask and make the best of this interruption to my life.

Nov 19 '16

Once again I need to remind myself there is no public for my writings. I must not allow free rein to my baser feelings. I must concentrate on the real purpose of my life—elevating my consciousness. I aspire toward a metaphysical plane of existence where my soul will feel more at home and where it can contribute to a metaphysical reality. There is truly pie in the sky for those who can find it. Salvation for me consists of a mystical consciousness. Reality is making something of one's spiritual potential. Illusion is blind commitment to material existence.

Went to a protest against the coming of a Dollar General Store to Sonoita (my current home). Dollar General is typical of America today: aggressive, dominating, cheap materialism—no interest in higher values. May the protest be successful. [It was not.]

Am reading Wm. Shirer's *Rise and Fall of the Third Reich*. It is revealing about the nature of the modern world—as was his *Collapse of the Third Republic* (France). We are all living in the aftermath of the World Wars of the first half of the twentieth century. If the USA continues its interventionist policies everywhere in the world, a third WW cannot be far off. It is no more suited to be the regulator of the world than were the imperialist European powers of the past.

The term 'God' needs clarification. As I use it, God means the metaphysical reality and meaning of the universe. That there is such a reality and such a meaning, I have no doubt. But I do doubt my ability—or any other individual's—to fully envision it. All I have is a *faith* in its existence.

What I aspire toward and what I am are two very different things. I have been mired in the swamp of the materialist worldview for all my life. It is hard to climb out of it. But the effort must be made. I would not mind contributing to contemporary culture if it were interested in what I have to contribute. But it is not interested.

Nov 20 '16

The central issue of the human condition is acquiring a metaphysical consciousness: in Christian terms, entering the kingdom of God. Once this happens, everything else of value follows—reining in materialist obsessiveness, concentration on developing the soul, loss of fear of death, unlearning bad habits and attitudes. How this consciousness is acquired, however, is a deep mystery. Christian clerics who glibly equate it with Christian dogmas have claimed it being 'born again,' courtesy of Jesus Christ. But where understanding is lacking, nothing is learned from facile labels. It is an inexplicable aspect of the human condition. That is enough for me.

The *ineffability* of metaphysical consciousness can be felt if not described. What is necessary is silence in place of verbosity. *"Wovon man nicht sprechen kann, darüber muss man schweigen"* (What one cannot describe, one must be silent about: Ludwig Wittgenstein).

Nov 22 '16

University philosophy is infatuated with the analysis of language. Symbolic logic, phenomenology, deconstruction, et.al. are the culmination of the identification of philosophy with logical positivism—the deification of scientific thought. Metaphysics is dismissed as a primitive form of mental activity. Ruminations about the soul are thought to be concepts without meaning since they are based on feelings rather than rigorous scientific thinking. They are based on personal self-indulgence, confusing imagination with hard reality.

Thus, the heart is cut out of philosophy. Few devotees of scientific thought in philosophy would have the courage to say what Wittgenstein said at the conclusion of his *Tractatus Logico-Philosophicus*. "We feel that even when all possible scientific questions have been answered [in philosophy], our life's problems have not been touched." For these, Wittgenstein felt, the proper approach is *silence*.

However, higher forms of reality can manifest themselves to an individual even if they are ineffable, meaning they cannot be expressed by language. This is the realm of *mysticism*, which ordinary philosophy must respect. I believe the proper role of philosophy is to prepare the soul to be receptive to mystical insight, remembering that trying to say what cannot be said is *unsinnig* (L.W.)—nonsensical, absurd. The concern with scientific method in philosophy is equally *unsinnig*.

My interest in philosophy at present is to prepare myself for mystical insights.

Nov 23 '16

For me, going into the city of Tucson is like going into an utter madhouse. I have had enough of madhouses. People swarming everywhere, shopping, shopping, shopping. Tucson is a vast, out-of-control bazaar. What are these people interminably buying? Why are they rushing about so frenetically? The buildings and streets are clean, but the people!—obese, slovenly, tattooed like Polynesian

31

primitives. Ugly fat arms and thighs shamelessly exposed. No one seems to have a care about their appearance, not to speak of their minds. It is with relief that I get back to my forest refuge in Sonoita. It is paradisiacal because there are very few people to be seen. May it always be so.

What do I really want from my life? I still do not have an answer that fully satisfies me. Self-development? Finding God? Mystical insights? All brave words, but only words. Straw, according to Aquinas. There is something inside of me churning, driving, forever changing, always discontent. All I really am sure about is that the society in which I live is not for me. It is why I need solitude and crave to be alone.

I write because it is a vent for my discontent and yearnings. Someday I will read all that I have written and try to make sense of it.

Nov 24 '16

Many writers have *infatuated* me during the course of my life. When this occurs, I read everything they have written, I become them mentally. Then the infatuation fades and I move on to the next one. Sometimes I return to a writer years later but usually not at the same level of infatuation.

These experiences have enriched my soul, but there comes a time when I should rely on myself and not depend on the thoughts of others. I believe this time is *now*.

"Purity of heart is to will one thing"—S.K. (There I go again!) I need to identify the one thing necessary to purify my heart. This one thing, I have now decided, is to *develop my soul*. Why I should wish this, what will become of my soul, what is the nature of the soul—all these are extraneous questions—interesting but not essential to answer. 'Develop my soul'—this is the categorical imperative that, in fact, I have been erratically pursuing all my life. But now is the *kairos*; even though there is no end to developing one's soul, now is the moment when it must be my central focus.

Writing this notebook develops my soul. It opens up unseen depths and hidden crevices. My soul expands as I compose it. All hail to the marvelous soul!—justification of the human condition.

Nov 25 '16
Family here for the holidays. Fine people all but their mental world is very different from mine. I must wear my terrestrial mask all the time. My granddaughter asked me if I missed city life. I said no, not at all, I had had enough of American society. That was the closest I came to lifting the mask.

Thoreau writes in his journal, "Silence alone is worthy to be heard...a night in which the silence is audible, I hear the unspeakable." Silence—the necessary precursor for mystical insight.

Right now, there is a paucity of silence in my household. What is the point of all the scurrying about that people engage in if their soul remains unexpanded? No point at all—madness, absurdity. But to expand the soul, one must be conscious of its presence. Reverence and love are the proper attitudes toward one's own soul—for the rest of the world, affection might be appropriate.

Animals are always on the move to obtain their food or to avoid injury to themselves—humans are that way because of societally-induced habits. Which are the wiser?

Fate has decreed that I have a wonderful companion in my life for the past 37 years. Without her presence, my life would be a far poorer thing. I don't know why I have been so fortunate.

Nov 26 '16

HDT noted in his journal that at age 34 years his mind had hardly expanded. He attributed this to the slowness of his maturation. I could have said the same at age 40 years. Since that time, my mind has slowly expanded and I trust is still doing so. My rate of maturation is considerably slower than was Thoreau's. This is nothing to be regretful about since neurological studies have shown that slowness of brain development ultimately leads to higher functions.

I am not a poet. My prose does not exhibit linguistic embellishments or flights of imagination. I rarely resort to metaphors. I try to express myself as directly and concisely as possible. In this, I differ greatly from 'successful' authors.

Most complaints of philosophers (including myself) about the faults of their societies can be attributed to the fact that the latter are in a state of decay. If one reads Seneca's descriptions of first century Roman society, it is clear that his society was *decadent*—for whatever reasons. The same conclusion can be drawn today in American society.

My public is myself. I cannot imagine a more desirable state of affairs or one that is more conducive to my personal development.

The family left today and I was able to doff my mask. What I gained from them in warmth and animal spirits, I lost by putting my soul on hold.

Nov 27 '16

My twenty-year old computer has finally given up the ghost. It is a blessing in disguise. It frees me from one of the last vices inculcated in me by society. No more compulsive reading of the news from around the globe—news that has nothing to do with my own self. Thoreau said the dichotomy in his society was nature versus the post office. Today it is the soul versus the laptop.

Last night in a waking dream I had intense sexual fantasies. They show me that my sexual drives are as strong as ever. I don't regret this state of affairs; I am no disembodied spirit. Since the creative heat is still in me, I have continued writing this notebook.

Nov 28 '16

Nations and the societies that compose them are like gigantic guilds. Their values are exclusively materialist in nature. A person whose soul is oriented toward a metaphysical consciousness will never feel at home in any society. He will become self-directed to the core and will eschew societal herd values. As for myself, this attitude is to be especially applied to my writings. The rest of me has long since lost any serious interest in participating in society. I have already paid my dues in full.

Nov 30 '16

A modern society provides electricity, potable water, sewage disposal, and medical care to its constituents. This is quite a bit more than the Roman 'bread and circuses' of antiquity. But it cannot provide for the metaphysical need. State supported churches are fortunately out of fashion. For his metaphysical needs, an individual must search out his own resources. In my experience, few do.

Even with my hand tremor, I am glad to be writing this notebook by hand instead of through the intermediary of a writing machine. [At the moment, I am transcribing it onto my computer.] There is a natural soul-hand linkage that is lost when utilizing a machine for writing. I think access to a typewriter—and all that has followed in its wake—has been associated with a downward tendency in literature. Machines may be good for copying but not for creating.

Writing down my thoughts is like extracting them from the metaphysical ooze that is my soul. I try to clean them up and make them presentable to a reader (mostly myself). The main thing, however, is to rescue them from disappearing. I derive great pleasure from this task. No doubt it is why the pleasure-loving Epicurus wrote over 300 scrolls!

The other day, my son brought me a box of books I had left behind in a former residence almost 40 years ago. Seeing them again was like a reunion with old friends of long ago. But it was not the same relationship I had with them in the past. Many books I had devoured with intense interest many years ago no longer interest me. Even my favored icons—Nietzsche, Berdyaev, Pessoa—have shrunk in my mind. Only Thoreau has retained his full stature for me; he was a superior individual, a great writer who was largely unrecognized by his contemporaries and even now his depth of mind is unappreciated. I feel I have penetrated into his soul; if he were to emerge from behind a tree in my private forest, I would relate to him at once as to an intimate friend.

Dec 1 '16

St. Augustine states that there are only two issues an individual has to face—God and his soul. Years ago, I narrowed this list to one, the soul. I am still of that opinion. Denial of the existence of the soul is denial of the reality of self. It is a kind of spiritual suicide.

The question of God is a more difficult one for me. I have never had a revelation establishing his existence to me. One can imagine a partially transcendental soul merging into a fully transcendental God. But this is just imagination, nothing more. I cannot accept the idea that something exists just because I like to imagine it.

All the arguments about the place of Jesus in a divine Trinity can be applied to me as well. If he were part Godlike, I can be also. It says in Ps. 82, "Ye are gods." Did not Jesus say to his followers; "God's kingdom is within you"? These are seductive assertions that appeal to me but to which I cannot subscribe my whole soul. For me, the idea of God is still an uncertain abstraction.

HDT mentions God often in *A Week on the Concord and Merrimack Rivers* but his true thoughts on the subject emerge when he writes, "I would give all the wealth of the world, and all the deeds of all the heroes, for one true vision. But how can I communicate with the gods, who am a pencil maker on the earth, and not become insane?" The same thought applies to all human philosophers and theologians.

Dec 3 '16

A Week is one of the most remarkable books in American literature. It was written during Thoreau's two-year residence at Walden Pond when he was 28-29 years of age. It describes the events of a boat trip he and his older brother John (since deceased) had made six years earlier. They had themselves constructed a dinghy-like craft, which they used to row upstream on the rivers into New Hampshire and then return. Both kept journals during their seven days trip. Henry's journal served as the basis for the book.

Thoreau's archaic English often seems incomprehensible to the modern reader. It must have been the same to his contemporaries since the book only sold a few copies. It is filled with imaginative flights of philosophic thought that require much concentration by a reader—as well as a literary background. The concentration is well worthwhile, however, because the book contains some of the most profound commentaries on society one will find in any literature, religious or otherwise—albeit flavored with Thoreau's dry Yankee wit. He quotes from literary more than from religious sources to make his points, especially from long-forgotten English poets whose names will not be familiar to most readers. He is not bashful about quoting from his own poems, although it is often hard to tell which quotations are his own and which are from other poets.

Scattered throughout are interesting *'sententiae.'* Discovering them is like cracking oysters to find pearls. Thoreau is often undeniably garrulous so that a reader must do some scanning to come upon the pearls. I quote him:

> "The church is sort of a hospital for men's souls and as full of quackery as the hospitals for their bodies."
>
> "Scholars are wont to sell their birthright for a mess of learning."
>
> "He who resorts to an easy novel because he is languid, does no better than if he took a nap."
>
> "Men have a respect for learning and scholarship greatly out of proportion to the use they commonly serve."
>
> "It is a great pleasure to escape from the restless class of reformers. What if these grievances exist? So do you and I."
>
> "To one who habitually endeavors to contemplate the true state of things, the political state can be hardly said to have any existence whatever."
>
> "In my short experience of human life, the *outward* obstacles, if there were any such, have not been living men, but institutions of the dead."
>
> "I never read a novel. They have so little life and thought in them."

There are many more. It is amazing to me how little the conditions of American existence have changed over almost 200 years.

If these statements do not resonate with one's consciousness, it is best not to read Thoreau.

Dec 5 '16

Rereading what I have written about *A Week*, I have not done justice to Thoreau's mind soaring above the trivialities of daily life. When he wrote *Walden* some years later, he was aiming at an audience who wanted to know about his life at Walden Pond; but with a *Week*, he was pouring forth his spacious soul. For that reason, it is a privilege to read the latter. It is too bad that so few read it.

Walter Harding, an eminent Thoreau scholar, wrote: "*Walden* is a far superior book to *A Week*." I find the reverse to be the case. *A Week* inspires me while *Walden* only instructs me. Meaningful instruction is no small thing, but inspiration is the rarest of literary experiences.

HDT spoke well when he wrote how vast is the disproportion of the told to the untold, of the sensed to the unsensed.

> Unless above himself he can
> erect himself, how poor a thing is man.
>
> Samuel Daniel (?), quoted by HDT in *A Week*

Thoreau says the 'poet' writes for his peers alone. But what if there are no peers? Must he be quiet? Or can he write for himself alone? Better yet, he can *create* his soul *th*rough his writing.

Dec 10 '16

Unfortunately, most higher thought proceeds from a metaphor. Thus, I believe each form of life from the microscopic bacterium to the profoundest Homo sapiens is like a wavelet breaking upon the sandy shores of the globe, shedding its refuse, and finally returning to the vast ocean from whence it came. Who knows what special substance from the shore each wavelet brings back to the ocean? But I know what my personal 'wavelet' will bring back—my developed soul with which a metaphysical ocean will be refreshed. Need I say the name of this metaphysical ocean is *God*?

Dec 15 '16

Back in Alamos. Very warm and balmy, good for my old bones.

I am reading again the Upanishads (Yeats trans.). I wish I could shed myself of the social pressures the way these Hindu sages must have done three thousand years ago. At least I am clear I do not belong to the American world of letters. Whether it be for lack of literary or academic credentials or disinterest in what I have to say, I have no place in the contemporary literary world. My literary universe is myself. This attitude fits in well with the Upanishads' worldview.

Dec 16 '16

Night thoughts. Where do they go to when they disappear by morning? Or do they not disappear and are merely buried in my mind? I do not know.

A person with a *metaphysical consciousness* becomes conscious of a *metaphysical reality* existing beyond the material universe. He can call this reality 'God' if he wishes—or by any other name. But if he does not develop this special consciousness, his mind will prematurely deteriorate. He will become senile or insane. One might say the choice is between awareness of God or lunacy. Nietzsche rejected God and fell into madness.

If, however, one is a shallow materialist, the problem does not exist—as is the case with other animals.

Dec 17 '16

I am tremendously impressed by the profound pantheism of the ancient Hindu scriptures. Although the English translations of many sections are often incomprehensible to me, there is an overall message of the oneness and ubiquity of *Spirit* (Self, God, Lord). It is intellectually satisfying in a way that the Abrahamic monotheisms are not. Spinoza, 2000 years later, put forth the same conceptions in a mathematical framework (for which he was attacked as an atheist). I add to all this that the human soul can enrich the universal spirit.

Besides the superior pantheism of the forest sages who created the Upanishads, these individuals were devoted to learning and teaching—admirable qualities indeed. And even before the antique Greek philosophers, they *lived* their convictions.

Conversed yesterday with Father X. We both agreed that America is rotting within because of unrestrained materialism and extreme factional hatreds. The analogy with pre-World War II France is striking. The way out is not clear.

Meanwhile the shallow sociality of expat Alamos bores me. Here also I crave solitude.

One might think that my rebellious attitudes are more appropriate for a youthful person, at least in the first half of one's life—but not from an octogenarian like myself. Most of the important thinkers of the world expressed themselves far earlier than I have. But that is the way I am. The banana tree takes many years to produce ripe fruit.

Reading most novels for me is like falling asleep (confirming HDT). If I want to sleep, I prefer having my eyes closed.

Dec 19 '16

A Statement of Faith. A thoughtful person with a *metaphysical consciousness* strives to become conscious of an ultimate metaphysical reality (often called God). If this does not occur, he will either shrivel up mentally or go mad. This reality cannot be ascertained through the senses. It cannot be seen, heard, or felt. The only access is within one's soul. God can only be found within one's soul. Worship consists of bringing His reality into consciousness. No intermediaries can accomplish this task. Proper worship is beneficial to the soul.

If one tries to be too explicit or to read earthly matters into the metaphysical reality, consciousness of it disappears. The large picture is all that can be meaningful to a human being.

Keeping this notebook is my saving grace, my lifeline to sanity.

Dec 21 '16

Reading about Girolamo Savonarola, the fiery priest who upended late 15th century Florence. The similarities between him and the Galilean Jesus are quite striking. Both at a young age exhibited an exceptional level of intelligence, both became profoundly spiritualized early on, both moved into a life of preaching—Savonarola as a Dominican friar, Jesus as an independent figure. Far more information is available about the early life of Savonarola: he was influenced by his grandfather, a man of deep religious sentiments and repulsed by the clerical corruption in Italy at the time. The evangelists, particularly Luke, portray the youth of Jesus as immersed in study of the Hebrew sacred scriptures. Later, if one can believe the gospels, he embarked on a vision quest in the desert.

Both Savonarola and Jesus finally entered into a life of powerful preaching against the established order, particularly the corrupted clerical hierarchies of their time. This finally culminated in their horrible deaths. But Jesus' life became the impetus for the development of the most important religion of all times, while Savonarola has become a footnote in Italian history—portrayed as a fanatical, puritanical priest, bent on destroying the artistic life of Florence.

Jesus' life needs no defense, but Savonarola's should be rehabilitated from conformist scholarly studies and be recognized as an important event in European spiritual history. (I can't help thinking that Savonarola must have been driven by some inner demon to rescue Florentine society from 'sin.' Some outstanding people died because of him. He would have been better advised to develop his spiritual insights and give them to the world by his own personal example. Ditto for Jesus.)

All this writing about history wears me out. Is it appropriate for my notebook? What have I gained for myself? Maxims: Avoid hubris. Concentrate on self. Form few relationships. Still, I can't help admiring the courage and audacity of the above two figures. Like Savonarola, I think I would give way under torture. The greatest of Jewish prophets was not put to that test.

Dec 22 '16

I feel my physical capacities draining away. Vision poor, hearing impaired, tremor increasing, sexual performance nil. I can't run anymore and my balance is precarious. If I were a snake, I would have long since shed my old skin. All quite sad. But my interior self is still alive; wondering, wanting, wishing, writing. My soul still has its vitality. What will become of it at the end of my life?

My essay, "The Art Form Called Philosophy," has appeared in an electronic journal (Philosophy Pathways). I am mildly pleased but not overly so. The intense gratification of seeing my writings in public display is behind me. However, in recompense, I derive great pleasure from being able to place my thoughts on blank pages. Why this is so, I do not know. I don't expect or even want other people to see them. But the desire to do so is so strong and so constant that I feel it must have some significance. "Richard Schain, *creator* of thought." Perhaps that is its significance.

Dec 23 '16

The wild area behind our house in Alamos has been transformed into a public park. Instead of narrow trails through the forest, there are wide crisscrossing pathways. People are coming to use them with their dogs and bicycles. My Rhodesian Ridgeback Simba does not like other dogs, so I have to be vigilant. I hate putting him on a leash. It's not the same free and easy walking as before. Civilization has encroached upon what used to be a wild area. Irrationally, I feel imposed upon. Where civilization moves in, the freedom of the individual is limited. I know if there were no civilization whatever, I could not live here. I would have no food, water, or shelter. Hostile Indians or outlaws would kill me. I can't exist without some degree of civilization so I have to put up with it. But the less the better for the well-being of my soul.

It must be conceded that my money buys me some freedom from the oppressive effects of civilization. Pessoa knew whereof he spoke when he wrote of the freedom of the anarchist banker.

Dec 24 '16

One reason I am glad to spend the winter in Alamos is to escape the insanity of Christmas commercialism in the USA. But it is creeping into Alamos also as are most of the evil vices of its northern neighbor. 'Semana Santa' (Easter) used to be the main 'religious' holiday in Mexico; now 'Navidad' with its gauche tinselry, endless caroling, and irrational gift giving of things most Mexicans cannot afford to buy is outdoing Holy Week. Pretty soon Santa Claus will make his appearance here on horseback pulling a load of gifts for good *muchachos* and *muchachas*.

The main problem I have with Henry David Thoreau is the apparent lack of sexual impulses in him. He never seems to be distracted by *eros*. As far as I can tell, his only significant female relationships were with an elderly aunt on an intellectual basis and with Lydia Emerson, the wife of Ralph Waldo Emerson. It is remarkable that Emerson allowed Henry, a young bachelor, to live in his home with Lydia for over a year while he travelled about in Europe. Lydia was attractive, sensitive, and intelligent—qualities that he might have guessed would endear her to Thoreau. However, Emerson seemed to have no qualms about the arrangement. Lydia and Henry maintained an intimate correspondence after the latter left the Emerson home. It is unlikely their relationship became physical but we will never know for sure.

I really have great difficulty understanding this aspect of Thoreau's personality. Unlike Walt Whitman (whom he once met), he seemed to have no homosexual inclinations. He seems to have been utterly sexless. No doubt this lack of understanding is a limitation of my mentality. (I have only freed myself from *eros* by advanced age and then not completely.)

Free of the constraints of writing for publication, my mind flourishes. Thoughts spring forth like mushrooms in a damp forest— a very pleasurable state. Yet it is odd that my best thoughts emerge when I am in bed at night but are not as wonderful when I write them down during the day. It is one of the problems of creative writing.

Dec 27 '16

People were interested in me when I was filled with youthful vitality and promise; they were interested when I was a successful academician. Women were interested when I was socially important and exuded masculinity. Now that I am an old man and possess none of these qualities, no one is interested in me. My essential self that has emerged in full bloom holds no interest for members of the society in which I live. Perhaps this is as it should be since I have little interest in them either. All my interest is focused on the *Ultimate Reality* of which I wish to join and contribute myself.

I read the Hindu scriptures (Upanishads, Bhagavat-Gita) in all translations I can find. For me, they are superior as sources of metaphysical wisdom than is the Judeo-Christian Bible (I can't abide the God of the Old Testament) or even the antique Greek philosophers. But I think Hindu scriptures do not pay enough attention to the importance of experience and the development of personality. Comprehending "Atman is Brahman" is only a part of a fulfilling life. Perhaps the forest sages knew this but thought it was self-evident. However, in our experience-deprived, machine-dominated societies it needs emphasis.

Sometimes I think what is the good of all my daily scribbling. But what's the good of wanting sex or wanting to climb a mountain.

Writing is something I want to do. No other justification is necessary.

Fortunately, fame as a writer has not come upon me. What would I do with unpleasant or foolish intruders into my life? Gone would be the freedom of my anonymity. May my good fortune remain for the rest of my life. After that, *n'importe*.

When the wellsprings of my mind run dry, I may return to the poetry of my earlier days. Then I can concentrate on the language.

Time to stop scribbling!

Dec 28 '16

The principal social feeling I have at this time in my life is disdain verging on contempt. These feelings act as a shield for my soul. It may not be a happy situation but, given the society I live in, it is a necessary one. The ancient Greeks thought that a warrior who abandoned his shield was beneath contempt. Only senility would deprive me of my shield.

The self-destructive universal love preached by Christianity is not for me—and may be an induced senility.

Dec 31 '16

The ancient and still extant *caste* system of India accepted the reality of order of rank in society. The weak points were its hereditary nature and the evil category of untouchables.

I have not and cannot live up to the high ideals proposed by Thoreau. I'm not even sure I would want to. But they are of a higher caliber than the Christian ones. And his scathing criticisms of his society are more relevant than ever.

My task is not to imitate Thoreau but to try to survive as a free spirit in the anthills in which I live. All my energies are required for this task. All the decisions I took regarding marriage, career, and family haunt me now. How could I have taken such wrong paths. I didn't lack intelligence, I lacked the character to strike out on my own. And now? I hope I have more integrity in my life but I'm not sure. I'm afraid I can't say as Thoreau did at the end of his life, "I regret nothing." All I can do is repent for my past weaknesses. That must be worth something. The Ultimate Reality will judge me.

If composed honestly, an *intimate journal* can point an individual in the right direction for his life. Otherwise, it is easy to lose one's bearings in the jungles of the modern world.

January 1, 2017

Went to a New Year's Eve dinner party last night. The food was good but the conversation stultifying. Three hours at a round table with no possibility of escape! I was relieved to be able to finally return home to the pleasure of my own company.

HDT seemed to view 'Nature' as primary and his 'self' as secondary. I have the opposite view; my 'self' is the main focus of my life, nature is subsidiary. It is my responsibility and my joy to develop myself to the maximum degree. I have tried to follow all possible paths to this end: travel, reading, relationships, experiences of every kind. Writing has been an especially important way of self-development. Epicurus said it is never too early or too late to engage in philosophy. I think he was really referring to self-development.

After much vacillation, I have come to think that preoccupation with the idea of God is a distraction from the main purpose of one's life. At the end of life, one can confront the Ultimate Reality. Before that, developing one's self according to one's own lights is the only important issue.

Leisure and solitude are my main requirements for self-development. When it comes right down to it, the 'self' (soul) is a metaphysical entity and requires a metaphysical milieu.

Jan 2 '17

I have spent virtually my entire adult life living with one or another woman. During the brief period when I lived alone, I was always in search of a woman with whom I could share my life. I used to attribute this to my sexual drives, but I could have satisfied these without total cohabitation. Now at this late stage of my life, I think I am no longer capable of living without a woman—just as an inveterate bachelor reaches a point where he is incapable of living with a woman.

I have meditated on various reasons to explain my need for the opposite sex. None of them really satisfy me. The plain fact is that I feel *incomplete* living alone and require a woman to whom I am attracted erotically. This last proviso is essential; I am repelled by the idea of living with a woman who is unattractive to me. Why this is the case, why I do not feel complete in myself is still a mystery to me. I look at the life of Thoreau and am amazed at his self-sufficiency.

The question of family and continuation of lineage is an entirely separate issue. I have never had the desire to be a *paterfamilias* or to propagate my surname. Given the state of overpopulation of the planet, it seems absurd to me to want to add to the problem. There are enough of those who are only too happy to do so.

Jan 3 '17

I regard the proliferation of computers, 'laptops,' 'tablets,' 'smart phones,' and the like as analogous to the plague of mind-altering drugs having such an adverse effect on today's societies. These poisonous 'communication' devices produce addictions that are just as destructive as those of heroin or cocaine. People have lost the capacity to think on their own without the incessant stimulation from computerized devices. Youth seem not to be able to exist without some device feeding trivial information into their minds. These devices are used to avoid the solitude that is necessary for personal development. They rarely have anything meaningful to communicate to others. All this noise fed into the brain causes a shriveling of one's soul. But since few people today are aware of their souls, the situation does not disturb them.

However, I am disturbed by it. I cannot watch, without a feeling of revulsion, human beings glued to electronic devices as if they were inhabitants of an opium den. I myself refuse to take anything seriously I see or hear through an electronic device. It is my small way of registering my objections to the degenerate habits of society,

Personally, I consider gazing at electronic screens, which I do occasionally, as analogous to watching animated cartoons. It is mildly entertaining, but it is necessary to prevent it from becoming an addiction. That would be disastrous.

Jan 5 '17

Once more, I have been poring over the Upanishads and Bhagavat-Gita. Once more I am impressed by their metaphysical profundity, which leave western religions far behind. What can be said about the progress of world culture when one realizes these writings date from at least 2500 years ago?

However, I have one stumbling block with them. What is the point of self-enlightenment if the end result is merely the return to a pre-existent Ultimate Reality (Brahman), a Reality that is unchanging, eternal, and perfect in all ways. Would it not have been better never to have been born at all and save a lot of trouble? There is a certain futility to a long cycle of births and rebirths, only to culminate in absorption of the individual self into an already perfect and limitless divine Self. Something within me resists this viewpoint. I feel there is a *meaning* to my own spiritual development beyond mere absorption into a great unitary Self. I feel something significant is accomplished by my personal development beyond merely escaping the karmic cycle. What is this *something*? I do not know any details but that does not mean it is illusory. I believe I am contributing something unique to the Ultimate Reality that It did not possess before. My own interior self that has emerged during my lifetime is unique. I may not be able to reach the metaphysical profundity of the Vedic seers of yesteryear, but I am special in my own right and can contribute to the Ultimate Reality. This contribution should not be ignored.

Jan 6 '17

Sometimes I get so discontented and restless in my social circumstances that I think insanity is the only way out. Then I could rant and rave to my heart's content. I haven't ever taken that route, but it may come to that yet. However, the trouble with insanity is that it is a one-way street. There is no turning back.

Jan 8 '17

I am adjusting to the realization that I have no connection with literary or philosophical circles anywhere. There are some electronic contacts with individuals but these don't amount to much. No personal associations whatever. By choice, I am no longer an academic so academic circles are ruled out. My books don't sell so I have no credibility in the literary world. All this leaves me with an extreme sense of isolation.

There are advantages to this state of affairs. I am free to develop and express myself according to my lights. I do not have to answer to critics, confreres, or a public. I can distance myself from the decadent ills of my society. These are no mean advantages and I treasure them.

The disadvantages are largely psychological in nature. Like all human animals, I would like a feeling of being part of some herd. This I do not have. Since I receive no approval as a writer or philosopher, I sometimes feel myself to be just a ridiculous mediocrity. Mediocrities do not have any impact on their society.

No amount of personal reflection on myself or the world can do away with this possibility. I have to live with it—along with the faith in myself.

Occasionally, I have been told I would benefit from critiques of my writing. I can honestly say that I don't believe I have ever received one word of value to me from the rare 'feedback' that comes my way. The books that I have chosen to be my lifelong companions are enough feedback for me.

All in all, I am satisfied with my fate in life. Even up to the present time at my advanced age, I feel that I improve myself daily. I can't imagine myself as a prominent professor or a celebrated author. I have learned to appreciate my lone wolf status. When I read programs of important meetings or hear of honors bestowed upon famous writers, I feel a sense of superiority stemming from my solitary circumstances. Others may see this as rationalizations of a failed writer, but I enjoy the feeling without having to analyze it. I consider my life to be a success. *Amor fati* is my aspiration, one that I have lifted from Nietzsche.

I have tried to define for myself the type of thoughts that are going into this notebook. The best I can do is to say they are thoughts I do not discuss with anyone (except my wife since there are few thoughts of mine I have not confided in her). This only shows how shallow are the interactions of my social life. These have nothing to do with the real issues that affect me. It is why I am bored so often in social situations, but never when I am alone and have "the storehouse of my soul" (Antisthenes) to fall back upon.

Jan 10 '17

The only way an independent philosopher today can get his work published is by paying himself for the expenses of publication. Honest pay for honest work. It would only be deceiving commercial publishers to lead them to believe they might make money from his writings. A literary agent once told me it would be violating his 'professionalism' to recommend a manuscript to a publisher without any 'platform' for the author. He was right; the responsibility of literary agents is to bring to publishers works that will *sell*. My writings do not fall into that category. I march to the beat of a different drum. I am not looking for charity. So, the only alternative has been to pay my own way. If an independent philosopher can't do that, he shouldn't expect his writings to be published.

It has always been this way. Kierkegaard and Nietzsche had to pay themselves to bring out their writings. When they ran out of money, they died or became insane. Schopenhauer had independent means allowing him to publish his opus magnum *Wille und Vorstellung*. In earlier times, there were patrons who subsidized philosophers whom they considered worthy of support. The Church subsidized the scholastics. Today, there are no patrons for philosophy and virtually no independent philosophers. They all seek refuge in universities and must follow academic codes. The world is following the American way in philosophy as they once did the German way. But academia devitalizes philosophy, which is in a markedly lifeless state at the present time.

So in spite of the snide caviling of professional litterateurs, I continue to pay my way for publication of my writings. When I leave this world, I hope to hear a voice saying, "This is one of my sons in whom I am well pleased."

For someone like myself, constant exposure to society would lead to the *necessity for insanity*.

Jan 15 '17

When Melanie and I first visited Alamos in 1991, it was a sweet little town, horses everywhere on cobblestoned streets and much ease of walking, even in the busy squares. Automobiles and trucks were only occasionally to be seen. It was a quiet bucolic place. Now, 26 years later, all has changed. Motorized vehicles have taken over the town. It is difficult to walk on the streets of the central areas because of constant traffic. The noise from car radios and defective mufflers (or no mufflers at all) is deafening. Many of the trees lining the streets have died, probably because of exhaust fumes. Alamos has been transformed by motorized vehicles, much for the worse.

Alamos is only a tiny microcosm of what is happening all over the world. The internal combustion engine has taken over the life of cities. (Venice is the solitary exception, protected by canals replacing streets.) There seems nothing anyone can do about it, other than to develop a few token pedestrian thoroughfares. Even that has not happened in Alamos where the only streets escaping the scourge are occasional side alleys, too narrow to admit vehicles.

The evils of motorized transportation is only the most visible problem of modern life. Drugs, legal ones prescribed by doctors and illegal ones provided by traffickers, are a dominant element in advanced societies. The same is true of the ubiquitous electronic gadgets that make 'entertainment' rooms resemble opium dens without the odor. Sex and violence are the principal themes. The obsession with worldwide news has replaced more meaningful local news. Meaningless communication of meaningless messages abound. It is distressing to see how people cannot sit for more than a few seconds without pulling out a handheld communication device. Their own thoughts seem never to be enough. Everywhere there is to be seen what only can be regarded as a downward trend of society.

Millennia ago, Hebrew prophets foresaw doom for Hebrew societies based on their observations. It is hard not to think that if Isaiah, Jeremiah, Hosea, and the rest of them lived today, they would prophesize the same fate for the societies of our times.

Jan 17 '17

I have been reading much in early nineteenth century English novels—Jane Austen, Anthony Trollope, Charlotte Bronte, and, of course, Charles Dickens, especially *The Pickwick Papers*. I am struck by how their characters exhibit the full range and depth of human thought. They appear superior to the usual characters of contemporary real life. This in spite of the so-called psychological progress made since these novelists wrote their books. They did not have motorized vehicles, electric light and power, computers, television, air travel, and a host of other modern appurtenances. Yet they lived (albeit not as long—a benefit to the world) and thought and acted as least as well, perhaps better, than the people of today. What has been gained from all the technological 'progress'? Certainly, increased stress and tensions. The tempo and demands of daily life have been increased to an inordinate degree. People are over-stimulated to no purpose. Thoreau wrote that the 'means' of life have been greatly developed, but the 'ends' not at all. He thought that in the mid-nineteenth century. What would he say now? People do not think about the purpose of human life. They are not capable of doing so. They procreate, make money, raise families, and that's about it. Do-gooders proliferate but what good they do is questionable. The people of the world are carried along by the torrents of the machine and information age to a destination for which they are totally unprepared. This, I think, accounts for the contemporary 'denial of death' of which so much has been written.

Mr. Pickwick at the end of his peregrinations stated that their principal purpose was "the enlargement of my mind and the improvement of my understanding." Few can say the same of their life today.

My mind is filled with thoughts at the oddest hours. It is all I can do to recover some of them for this notebook. (Some I have not yet dared to write down.)

Jan 18 '17 – Confession

I am often affected by sexual fantasies. These could be regarded as the perversities of a dirty old man, but I think that is rather too simplistic a point of view. It is better explained by a basic *defect* in my nature that I constantly strive to deal with. This was Plato's explanation of the reason for erotic attraction. I must not be a person complete in myself. The male condition is not complete so that it needs to join in special ways with a special female. The effort must be made.

The sexless Mr. Pickwick does not evidence erotic desire— probably because Dickens wrote the story in his twenties without any knowledge of the state of older people.

Jan 20 '17

Trying to increase my activity with walking, jogging, calisthenics, etc. The only way it is worth living beyond my current age (86 yrs.)

is to maintain my motility. Motility is independence and freedom; without freedom, life for me would not be worth the effort.

I can hardly recognize any similarity between the youth I once was and my current self. According to physiologists, my body is constantly changing, breaking down and reforming; similarly, my mind has no resemblance to its former state. Wherein, then, is the continuity of my life? Myself as *organism*—this concept provides the necessary continuity, but 'organism' is an ill-defined term that is hard to define physiologically. Biologists haven't the least idea of the motive force behind living organisms. They describe in infinite detail their origins, mechanisms, and functions but the reason why they arise and why their existence eventually terminate, they do not know. It is another one of the mysteries of nature.

I believe chastity and vegetarianism are dubious habits for human beings at any age. They are certainly not features of my life. It is better for me to eat meat than to always yearn for it, better to be sexually active as much as possible than to 'burn'—in the words of St. Paul.

It is quite clear that sexual activity for me is unrelated to procreation, much as urination is unrelated to sexual orgasm. Merging with a female erotically does not have as its goal fertilization of one of her ova. It is an act of union in which one strives for wholeness. The orgasmic feature culminates this union.

Nature may have its own agenda but I do not always pay attention to nature. All this can only be understood as a form of *mystical* activity.

When the impulse toward eroticism is gone, one desiccates like an old fig. The real challenge is what to do with the impulse. To paraphrase Epicurus, one is never too young or too old to act upon it. There are always opportunities and new modes of expression.

Jan 21 '17

HDT wrote that one should move from the animal state to the divine one, but I say animal impulses are the *marrow* of the divine in human beings. Intellectual activity should be looked upon as the crowning touch for animal impulses. Without the latter, intellect and understanding are empty vessels. I now grasp why Aquinas collapsed intellectually and Spinoza was driven to end his life (in my opinion.)

The state of erotic desire is more important than the means chosen for its fulfillment. It is the signal of human vitality. Desire underlies everything (read Jacob Boehme). Just as one's appetite for food can never be permanently satisfied, so erotic desire can never be permanently satisfied. Erotic fulfillment is for the moment.

My notebook has finally come alive! Now I must do the same.

A truly intimate journal acts as an enabler for the fulfillment of life. It serves as a compass, rudder, and eyeglass, all rolled into one.

Jan 22 '17

Gratitude, fidelity, duty, *agapé* are important features of the human personality. However, they must take second place to the forces that well up from the depths of one's being. Survival and sex represent these forces. A third, often overlooked, but no less important as Aristotle asserted, is the desire to *know*.

Jan 23 '17

A serious problem of aging, one that I know well, is the gradual loss of energy that it entails. I barely have half the energy I had as a young man. Besides that, there is the inexorable decay of physiological functions. Strength, digestion, excretion, coordination, and so-called 'normal' sexuality are some of these. These losses tend to produce a certain demoralization in the aging individual. But I think as long as there is enough energy there to power the big three of human life—survival, sex, and the desire to know—one can obtain sufficient gratification from living while awaiting the peak experience of spiritual existence—transition to a new state of being.

The imperialism of Europe and its American offshoot lives on. Gone are the military and colonial forms of imperialism; in their place are economic and spiritual imperialisms. Missionary Christianity is vying with Islam for spiritual domination and will probably win out because of the technological superiority of the Christian world.

The United States now has a new president in the form of an emperor-like business executive. President Trump and his model wife make a regal pair. Unlike many others, I am not unhappy about their presence in the White House. It is a welcome change for me from the self-serving politically correct politicians of the past. The country needs some radical changes. Now let us hope Trump will do his job properly. I support his idea of 'America First' as his guiding theme. America should not direct the rest of the world or assume responsibility for it, just as individuals in a community should not direct or assume responsibility for other individuals.

Jan 24 '17

I am occupying an increasingly minor role in management of my affairs and the affairs of my marriage. Perhaps this is as it should be. The fact is that I have difficulty being interested in them and do not have the computer skills that are increasingly necessary. I am happy to hand them over to my capable wife. It may be that I am preparing myself for the great transition.

At the present time, this notebook is the sole focus of my thoughts. Gone is the desire to publish my writings, which I now see as a lesser phase of my life. I have made my contribution, such as it is, to society. It is time to leave off being a creature of the literary industry and to move to a higher function in my life—developing all the capacities of my soul. Creating this notebook is an important aspect of this task.

Jan 25 '17

The Delphic maxim "Know thyself" (*Gnothi seauton*), of which so much has been made in the history of philosophy, boils down to one principal insight: know that you are a metaphysical soul distinct from the material domain. All the psychological ramifications of one's nature are derived from this key awareness.

I think the high point of American thought was the period 1835-1861, up to the onset of the War Between the States. Emerson, Thoreau, Poe, Whitman, Melville, and Hawthorne produced their epochal works. During this time, the transcendental movement emerged with a host of interesting writers. The violent, blood-drenched Civil War marked a sharp downward turn in American culture. The country became increasingly materialistic and militaristic. Literature turned to social or psychological issues; philosophy became irrelevant to American life. Transcendentalism was relegated to a footnote in the history of American literature; in academic philosophy it had and still has no currency whatever.

The spirit of America did not recover its cosmic and spiritual qualities after the Civil War. Thomas Edison and Henry Ford represented the heroes of the times; Emerson and Thoreau were forgotten. In the twentieth century, Robinson Jeffers played the role of Jeremiah to Americans—but, like the Biblical prophet before him, was either ignored, castigated, or ostracized. No one took what he said seriously.

Jan 26 '17

I cannot help thinking humanity is turning downward in terms of 'spirituality.' Everywhere technology and robotization advances. Who knows where it will all end? Ultimately, human beings may become like ants scurrying over the face of the earth, building huge supraterranean or subterranean structures, but devoid of spiritual consciousness.

What is 'spiritual'? People do not appreciate its meaning. It is not morality, not charity, not prayer, not erudition, or intelligence. It is the special quality of *metaphysical consciousness*, realizing that *spirit* is the dominant reality in the universe and that the Ultimate Reality and the soul of individuals are coextensive. The succinct Hindu maxim, *Atman is Brahman*, sums it up. Hindu religious consciousness is superior to the Christian version.

Out of the saga of humanity may emerge a few individuals who qualify as spiritual and who justify the human race. Finding them is like sifting gravel in search of precious metal. My simple descriptions may be inadequate to describe the reality, but that something like it occurs, I believe with all my soul.

Jan 27 '17

The deep-thinking philosopher Nikolai Berdyaev uses the term 'organic' in his writings differently than is the case in current usage. Organic for him is a characteristic of a society extensive in time, including both past and future generations. It must not be limited only to the present time.

With this concept in mind, I have the painful feeling that my present-day societal existence is *inorganic* as it is totally disconnected from my ancestry. I have absolutely no consciousness of my antecedents prior to my immigrant grandparents. I know they all lived somewhere in the Czarist Russian Empire (Poland, Ukraine, Byelorussia), but that is the extent of my knowledge. I don't know their language (Yiddish), their names, their occupations, where and how they lived, what they thought about, and what kind of people they were. I once saw photographic portraits of a heavily-bearded, grim-looking man and his equally grim-looking wife. They were said to be my great-grandparents, but nothing was told to me about them. I imagine none of their descendants who remained in the Soviet Union survived the German invasion.

It was an absolute rule of my family that Yiddish was never spoken in my presence. Consequently, I never learned the language that was the common idiom of all my ancestors for centuries. The occasional conversations with my grandparents were conducted in their broken English. We were never able to communicate in any depth. Much that I would like to know now, I never learned.

It is commonly said that America is a nation of immigrants. Therefore, my situation must be shared by most Americans. But I believe very few have had such an impenetrable barrier separating them from their ancestors. Most descendants of immigrants have some connection or knowledge with their past. I have none.

If Berdyaev is right in his conception of the organic nature of society, I have been grievously misused. In their zeal to promote my assimilation into American society, my parents inflicted serious damage to my personality. Perhaps I am akin to those 'hollow men' depicted by T. S. Eliot. I have spent the second half of my life trying to fill the void created by my well-meaning family. But intellectualization cannot completely substitute for 'organic' spiritual development just as malnutrition in early life cannot be fully compensated for by later overnutrition. I have had to learn to live with myself as I am.

Jan 30 '17

This notebook is my spiritual testament. Others may think who am I to produce a spiritual 'testament'? If it lay in a gutter, they would not bother to pick it up. However, it is an important part of my life— perhaps the most important part. That suffices to justify its production.

I have published fifteen books during my life in philosophy—most at my own expense. All of them were directed toward a reading public, which, by and large, found few readers. But this notebook is directed elsewhere, only toward myself. I read what I have written as I write. This is an enormously important process for my interior development. It alone justifies my efforts. Here is a new role for philosophical writing—*personal development*. What more important purpose could there be for one's efforts?

Nietzsche wrote somewhere that he wrote because he had no other way of getting rid of his thoughts. There is truth to his confession, but there is more to it than that. When I write out my thoughts, I give them an objective reality they would not have in the kaleidoscopic whirl-a-gig that is my mind. *I create metaphysical realities.* How proud I am to be able to do this! Here is the true mark of *Homo sapiens.* What might become of them in the societal world is not my business—nor do I much care.

I have come to all this in the nick of time; for in a few years, the game of life will be all over for me.

Jan 31 '17

Here I record the titanic, earthshaking thoughts that have emerged in my mind. But, meanwhile, my outer life serenely flows on, seemingly undisturbed by the activity within. Yet it is all part of the same '*me,*' the same Richard Schain. The situation is reminiscent of volcanic soil, where underground rumblings can go on for centuries without disturbing the activities on the surface. Yet one day, a volcano may erupt with all the power of long suppressed forces. An individual may go berserk, destroying his life, and changing the life of those around him. Nietzsche's creative activity exploded into insanity. I do not wish this to happen to me. Some of my interior forces ought to be gradually released. Easier said than done! Perhaps senility will relieve me of the threat.

My freest writing is done in the middle of the night when my mind has been washed clean from the mundane pressures of the day. Then I have to put a cap on my thoughts in order to return to sleep. Too bad that this is the case; but there it is.

The Alamos Music Festival is finally over. To me, it was more like a release of maniacs from their madhouse. Thousands of them pouring into our little town. A constant flow of alcoholic beverages—mostly cheap beer. The noise and tumult are unbearable. Any resembling to genuine music appreciation is purely coincidental. The *hoi polloi* are told they are listening to great music and they respond vociferously. It is disturbing to me to see that the music emperor has no clothes.

Feb 1 '17

Seeing that the end of my life in the world may not be far off, I feel it is proper to give an accounting of it to myself. An external observer would see many negative features to it, which I will try to enumerate:

– In an academic medical career of over 20 years, I can think of no real accomplishments. I left it with a sense of relief.

– The failure of my first marriage

– Very few friends—only one whom I could consider close

– Weak relationships with my sons and grandchildren

– No meaningful community connections or service

– Never any charitable contributions

– My life as an independent philosopher has had no discernable impact. My published books do not sell. (However, they could be treasures for those whose minds run in channels similar to mine.)

I can list only one definitely positive feature—my second marriage with Melanie Dreisbach. I believe my wife and I are devoted to each other.

Objectively considered, my life could be judged a virtual failure beyond the mere fact of supporting myself. But there is more to it than might meet an observer's eye. *I have developed my soul.* This may have little meaning in a strictly materially-minded society, but it means much to me. I think this is all that counts when one makes the great transition at the end of life. I have an intuition, a hunch' one might say, that there is an ultimate metaphysical reality, commonly called God, who will 'benefit'—using this word in the widest possible sense—from what I have made of myself. I cannot call this a 'faith' since hunches do not qualify as faith, but I think my hunch is well founded. If I am right, then my life will have been a success, more than that of skeptics who are 'successful' only in society. Of course, in the anti-metaphysical society in which I live, no credence will be given to my hunch.

There are several discussions in my books, especially *Souls Exist*, about what it means to develop one's soul. I will not repeat them here. Suffice it to say that in the last half of my life, I have done my utmost to accomplish this task. This should make up to some degree for my failure to address it in the first half. In any case, I am prepared to meet my maker.

My mind is exhausted, a break is necessary.

Feb 4 '17

Analytic philosophy today is akin to spiders weaving their webs—useless to human beings, including analytic philosophers, except to university faculty who need publication for academic advancement. Philosophy as I understand it, arises out of the life experience of the philosopher. Without an experiential grounding, it is useless verbiage.

If I must define my philosophy, I would call it 'existential metaphysics'. It is a ponderous term, but descriptive.

Feb 6 '17

The writers of the Pentateuch, and later Thomas Aquinas, say, "God is." I say, "I am." Is there an identity between these two statements? This is a question needing clarification. The issues of God's will, faith, love, justice, piety are distractions from this central question. If God *is*, I certainly have no idea of what he may want—if anything. Wanting is a human trait. But I would like to know how to establish a relationship with him.

Discussing these questions with Father X. makes me realize we live in different thought worlds.

I note that I am often sleepy during the day. Is it my age, my dinner glass of wine, or is it simple boredom? Perhaps a combination of all these things.

Feb 7 '17

Jesus, quoting Hebrew Scriptures, says one should love God with all your heart, all your soul, and all your strength. He seemed to feel God was his father—but I don't. How do you love someone or something with which you have no relationship? I might as well try to love the images of the Virgin Mary that are at many corners of my neighborhood. It would be like developing an infatuation with a piece of sculpture or a portrait. I remember expressing a different opinion earlier in this notebook but I retract it.

In the absence of any new experience, I cannot say that 'God' is anything more than a concept in my mind. It seems to me to be a form of spiritual masturbation to be in love with an illusory concept. Once and for all, I must cease occupying myself with this concept and concentrate on preparing for the Great Transition.

Preparing for the Great Transition:
- express myself freely
- read and reread metaphysically significant writings
- seek out metaphysically-oriented individuals
- avoid acquaintances who bore and exhaust me
- remember that my relationship to the universe is the same wherever I may live.

Significant experiences for me are becoming increasingly difficult to obtain. It is regrettable but there is no help for it. The downward trend of society is evident everywhere. If there is no metaphysical dimension in the universe, I am a lost soul.

Feb 15 '17

I am aware of an ever-present desire of mine to reach out toward a reality that is outside of myself. It is why I seek out individuals with a metaphysical orientation: priests, philosophers, devotees of religions of whatever stripe. Individuals without a metaphysical orientation are of little interest to me. My readings now are exclusively directed toward religious writings. Any type of worship, prayer, or meditation interests me as long as it expresses metaphysical yearnings. It must be based on a sense of a metaphysical reality underlying the physical world—and the desire to associate oneself with this reality in any way possible.

All purely worldly activities soon bore me. I soon feel they are without real substance. I have to socialize occasionally, but I need a mask to function. My soul is elsewhere. I have a feeling of friendship for a few people, a deep affection for one, but it is with an Ultimate Metaphysical Reality that my desires lie.

Every time I hesitatingly conduct affairs via the all-pervasive internet, I become aware of the increasing robotization of human society. Computer programs are fast replacing people—all in the name of efficiency, but really in the service of producing more billionaires. Where will it all end? I would like to say *ohne mich* during my remaining years, but I cannot. I am caught in the spider webs of the modern world.

My writings teach me, train me, sustain me, *elevate* me. Readers are superfluous.

Feb 16 '17—Religion commentaries
Between the fairy tales of Judaism/ Christianity and the dream states of Hinduism/Buddhism, there is no major religion worthy of free-

thinking individuals. (Neither is Islam, which is a slave religion.) A free man or woman is compelled to *create* his or her own metaphysical belief system.

The only books of the Bible in which I maintain an interest are Isaiah, Ecclesiastes, Song of Songs, a few Psalms, The Book of Wisdom, and the Gospels. As far as I am concerned, the rest can be safely consigned to the archives of seminaries.

The two outstanding figures of the Bible are Moses and Jesus. However, they had their faults; Moses was a religious dictator and Jesus exhibited a tendency toward mystical megalomania. It would be better to admit their limitations.

Much as I admire the ancient Vedic scriptures, I am not prepared to give up my personality for trance-like states. It is all *reality* I crave, not self-induced trances.

Feb 17 '17

A nasty little devil once asked me, "Why do I publish? Do I unconsciously seek fame?" Immediately I answered, "Please, you little devil, none of your evil psychological innuendos." He then left, grinning unpleasantly. I should have said to him, "I only deal with metaphysical issues, not psychological ones. These latter are beneath me. They have to do with the excreta of the mind. For this, one needs plumbers, not philosophers."

Feb 21 '17

Had an intense two-hour discussion with Father X. today about one's relationship to God. We had a remarkable coincidence of views considering our hugely different backgrounds and stations in life. His Roman Catholic training does not seem to interfere with the meetings of our minds. I think he must be quite an unusual priest. What strikes me about myself is my alertness and concentration throughout our discussions. Gone was my habitual boredom and drowsiness. We were attending to what is of vital interest to me—my metaphysical situation.

I said to X. that I have come to believe my yearning for the Ultimate will not be satisfied in this life—and hope it will be at the Great Transition. He was silent on the question. Good Catholics are supposed to find God in this life. But he didn't object to my ideas on the subject. Perhaps he agreed with them.

Feb 25 '17

Planning to reread Kierkegaard to see what I can learn. I know when he writes 'Christian,' I can substitute 'metaphysical'; whenever he says 'Christianity,' I can think 'metaphysics.' With these minor alterations, I learn much from S.K. He is one of the greatest thinkers of all times.

Feb 28 '17

In the midst of all the hustle and bustle of preparing for departure for France, I still am aware that I am completely isolated from the contemporary world of thought. If there is a 'noosphere', to use Teilhard de Chardin's terminology, I do not exist within it. My ideas and writings interest no one in that world. I participate in no cultural, educational, or religious events. My intellectual isolation is virtually complete.

This situation is either a horrible deprivation or a source of great strength. Likely it is some of both. Given the present status of the society I live in, I definitely prefer it this way.

I have once again given up the futile idea of looking for God outside of myself. It is my own soul that must be the focus of my attention. If God is to be found, He must be somewhere in it. However, instead of Atman=Brahman, I feel Atman→Brahman. This conclusion is a great relief for me.

The problem with the society to which I have been exposed is that the spiritual element of existence is divorced from the material element—and the latter is totally dominant in an age of machines and computers. I am unable to be interested in anything devoid of a spiritual element. Teilhard thought that spirit can be found in everything, but my experience is that it is confined to the animate world. I am willing to believe that an *anlage* of spirit exists in an amoeba, but in a computer or internal combustion engine, no! A thousand times, no!

I am sure that my double mental life has an inhibitory effect on my spiritual development. I wish it were otherwise, but I have made my bed and must occupy it. Things could be worse—I do not think I would flourish in a state of poverty or in a mental institution. Even worse, I might be confined to a professor's life in some institution of 'higher' education.

March 3 '17

The only philosophers that now interest me are those who write *existentially*—namely, expressing the philosopher's own *personal* experience. These are hard to come by as most philosophers today express themselves analytically. The few I have come across include Kierkegaard, Thoreau, Stirner, Nietzsche, and Berdyaev.

I think reluctance to fully part company mentally from institutional Christianity has inhibited the development of many otherwise profound thinkers. Among these, I include the Scholastics, Kant, Kierkegaard, Berdyaev, Tillich, Jaspers, Heidegger, Teilhard. There are others too numerous to mention. Jewish philosophers are not so inhibited but have their own problems to contend with such as the sacred Pentateuch (Torah) claiming Jewish exceptionalism and the need to obey 600 plus commandments.

Mar 6 '17—Attempt at an understanding of the metaphysical universe

A *transcendental ultimate reality* exists everywhere. It is always trying to enlarge itself, physically as well as metaphysically. Astronomers say the physical universe is constantly expanding. The means for metaphysical expansion is *animate* life. Every living individual organism, from an amoeba to Homo sapiens, represents the transcendent reality (i.e. God) expanding himself. In human beings, this is called spiritual development. It is really God seeking to expand himself metaphysically.

God as spirit in individual humans is referred to as their *soul* and, as stated above, represents God in human form striving toward his metaphysical development. When the physical body of an individual wears out, death ensues, which represents the departure of the soul. This soul, which has been a manifestation of the spirit of God in human form, may transfer itself elsewhere, the details of which I cannot envision. But the recognition of the possibility of *metempsychosis*, transfer of a soul to another organism, was one of the features of Hindu higher thought, along with the concept that Atman (soul)=Brahman (God).

Buddhism is an outgrowth of Hindu higher thought. The superstitious elements of Hinduism are discarded and there is an emphasis on achieving tranquility. But like Hinduism, there is no awareness of an ultimate reality striving for development. Entry into *Nirvana* represents a totally static view of a dynamic universe. A similar statement can be made of Spinoza's worldview and most other pantheistic philosophies.

As depicted in the synoptic gospels, Jesus approached the point of view that his own soul merged into that of God—for which the Jewish religious establishment accused him of blasphemy. Thereafter, the doctors of the Christian churches clamped down on any creative development of these thoughts of Jesus—leading to a petrification of Christian philosophy.

For me, the transcendental ultimate reality (God) is like a huge cosmic amoeba extending its pseudopods into every life form, pulling back from those worn out and pushing forward into fresh new ones. Like God of the physical universe, metaphysical God is in an expanding mode of existence. There may well be laws of metaphysical existence analogous to the laws of gravity and thermodynamics, but we human beings have not been intelligent enough to discover them.

I do not allow anyone or anything to tell me how to think or to behave with respect to the important questions of existence. Not Holy Writ, not a Pope in Rome, not the Torah, not any authority other than my own soul. If I do not come to an understanding of the importance of something *on my own,* the understanding is useless to me. I regard my soul with reverence, as I believe it is a vehicle for the development of the transcendental ultimate reality.

When I am expressing my thoughts, as I am now, I am participating in its development.

"Honi soit qui mal y pense."

Mar 7 '17

"Shma Y'Israel, Adenoi, Elohanu, Adenoi, echod." This is my recollection of the famous '*Sh'ma*' that every Jew is supposed to recite at eventful moments of his life, most especially at his impending death. It means, "Hear O Israel, the Lord thy God, the Lord is one." This is supposed to convey the oneness of God and his supremacy. The ancient Hebrews made much of the oneness of God—monotheism—as opposed to the prevalent polytheisms of their times—a feeling I have recently become aware of in myself.

"Beauty will save the world," said Dostoevsky in one of his novels. I wonder if it is true? The beauty of the French and Italian Rivieras where I now reside may support his statement. Looking out my window in Vielle Menton at the Mediterranean Sea brings his thought to mind. I am not able to do justice to its beauty but many others with the proper literary talent have done so.

Jean-Jacques Rousseau commented on the jealousy of philosophers. He said they would prefer to have their ideas sink into oblivion if they did not receive credit for them themselves. This is as true today as in the era of Rousseau and compares unfavorably with the lack of egotism of ancient Hindu and Hebrew thinkers. There seems to be an inverse relationship between literary egotism and metaphysical consciousness.

A culture should be in some manner transmitting the important thoughts of its thinkers. If it does not do this, it will surely disappear.

Mar 8 '17

My distrust of the medical establishment is limitless. The sly mendacity of its representatives is a sign of the decay of our culture. It seems to me that the entire edifice of modern medicine is purely self-serving for the doctors, pharmaceutical companies, hospitals, medical supply companies, insurance firms, and the ever-present hordes of lawyers making their living from malpractice claims. The cost of medical care has become astronomical and threatens to bankrupt the nation because of its support of the system. A gullible public puts its faith in doctors in a manner that is analogous to the trust Roman Catholics once put in their priests. The latter trust is far better founded than the blind acceptance of the dictates of physicians.

One striking example of blind faith with which I have personal experience is the treatment of 'high blood pressure.' A fabulous amount of money is spent on ever-changing medications to reduce blood pressure (not to speak of expenses connected with visits to the physician, laboratory tests, radiography, etc.). All this based on statistics purporting to show that life span is reduced by high blood pressure. The gullible public is unaware of the maxim, "There are lies, damned lies, and statistics." Perhaps there is a small number of individuals whose life is prolonged by use of drugs that reduce blood pressure. These are the ones that skew the statistics. On this is based the gigantic hypertension-treatment industry.

The drugs utilized for treatment of high blood pressure are not innocuous and produce frequent side effects, not to speak of a general lowering of vitality since their effects are not limited to blood pressure. The effective circulation of blood is essential to bodily health; who knows what subtle effects the reduction of blood pressure may produce? Diet and exercise, which are markedly beneficial to health, are usually only given lip service by physicians. The U.S.A. has only recently relinquished its position to Mexico as the most obese nation in the world—which latter usually dutifully follows in the footsteps of its more affluent northern neighbor.

The arrogance of physicians in thinking they are wiser than the wisdom of the body is remarkable. Blood pressure is necessary to maintain the functions of bodily organs, especially of the brain. The level of pressure needed is regulated by the body—generally, the older one is, the higher the pressure needed to adequately supply one's organs. But the medical profession in its arrogance has decided that the body doesn't know what it is doing in one third of the population and floods it with highly potent drugs. One day all this will come to light and the widespread treatment of high blood pressure will go the way of bloodletting, routine tonsillectomies, surgical treatment of any hernia, and prolonged bed rest for all kinds of illnesses.

Enough said!

Mar 10 '17

I but have been rereading the nineteenth century journal of Alfred de Vigny. He was an independent thinker and gifted writer. I don't know of any intimate journal, memoir, diary, or the like that can compare with his depth and scope. He fearlessly expressed himself on the major issues of human existence, especially his own. God, morality, fame, immortality, democracy, and more. Camus must have read de Vigny's journal—there are similarities between the two writers, but de Vigny is more incisive, less wordy, and more genuinely *existential*. The problems he wrestled with are the same ones I wrestle with. And we have the same attitude toward the 'public.' I have adopted his succinct phrase regarding potential readers of his writings, *"Attrape qui peut."* If there will be some readers of our works, it will be good. If not, it will also be good.

Leafing through Etienne Gilson's *La Philosophie au Moyen Age.* Reading Gilson is like drinking a thin chocolate malted soda. It goes down easily; afterwards, one has the sensation of not being satisfied with the bland experience.

Mar 11 '17

I feel that I turn to other writers too much in this notebook. It is an escape from looking deeply into my own soul. If I cannot find anything to say meaningful for myself, I should remain silent. Silence is much superior to literary garrulousness.

In the early dawn, I look out from my window upon the silent beauty of the Menton shoreline, devoid of vehicular traffic. The experience is uplifting. How much better this world would be without the ever-present noise of internal combustion engines. Noise drowns out interior development, which is why I hate it.

Mar 13 '17 – A Summing Up

When I review what I have written in this notebook, I am aware of a pervasive pessimism, negativity, and feeling of alienation in it. Yet, objectively, I have been favored by fortune to a degree few others can equal. Here I am at 86 years of age, in good health, fully functional, and with mental faculties that have never been better. I am financially well-off, have an intelligent, attractive wife who is devoted to me, own two substantial homes in Mexico and Arizona, and travel the globe at will. At this moment, I am writing in an ancient apartment overlooking the Mediterranean—a paradisiacal location. What more could anyone in my position possibly want?

Yet in the depths of my soul, I feel vaguely discontent. What is wrong with me? What is it that I am missing? I can point to faults in my upbringing but not nearly as severe as others have endured. I suffered as a child in an anti-Semitic neighborhood but this was long ago and the feelings of ostracism have long since dissipated. I was ill-suited for the academic career I entered into at too early an age, but this is no longer a factor in my life. The fact is that I feel ungrateful for complaining about anything in my fortunate circumstances.

Nevertheless, and in spite of the above, I am discontent. Certainly not for a lack of recognition of my writings for which I would only be contemptuous (contempt comes easily to me). Not because of my lost youth spent on unworthy activities since I have long since corrected that. Not for lack of a meaningful homeland as I value my existence as a pilgrim in this world. No, I am sure that none of the above explains my discontent. I feel in my heart that what I miss is a connection to what I have termed a 'transcendental ultimate reality', otherwise known as God. This feeling is not based on any rational or empirical reality. As far as I can tell, it just sits in my psyche, without any discernable antecedents. I yearn to feel some connection to a metaphysical reality beyond myself. It is a *metaphysical need* for me. I don't know if others feel this need (Schopenhauer says it is ubiquitous), but that is not important—that I feel it is enough for me.

I was raised without any significant religious influences; thus, my feeling cannot be attributed to a childhood indoctrination. A scientific worldview was dominant during the first half of my life (my father was a science teacher). I turned to philosophy to find wisdom, not to find God. (The former, however, often leads to the latter.) My yearning for a connection to God has only appeared during the last few years.

Some might think that as my allotted time on this earth comes to an end, I look to an imaginary God for salvation. It's possible. But I have no awareness of fearing death, no desire for immortality, and certainly no apprehension about what might be in store for me upon my demise. In fact, I have a certain curiosity about what I have named 'the Great Transition of the Soul' and what it might entail.

No, I just yearn for some kind of relationship with God without any hidden agenda. Moreover, I have a sense that God might wish a connection with me. Spiritually and intellectually, I have something to offer. I don't believe that God is all-powerful, all perfect, and without any need of further development. He may be moving forward just as everything in the universe is moving forward in some way.

Faith for me means an uninhibited yearning for God in my life. The mental castles in the air built by theologians hold no interest for me. They seem to me to be without foundation. The one maxim in Deuteronomy, repeated by Jesus, "love the Lord thy God with all thy heart, all thy soul, and all thy strength" is a worthy goal for one to strive toward spiritually. I am still trying to live up to that commandment. The rest is just the history of human mental wanderings.

I have a suspicion, however, that it is not possible for human beings to be metaphysically fulfilled on earth. Yearning to know God may be the best that can be done. It is equivalent to loving him.

Mar 15 '17

I am now too old to have an impact on society—neither the one I live in or any other. Every time some young person on a bus or train gets up to give me their seat, I am reminded of my age. I think why is this person giving me their seat? Then I realize how old I must look to them. People may give me their seats but they do not take my thoughts seriously. I would rather they keep their seats and listen to what I have to say. Then I wonder if it is time for me to leave the banquet table of life?

It is not just my age, however. There is no society I have ever genuinely fit into at any time in my life. Consequently, I have never genuinely been successful anywhere. The society I was born for does not exist. This is the reason I search for a metaphysical dimension of existence for which I may be better suited. In a word, I yearn to find God. The Hindu holy men who authored the Upanishads did not think this is a vain effort. Nor did Abraham Joshua Heschel in his inspirational book *Man Is Not Alone* (1951). I hope they were right. But the very fact that I express some doubt reveals that my faith in the availability of God does not rest on a solid basis. I would like to believe, however, that an individual's aspirations are a better guide to reality than his beliefs or behaviors. Behaviors are often misguided and beliefs unreliable.

Nevertheless, one must choose beliefs and act on them. Even if I am unsure that my present nomadic way of life is the best for me, I have commitments I cannot abandon. Things could be worse.

The beauty of Menton has not been obliterated by the noise of vehicular traffic or the greed-induced high-rise buildings that line much of its coastline. But one cannot build on the Mediterranean or on the jagged mountain ridges that surround it. So far the sea is not congested with motorized boats. This small piece of the world still has great appeal. Nature and climate here are kind to human beings. I am blessed to be here.

Mar 16 '17

The Harvard Review of Philosophy has declined to publish my essay entitled, "The Art Form Called Philosophy." I really did not expect otherwise. Why would an academic journal publish a far-out article by an unknown independent philosopher? Better to maintain my pristine state of invisibility.

I have not written in this notebook of my relationship with my wife Melanie. Some things are too deep and too profound to put into mere words. This statement will have to suffice.

Mar 17 '17

I am going to break my vow of not quoting other writers in this notebook. It is because *Man Is Not Alone* by A. J. Heschel profoundly deals with an issue close to my heart—man's relationship to God. This book is not your usual religious tract, full of moralistic cant. Heschel is at once existential philosopher, theologian, Talmudical scholar, and talented poet. These attributes are rarely found in a single individual. He is passionately involved with the idea that man and God are closely intertwined in their being. Like a good poet, his writing is replete with metaphors; like a good scholar, he references his quotations (largely from biblical and Talmudical sources). Like most existential philosophers, he is repetitive, verging on garrulousness; but somehow this is not disturbing in Heschel.

The central message of the book is that not only is man in need of God, but also God is in need of man. Heschel's God is indefinable, ineffable, and is to be found everywhere and in everything, thus verging on pantheism. But he is also a personal God, concerning himself with every individual human being (especially if they are Jews). Heschel's anthropomorphism with respect to God is easily overlooked because of the passion and eloquence of his writing.

It has been exhilarating for me to again come upon *Man is Not Alone* after becoming aware of my own need to find God. I first read it twenty years ago when it only affected me superficially.

Reading it now has been a revelation—no doubt because it validates my own feelings. (I have had the same experience with Augustine's *Confessions*.)

However, I part paths with Heschel when he discusses the actual nature of man's relation to God. As a pious rabbi, God is the Lord for him and individual human beings are God's subjects whose fulfillment lies in obeying his will. What does he will for his subjects? Concern for the welfare of their fellow men (and women) expressed by morality and love. God needs *subjects* to carry out his wishes just as his subjects fulfill their own nature by obeying him.

All this is most offensive to me. Heschel's human beings are told to have reverence for everything except their own selves. But my first need—only followed later by the need to find God—is to revere myself, meaning to develop my soul. God must want developed souls, not subservient subjects. (If Heschel can indulge himself in anthropomorphisms, so can I.) I need to participate in expanding God's nature. As to whether all men participate in this process, I plead ignorance.

Heschel might have become another St. Paul if he consented to baptism and accepted Jesus Christ as his savior. But he never would have agreed to these terms. So he remains a strangely inspirational figure in the history of Jewish thought, deeply metaphysical in his nature and expressing his own special brand of Jewish theology.

Mar 19 '17

Sometimes I am awakened at night thinking I have a mortal illness and am going to die. It is my nocturnal hypochondria. It is usually triggered by some slight physical symptom I had during the day. All my daytime thinking that I have no fear of death, that I am ready for it, even look forward to it, flies out the window. I am gripped by a terror of dying; I am like a wild animal, wanting to live at all costs. There are at other times sexual or aggressive fantasies, but the desire to hold on to life is paramount. When the morning comes, the beast crawls back into its lair—then I revert to my 'normal' self.

This beast frightens me. Which is the real me, my nocturnal or diurnal self? Or am I a split personality; something like Stevenson's Dr. Jekyll and Mr. Hyde? My age has only accentuated my nocturnal fears and produced more vivid fantasies. I do not think I need a psychoanalyst; I need 'God' to help me surmount my animal self.

Mar 20 '17 – Migration to Ventimiglia

There is a constant flow of mostly black African migrants at the railroad station of Ventimiglia, just across the Italian border from Menton. Some wander onto the platforms thinking they might jump on the train going to Menton, eight minutes away. However, they are usually shooed off the platforms by the Italian police, or, if they manage to get on the train, they are intercepted by French police on the other side and sent back to Italy. It is a sad human spectacle.

They often have a hunted look about them. But, they are comfortably dressed, have full backpacks, and usually brandish cell phones. These have been provided to them by private organizations, besides giving them food, shelter, medical, and even psychological services. Their physical needs have probably never been so well met in their homes in Africa.

But what then? Who will hire them—and for what type of work? How will they cope with societal expectations? Will they find women with whom they can socialize? What kind of life will they lead in Europe? Many want to go to England but it is unlikely they will ever reach that destination. The ones I have seen are coal-black, clearly setting them apart from the native population. It seems to me they don't belong in Europe. They should find their place in Africa. But that is not what they want and the whole system of rescuing them and providing for their immediate needs ensures that the migration will continue. However, the Italian coast guard and the well-meaning NGOs will not help them adapt to existence in Europe. A life of welfare or crime or drugs is likely to be the fate of many of them.

Mar 22 '17

Yesterday, Melanie and I went to the Chagall museum in Nice. It was an inspirational experience. Marc Chagall was that rarity today, a truly spiritual artist. It is why his fame and importance steadily grow, while that of his contemporary Picasso, whose soulless work I detest, steadily diminish.

I believe the only true culture is a *spiritual* culture, a culture that develops one's soul and helps relate it to a transcendental reality. There is no subject more needful of an approach reflecting the artist's own existence. Otherwise, one is weighed down by meaningless values and traditions. People should not order their life on such a basis. The only spiritual expressions that affect me stem from the personal experiences and personal judgments of those who express them.

It must be said that everything that comes under the heading of 'secular' (i.e. materialist) culture eventually degenerates. The visual arts become trivial distractions, literature becomes shallow amusement, music becomes barbarous noise, and electronic screens provide either unnecessary information or sex and violence. There is no essential purpose to secular culture and thus it must degenerate.

Spiritual culture should not be confused with religious institutions or their idols. The Roman Catholic Church is a prime example of secularization hiding behind a facade of spirituality. Seventeen hundred years ago it modeled itself along the authoritative structure of the Roman Empire—and it has hardly changed. Protestant religious institutions are little better, substituting a 'holy' book, the Bible, for the Catholic hierarchy.

Spiritual culture requires an individual to develop his own relationship to the metaphysical dimension of human existence. If people are incapable of engaging in this task, they can relegate it to a religious authority, but they should not delude themselves that they are participating in genuine spirituality. For this to happen, creative individual spiritual effort is required. This is what I have found in my own life and therefore this is what I believe.

Mar 23 '17

As I look out my window onto the Mediterranean and see the escarpments of the Maritime Alps jut down to the sea, the imprint of human civilization seems miniscule. Civilizations have come and gone in this area for millennia. The ancient Greeks were here for two centuries, then the Romans for five. The latter built a remarkable civilization with their theaters, baths, excellent roads, and stability of life. But it passed as all have passed. The Grimaldi family of Monaco possessed the area I live in for also almost five hundred years until the French Revolution and Napoleon dispossessed them. It has been a part of France for a relatively short time (since 1860). Mussolini annexed Menton into Italy (Mentone) during WW II, which was probably the shortest annexation in the long history of the city.

It will all end sometime in the future. At the longest, the sun will grow cold (or burn up) and life on the planet Earth will end. More likely, however, overpopulation or climatic changes will earlier end civilizations as we know them. If there is not a metaphysical dimension to human existence, culture is a meaningless phenomenon—merely a diversion to while away the time during the brief life of human beings.

Mar 24 '17

I recently acquired a book for two euros at an outdoor market of Menton. It was *Saint Thomas d'Aquin, Maître Spirituel.* The author (J. P. Torrell), a professor at the University of Fribourg and a Dominican priest, makes a case for Aquinas' view that there is a strong human need to relate himself to 'God.' Obviously Torrell shares that view. However, his task is complicated by Christian doctrinal requirements for justifying a divine Trinity, including the unique divinity of Jesus of Nazareth.

Torrell presents the usual views of faith in an almighty deity and the helplessness of human beings left to their own resources. The only thing man can do alone is worship his Trinitarian creator, accept the words of God in Holy Scripture, and hope for salvation. Philosophy is an avocation whose sole purpose is to buttress faith. It appears that toward the end of his short life Aquinas lost interest in writing philosophy, regarding it as so much "straw."

I see things differently. I prefer to envision 'God' as an elder brother rather than as an authoritarian father. I view Jesus as a Jewish prophet, perhaps the greatest one of all, but not as God descended to the planet in order to save mankind. I don't mind anthropomorphisms attributed to God as long as they don't make him a dictator over my life. *Reverence for one's own soul is the key to a truly spiritual worldview.* I try to remember the ultimate wisdom of Vedanta, "Atman [soul] is Brahman [God]." One must go beyond Aquinas and Torrell.

The need for a Trinitarian concept of God is due to the perceived necessity of establishing the divinity of Jesus and of maintaining the authority of the Catholic Church in interpreting Holy Scriptures. Protestantism has thrown out the latter but maintained the former. Regarding Jesus of Nazareth, the criticism of Gotthold Lessing still holds true in my mind—the impossibility of transforming an historical event into a universal truth.

Mar 25 '17

Many thoughts are flying around in my mind today. During a bright morning shining over the blue Mediterranean (there are many such in Menton), I aspire toward the worldview of Zen Buddhism—mindfulness toward *every* aspect of existence. At night, I am caught up by the metaphysical mysteries of Vedanta. I also make some room for Tantric worship. There is not much space left for the obsequious Abrahamic religions. In any case, I don't really want to approach God physically, metaphysically, or otherwise, because then I might die to the world—and I'm not quite ready for that. There are no simple solutions to the human condition...nor should there be for living human beings.

The more I think, read, and write, the more developed my mind becomes. Why not? If an athlete improves his performance according to the time he spends training and practicing, why would not the mind (soul) improve as a consequence of its creative activity? The universal laws that apply to physical performance should especially apply to mental performance. Woe to those who put brakes on the minds of human beings.

Mar 26 '17

I have given over management of all our personal affairs to my capable wife. There are many reasons for this act; her superior ability to handle the requirements of modern life, my age and infirmities, my computer illiteracy, her natural abilities as a practical 'doer' and mine as a 'thinker.' All this would make the arrangement seem quite sensible...and yet...and yet I am unhappy about losing the independence to handle my own life myself. Fundamentally, it is not a desirable situation. There is too much on her delicate shoulders. I feel guilty; I think I should be living in a studio apartment with paid secretarial and maid services. What to do? I don't have an answer. A wrong solution would be turning to alcoholic spirits.

Perhaps a timely demise will take care of the problem.

Mar 28 '17

Went down the Nietzsche path on the Riviera from Eze to Eze-sur-Mer. The views of the sea, mountains, and sky are awesome.

Physical reality seems unchanging here; I am sure what I saw was exactly the same as Nietzsche saw it. Humanity has an ant-like quality scurrying over the face of the earth. The ants come and go; the earth remains.

The great Scholastics of the medieval era—notably Bonaventure and Aquinas—knew that it was only the metaphysical nature of human beings that was significant about them. It is necessary, however, to free Scholastic thinking from the shackles of Christian dogmas. Otherwise the metaphysical baby will be thrown out with the Christian holy water!

Nietzsche first achieved fame because he was a German philosopher who had gone mad in Italy. His fame progressively increased as a result of the machinations of his sister Elizabeth—whom he had grown to despise while he was still sane. I am not prepared to make such a sacrifice for my writings. I reflect, I write, I publish—then *l'attrape qui peut*. This seems to be to be an eminently sensible attitude for an independent philosopher.

Mar 29 '17

It is not enough to love God—He already has had enough servile admirers who probably bore him to distraction; He does not need any more. One must bring something of value to God, something that enhances his existence. The concept that he is perfect and unchanging is unsustainable. Change is the fundamental property of all that exists; why should it not be true of God as well? If he is somehow beyond existence, then we can have nothing to do with him—as Epicurus concluded.

What have I to bring to God? Unrestricted love is generally unrequited love. Just because some Jew from antique Tarsus thought it was the be all and end all of human life does not mean I must think the same. If there exists an almighty, all knowing, perfect Deity, there is no reason to believe He would concern himself with me. That is pure wishful thinking and a heritage from Jewish exceptionalism where God showed compassion for his chosen people. To rely on his 'compassion' is just naive anthropomorphism.

April 1 '17 (April Fool)
It seems to me that metaphysical and physical development are interdependent. No real wisdom is possible without progress in both realms of existence. If the Psalmist was right that it is the fool who thinks there is no God, it is also right that the man who lives without wine, women, and song is also a fool.

April 2 '17
Paid 10 Euros to visit the 'Museum of Modern and Contemporary Art (MAMAC) in Nice. The huge building is ostentatious, overwhelming, typical French 'Monumental' architecture. I hesitate to express what is in my mind about its contents. They confirm my opinion that secular art inevitably tends toward degeneration. The

'*École de Nice*' is to my mind the '*Égout de Nice.*' A quotation attributed to Hermann Goering (I use any sources) comes to mind, "When I hear the word culture, I reach for my revolver."

It was far more rewarding to have a coffee outside the museum at the enchanting Place de Garibaldi.

April 3 '17

It strikes me that life in Menton is decidedly *sensual*. Everything conspires to please the senses: the expanse of the Mediterranean, the fantastic mountain views, the warm breezes, the opulent gardens, the shoreline promenades. Food of every type to please the palate is everywhere. And, of course, the abundance of fine French wines.

Concern for the metaphysical dimension of existence seems out of place here.

April 4 '17

The Hindu sages of antiquity have always fascinated me. These forest '*rishis*' all came to the same awareness of an ultimate reality underlying the constantly changing human soul and constantly changing material world around it. It was a great era for the 'perennial philosophy,' one that has never been equaled, even by the ancient Greeks. The Hindu sages asserted that the ultimate reality of the universe is to be found at the core of the human soul. The phrase "Atman is Brahman" encapsulates their discovery.

The rishis concluded that fulfillment in life for human beings consisted in losing oneself in the Ultimate. This could be accomplished in various ways, but especially through deep continuous meditation. The term 'attaining Nirvana,' popularized by Buddhism, refers to this transformation. The metaphor "all rivers empty into one ocean" describes the process. These unknown forest sages who produced the Upanishads, the primary source of Hindu metaphysics, felt the supreme goal of human life was to attain metaphysical being.

While I have the highest regard for Hindu sages and have come to many of their fundamental concepts on my own, I find something suicidal about losing oneself in metaphysical being. Is the development of the human personality with all its desires and vicissitudes merely a punishment for being born? Is it to be discarded as soon as possible? In fact, there is a facet of Hindu metaphysics that sees human life merely as a game originated to amuse the gods.

I do not care to give up my hard won self to an ultimate reality, no matter how alluring the prospect. I refuse to reject my role in the physical universe while life exists within me. The physical world is my teacher. Instead of conceiving my soul as a river emptying into an ocean, the metaphor I prefer is a condiment added to the cauldron of primordial soup. The condiment does not vanish in the soup but adds flavor to it. A developed soul on joining deity *enhances* it.

My conviction is that it is important to progress beyond the 3000-year-old insights of the rishis. I believe the purpose of my life is to fulfill the godhead, as well as myself. Others can call this conviction the ultimate hubris (assuming any attention is paid to it at all), but it is what I have come to believe.

The question arises as to whether there is any *reality* to the thoughts expressed above—or are they just the product of a febrile and fertile imagination? The fact is, however, that I am quite poor in imaginative thinking. My mind tends to hew toward hard reality. Therefore, I cannot help believing there is at least some degree of reality in what I have painfully represented.

I do not have 'faith' in what I have set forth. I don't think human beings should ever have faith in their metaphysical ideas, no matter how they have arrived at them. To think there is a nucleus of truth in them is more than enough.

Expression of these thoughts has been difficult for me and I do not intend to return to them again. The capacities of my mind are barely adequate for the subject.

April 5 '17

At night, the flickering lights along the shoreline of Menton remind me I am still alive. I can still appreciate beauty, still have the gift of sensual life. To hell with the Hindu sages!

April 7 '17

More night thoughts—For an unknown and aged philosopher like myself, there are three choices:

1. Death by suicide. Take my termination into my own hands.
2. Descent into madness. Very unpleasant, with people staring at you.
3. Continuation of the present existence.

In the absence of compelling health reasons, 1 is beyond my ability to carry out; 2 is too degrading; 3 is what remains. How many years are left for me? One?, five?, ten?, even 20? The thought is mind-boggling.

Failure in worldly affairs has dogged me all my life. I am not able to escape this realization even if I regard it as a badge of superiority. Like a judgmental God who has ignored me, society too has ignored me. Therefore, I ignore that God and I ignore society. Silence for silence, dislike for dislike, contempt for contempt. May the Ultimate Metaphysical Reality have mercy on me.

I must stop writing now or (2) will ensue. But if I don't write at all, I fear the worst. The fate of Nietzsche looms up before me. Still, I have a devoted wife, alcoholic spirits, and good coffee. I have money. Nietzsche had none of these supports. I should be able to survive.

April 8 '17

New outlooks—The human beings that compose society are only one segment of the various fauna that populate the planet Earth. Adverse judgments about them are not appropriate. One does not criticize tigers for killing other animals, rabbits for breeding, pigs for smelling bad. There is no reason to criticize human beings for their attitudes and behaviors. They are what nature has made them to be. History bears out the observation that human behaviors do not change during the course of civilization. The style of the behaviors may change but not the substance. Whatever progress occurs is in technology, not behavior.

I regard myself as a mutant outside the category of so-called *Homo sapiens*. I do not fit into human society; appearances to the contrary, I have never fitted in. But I too am what nature has made me so I ought not to be hard on myself. I should be satisfied to be a spectator of the human comedy, and be grateful for the beneficial things that have come my way.

As far as my 'metaphysical need' is concerned, there is only so much I can know. I must not forget my position as a tiny grain in a vast universe and not expect too much for the metaphysical need. A sense of wellbeing is the main goal in life. One should know that the wise Epicurus defined philosophy as the highest form of pleasure, i.e. wellbeing. In our stress-burdened world; more attention needs to be paid to his thoughts.

Perhaps I will arrive at a closer sense of God in the future, but I am not going to concern myself about it at the present time.

April 9 '17

Death ushers in the great unknown event. If my soul approaches, it will do so not as a suppliant but as a gift-giver. My soul will be the gift. I believe God is in need of fully developed souls, not merely pious ones.

If you, religious reader, ask me how I know all this, I respond how do you know that human beings ought to follow God's will? If you cite tradition and learned doctors of churches, I say I have no confidence in tradition or learned doctors. If you fall back on your own revelation, I will say I too have had a revelation, one that is very different from yours.

April 15 '17

This notebook is overturning my life! memories! memories! memories!—roads not taken—opportunities missed—character defects—no fool like an old fool—it's too late. Time to say good-bye.

I can't write everything on my mind—too distressing for me.

April 18 '17

I have recently read *Le Kabbaliste de Prague* by Marek Halter. He has one of his characters write that only Jews believe a new man can be created with words. He cites Marx, Lenin (?), and a Prague rabbi Malta Ral. There are others he might have mentioned—notably Saint Paul and Sigmund Freud. Of course, it is not only Jews, but all exponents of religions, founders of political parties, and charismatic leaders of various types who think they can produce new men with their words. They assume that the new men will be better human beings, but experience has shown that this is not the case. Fanatics, hypocrites, demagogues, and self-serving types of every stripe think they can change men by their words.

Words certainly have their importance, but I think their importance is largely limited to the person who expresses them. Words expressed give substance to the thoughts of individuals and stamps their souls with their meanings. I believe I have become the person that I am through the words I have written down, read, and reread. Words for me are highly important. Whether one's words can have a similar effect on others is a dubious proposition and surely not at the same level as for their authors.

Much depends on the purposes of those who create language from words. When a writer writes to amuse, instruct, or otherwise divert readers, what I have written above does not apply. Entertainment and instruction have their own values. But for the creative writers who seek the wellsprings of existence, their words are largely significant to themselves alone. This ought to be the case for any serious writer who, in the words of Nietzsche, *has reverence for his own soul.*

Reverence for the soul is reverence for the *metaphysical self.* This kind of reverence is difficult to achieve because people tend to see themselves as others see them. For example, I am seen by others as an unsuccessful writer, a failed academic, and an out of touch philosopher. All I have to recommend me is longevity, a devoted wife, and a bank account (accumulated I know not how). All in all, adding up to a pathetic old fool in the eyes of a critical observer—should there ever be one.

Yet I have been faithful to my role as an independent philosopher for which I give myself credit. I cannot say it reaches the level of reverence but I am still working toward that end. *Honi soit qui mal y pense*!

April 19 '17

At my age, one looks back much more than forward. There is much more to see. The roads taken and not taken, the opportunities grasped and those missed, the failed enterprises; all these loom up in my mind. There is not a great deal to look forward to in the future.

I have a few maxims that I hold onto as guides: "live 'til you die," "love the life you live," "the noble soul has reverence for itself." However, these are only maxims, not life itself. So I keep thinking, keep writing, keep living, and hope all will turn out well in the end.

The history of Jewish thought is absorbing for me. I think I would have been more successful as a Talmudical scholar than in any of my past careers. Enlightened Jewish thought is existential in its core as evidenced by a philosopher like Abraham Joshua Heschel or a novelist like Marek Halter. I do not have the literary talent of these writers but my genius is similar. Sincerity is my dominant feature, a trait that is not held in high regard in the literary world of today.

My father taught biology in the Talmudical Academy of the Yeshiva University of New York City. It's too bad I did not follow in his footsteps—naturally not as a science teacher but as a Talmudist. Then I would have had some relationship with the Ultimate Metaphysical Reality— perhaps not a perfect one but at least a connection.

These thoughts keep rushing into my mind. What does it all mean? I would like to know before I die. I might even recite the *Sh'ma.*

April 20 '17

What do all my thoughts add up to? I think it is this: transition from the neuronal activity of my brain to my affective and intellectual states can only be regarded as *magical* events. Nothing in the laws of the physical universe can account for these events. They are like Aladdin rubbing his magic lamp to produce a genie possessed with magical powers. To ignore the magical nature of the brain-mind relationship is to ignore the most significant aspect of the human condition. We human beings are the product of a supernatural activity transcending the laws of the physical universe. Language is central to humanity, leading to the widespread belief that the word of God has created mankind.

If my soul (read personality, mind, psyche, whatever label one wishes) is the result of magical (read mystical, metaphysical) events, then anything is possible for it. Space, time, and the laws of causality are no barriers to magical activity. "What is impossible for man is possible for God." But someone has to rub the cerebral lamp to bring forth the genie.

Monistic philosophers prefer to ignore all this and claim that 'science' is not yet advanced enough to explain human mental or spiritual phenomena. Or to state as did Molière's doctor in *Le Médecin malgré lui,* that mental or spiritual activity are merely 'qualities' of the brain. However, hiding one's mind in the sand, ostrich-like, is no solution to the metaphysical needs of individuals.

What, after all, is the meaning of the terms mystical or metaphysical? For me, it means a dimension of existence beyond the purely physical. It is the destiny of *Homo sapiens* to enter into this dimension even if he does not understand its nature. He yearns for a *god-like* experience. I do not flinch from the expression 'born again' to describe this event. I only wish to assert that for me it has nothing to do with a so-called 'savior,' but has everything to do with the development of my own personality.

Success in my life is moving toward the goal of metaphysical consciousness. It is not acts of morality or piety or worldly accomplishments that is required of me, but a movement of my soul toward this end. This is what 'born again' means to me—and I think what it meant to the Jewish prophet Jesus of Nazareth.

N. B. I admit to leading parallel mental lives but I try not to go astray with either of them.

April 21 '17

Menton—Easter week. This town can be summed up as offering flesh, coffee, food, and alcoholic beverages. All in the context of perpetual sun over the blue Mediterranean. Today, youth is king here; the beaches abound with slender female bodies and smooth thighs. Everyone seems happy, but who knows what dark thoughts lurk below?

Would I wish to be young again? No more than I would wish to return to the quiet comfort of my mother's womb. I am made for higher things than the sensual pleasures of youth. If I do not find them, it will be due to my own inadequacies.

Nevertheless, the sexual wound is present throughout one's life. It can be ignored only at the expense of one's personality. In my opinion, repressed sexuality is the hidden factor in the Easter Menton scene.

I dreamt last night that I had died. Usually, I do not report my dreams in this notebook, but this one so affected me that I cannot help describing it.

I had just died. It was not due to natural causes but because I was involved in a secret geopolitical conspiracy. Everyone involved in it had died; finally, my time had come. I was aware that I had died but angry that my obituary had appeared in a newspaper. Someone told me that it was necessary so everyone would know I was dead. I accepted that explanation, but regretted I had not reached 95 years, which was my father's age when he died.

Finally, I woke up feeling very nervous. What did the dream mean? I haven't figured it out yet, but I will avoid involvement in geopolitical conspiracies. It is reassuring to me, however, that I was fully aware of myself after my death, suggesting that my physical demise had not abolished my existence. The partial nature of physical death was thus confirmed.

April 26-27 '17 – What the term 'metaphysical existence' really means for me.

1) The age-old 'metaphysical need' exists strongly within me. It is the yearning for something other than honors, wealth, sensual pleasures, the tiresome trivia of everyday life. The yearning can be thought of as seeking God, but I never feel it as such. It is just a yearning, a desire for something more in my life. I have tried the

religions known to me; they all finally seem to be a conglomeration of dogmas and rituals that do not satisfy my metaphysical need.

2) I have thought deeply about the nature of this need. It does not seem to be a seeking for any particular entity, whatever its nature. I have come to think it is a search for a *different dimension of existence* for myself, a metaphysical dimension beyond the purely physical. The mystical figures of historical religions seem to me closest to finding a new dimension for their souls. But their successes are temporary; they can never really escape their physical needs for food, shelter, and security that inevitably pull one back to the physical aspect of their existence. Without these supports, the most intense mystical engagement in yoga, meditation, or what have you will soon die. My yearning is not a death wish, neither is it a desire for transient mystical gratifications. Pathetic half-starved figures seeking metaphysical existence do not appeal to me. At least Buddhists make respectable compromises with biological needs.

3) The great Jewish commandment expressed by Jesus, "Thou shalt love the Lord thy God with all thy heart, all thy mind, all thy strength" has always had much significance for me. It is more satisfying to love than to yearn. "The Lord thy God" *symbolizes* to me existence in a metaphysical dimension. Jesus was a great symbolist; he spoke often of the 'kingdom of God.' One can love the kingdom of God without fully entering into it.

4) The desire to stay alive is one of the most fundamental of human drives. Other animals accept death more readily than do humans. Human beings, however, want to continue to live no matter what their age and health. With me, the desire to live and the yearning for metaphysical existence *coexist*. They are contradictory desires. In past eras, part of the aversion to death was the fear of what would come afterwards—hellfire, torture, devils, Dantesque infernos. These fears have largely dissipated through cultural enlightenment. Now it is total oblivion that is feared. Human beings yearn to leave behind monuments to themselves: artwork, books, structures, institutions, *children*. But leaving monuments behind is no substitute for timeless metaphysical existence.

5) I intuit that how one lives his life determines the fate of the soul. The Hindu concept of Karma gives voice to this intuition, as does the Christian dogma of the wages of sin. It is not necessary, however, to believe in rebirth into lower forms of life or in consignment of sinners to hell to apprehend that the fate of the soul is determined by how one lives earthly life. First, of course, one must be conscious of the existence of one's soul. This is a great problem in the era of flowering of science and technology. Second, one must be aware of a metaphysical dimension of existence, which a soul can experience during life.

6) The resolution of the conflict between physical and metaphysical existence lies in the Judeo-Christian commandment to

absolutely love God. But one must understand its symbolic significance. 'Loving God' does not refer to an entity, it refers to metaphysical existence. One can yearn toward this existence but it cannot be fully fulfilled in life on earth. Furthermore, the soul must be formed before it is capable of metaphysical existence. The experiences of life act to form the soul by stimulating spiritual consciousness and expressiveness. This is why, I think, human beings are so reluctant to give up biological living. A person *anticipates* metaphysical existence in the process of loving God but does not reach it. Such is my vision of the metaphysical realities.

7) The formation of the soul occurs through experiences, accomplishments, acquisition of knowledge, and especially through *expressiveness* of spiritual consciousness. The role of love, in all its forms, is to prepare the soul for love of metaphysical existence. Plato first expressed this concept millennia ago in his dialogue *Symposium*. The concept was widespread in the antique world. Aristotle wrote that life would not be bearable without 'friends' (i.e. soulmates). Escape from loneliness is an ever-present preoccupation of human life. Epicurus taught this in his philosophy, which is why his school lasted almost a thousand years. Healing of the sexual wound is a special aspect of love at every age. A man-woman erotic relationship tends to heal this wound but never completely. (Same sex love is beyond my ken, but its ubiquitous presence in civilization means it must have a significance.)

8) I believe the culture within which I live is spiritually degenerating. The successes of science and technology have expelled metaphysical awareness. The judgment of Thoreau that all energies are directed toward means and none toward ends is truer than ever. The only recourse of an individual is to stand apart—and that I have done. Cliques, guilds, and meaningless traditions are to be avoided. Much success in the contemporary world usually indicates failure of spiritual development.

'Culture' is ultimately based on words; images are a more primitive means of developing culture. 'Literature' refers to the culture of thought expressed through words. Thoughts can never be expressed absolutely accurately ("A thought once uttered is a lie," Tyutchev), but a sense of direction can be established. *Free and untrammeled expression of the spirit is essential for its formation as a soul* and its liberation into a metaphysical world.

April 29 '17

Our stay in Menton is approaching its end. I have no regrets. There is so much here to appeal to the senses that it is difficult to maintain a philosophical state of mind. In time, I suppose, I would adapt to the spectacular surroundings and then my familiar yearnings would resume once more.

Now, at midnight, under the influence of my troublesome insomnia, I feel the oppressive weight of society. The despiritualization of people seems irresistible. The digital revolution added to the industrial and scientific ones are producing soulless human beings. Superficial affability is no substitute for soul. My own soul has been corrupted by these events in spite of my efforts at resistance. Some may think all these thoughts are a product of my social isolation. But whenever I make efforts to lessen the isolation, my consciousness of the corruption of society intensifies.

I think the poet Robinson Jeffers was not far off the mark in considering the human race to be a failed experiment of God. Somebody must be responsible for this state of affairs. God is as good a scapegoat as any. If not God, who then? The thought is a frightening one in my insomniac state. Might Marcion have been right that an evil God rules the world? The Roman Catholic Church must bear responsibility for suppressing heresies that might express the truth of things. Gresham's law that bad money drives good money out of circulation is applicable to materialism versus spirituality. In the clash of ideological values in the world, Satan usually comes out victorious.

I see greed and deceit everywhere around me. The almighty dollar is king in America. In Menton, where this tendency (as euros) seems to be less than in its neighbor Monaco; there the huge high-rise condominiums and overfilled overpriced restaurants are examples. The natural spiritual yearnings of individuals have difficulty surviving amidst the downward press of society.

What Is To Be Done? is the title of a book by an action-oriented Lenin regarding the decaying Czarist autarchy. He had a definite solution in mind (which was no solution), but I have none for the problem I see. The most I can do is cultivate my all too weak spirituality and express my thoughts for my own benefit—and a few unlikely readers.

May 1 '17

If I were not afflicted with frequent insomnia, I might not have produced and written out my thoughts. Insomnia is a kind of blessing for me; it helps me form my soul.

Saw a film last night for the first time in years, *La La Land*. It was quite entertaining but depressed me afterwards. A significant relationship between two talented young people was abandoned for the limelight for each of them separately. Hollywood values at their finest! May the saints preserve me from the Hollywood mentality.

My two favorite literary figures are Sherlock Holmes and Hercule Poirot. If I could have created such characters, I might never have turned to philosophy. But this kind of literary creativity is beyond my capacities.

Sincerity is my Achilles heel. If I were not so damnably sincere, I could be witty and imaginative. "Never be sincere" was a motto of the Dadaists. However, I seem to be incapable of giving up the habit.

May 2 '17

My life as a philosopher has been lived without the slightest public recognition. I might have liked it at an earlier time, but now it would only be a burden. The opinions of others, no matter how distinguished or numerous, mean little to me. I have come to only rely upon myself for my sense of self-worth, which is the proper attitude in my opinion. Sometimes my books are entered into contests for the purpose of distribution, but not for public acclaim. As an ancestor of mine once put it in a different context: "Be of good cheer, I have overcome the world" (Jn:16,33).

May 4 '17

Again I say that my metaphysical yearning is to *participate* in metaphysical existence—not through subservient worship, slave-like obedience, fanatical blind love, and certainly not through analyzing spirituality as do the academics. My yearning is to become a part of the metaphysical universe, wherever that may be.

May 6 '17

Entering into metaphysical existence is a *change of state*, analogous to a liquid gasifying or to matter becoming energy. To be sure, these physical analogies are probably far removed from the situation of an individual entering into a metaphysical dimension. They merely indicate that changes of state often occur in the universe. Parmenides and Heraclitus were both right; nothing in the universe vanishes completely and everything in it changes constantly.

May 10 '17

Perusal of the Gospels in all the versions available to me, including the original Greek, has led me to conclude that the historical Jesus of Nazareth had the loftiest metaphysical consciousness ever vouchsafed to a human being. He called it 'the Kingdom of God,' which is perhaps a better term than mine. It is to the eternal credit of the Jewish people that out of them arose disciples who preserved his memory and teachings, albeit without the accuracy demanded by current historical standards. Nevertheless, the above is no reason to convert Jesus into a god and fill houses of worship with totems said to represent him. He was, first and foremost in my opinion, a human being—an example of what is possible for the human condition. There are pros and cons to his populism, in which it is not necessary to blindly follow him. I have no difficulty regarding him as the metaphysical Messiah that had been long anticipated by the people of Israel. Tragically, circumstances led his rejection by establishment Judaism—and then by the Jewish people as a whole.

May 19 '17

A new vision has come to me about why I write. Do I write for the public? Certainly not! For myself? In a certain sense, yes. But principally, I believe I write for 'God,' wherever he may be, within me or otherwise, so that he may know who I am. I do not think he will actually read what I write. I am not so naive as that. Rather I think he will *see* in a metaphysical sense what is in my mind as I write. If I didn't write, he would not know me. Thus, writing is an essential link between myself and God.

May 21 '17

I believe I had an encounter last night with the Ultimate Metaphysical Reality. It was a wonderful feeling of *intimacy* with something transcending myself, a feeling I have never had before. It lasted perhaps half an hour—then circumstances blotted it out. I hope it will return, but in any case, I will not forget the experience.

The world has been too much with me recently. There is no possibility of transcendental experiences under such conditions. I realize few people will take my experience seriously. This does not deter me from treasuring it. What else can be expected from a society composed of lemmings rushing to the sea.

May 22 '17

I feel a certain affinity with the great John Brown of Harper's Ferry fame. He had failed at everything he had put his hand to until he embraced the antislavery cause. To this, he gave himself over fully and without limits. In my mind, I have failed at everything I have tried to do until I undertook philosophy, which has been my salvation. The comparison is just.

May 23 '17

To reread: *The Prophets* by Abraham Heschel

The biblical Jews must have been a *metaphysically aware* people since they refused to give a name to God. The unpronounceable tetragrammaton YHWH was the most they were willing to do. Today, the name 'God' is bandied about as if he were a well-known CEO of a big company. The metaphysical awareness has been lost. Even the Jews of today freely pronounce the name of deity in their prayers for health, wealth, and family wellbeing.

May 24 '17

The Kingdom of Heaven, otherwise known as the Kingdom of God—this key concept of Jesus refers to the metaphysical dimension of the universe. There the spiritual people are first and the 'successful' people of the world are last. Why did he say this? The only answer is that God his father (the Ultimate Reality) made it known to him through mystical experience. This is what people need to know about the religious significance of Jesus of Nazareth. There have been none like him since. For me, he is a religious stimulus rather than a savior.

I wonder if Jesus derived his great powers from the fact that he spoke out his soul rather than writing it down.

May 26 '17

What do I want from my life? I want the metaphysical awareness of the Jews of yesteryear. But I also want to experience the world. Both are necessary for my wellbeing. Finally, I want to transcribe *Notebook* online before my capacity to do so is gone. I try to remedy its defects so that it will *look well* to whoever may notice it. Even more than my body, I want my soul to look well.

May 28 '17

I am more convinced than ever that developing consciousness of the metaphysical dimension of existence is the *most important* task for a human being. Meanwhile, however, I am weary of the adulation given to Jesus Christ in the vast Christian world. He may be a significant figure in the annals of metaphysical thought, but there were many before him and many after. Enough servile adulation!

Been reading Semyon Frank, the Russian religious philosopher, who waxes eloquent on God but is too righteously Christian for my taste. In the future, for my inspirational reading, I have decided to concentrate on two homegrown American mystics—Ralph Waldo Emerson and Henry David Thoreau. They are certainly equal to any of the foreign varieties and superior to most in that they emancipated themselves from Judeo-Christian overlordship. No philosopher who writes under the sign of the Cross is to be fully trusted—not by me anyway.

May 29 '17

As an octogenarian, I feel my mind has never been more versatile, more profound, more conscious of the real universe. Can this be true or am I deluding myself from hubris? I feel in my bones it is true and need to say so. My spiritual maturation has been excruciatingly slow. During the third and fourth decades of my life, I was a superficial, conventional, uninteresting product of my society. No one of any intellectual substance would have wanted to have anything to do with me. But beginning at about forty years of age, signs of interior development made their appearance and some genuine spiritual shoots emerged. Since then, my mind (i.e., my soul) gradually developed until at the present moment I believe I may have fulfilled whatever potential there is within me. Fortunately, my body and brain have maintained themselves sufficiently during this long period of incubation to allow the soul's development to take place.

HDT says in his journal (Aug. 8, 1852) that the entertainment of elevated thoughts unites men of whatever position or era (he does not use the word 'entertainment' in the modern degenerate sense). Thoreau was referring to the 13th century Persian poet Sadi to whom he felt a close affinity. In a like manner, I feel a close affinity to Thoreau even though his way of life was far removed from mine. Even further removed from me is Marcus Aurelius, the Roman Emperor, but when he writes that the fate of his soul upon death would be "either extinction or transmutation" (μεταστασις), I know we are kindred spirits, perhaps in some way even the same spirit. Of course, I have placed my faith in the second possibility; whereas Marcus, besides his role as emperor of Rome, was trained in rigorous Stoic philosophy and, therefore, permits both options open.

May 31 '17

I often receive electronic solicitations to display my books at so-called 'book fairs,' which are springing up like mushrooms all over the world. Besides participation in some of the most vulgar commercialization of literature, there would be a setting aside of scriptural advice, "Speak not in the ears of a fool, for he will despise the wisdom of your words" (Pr. 23:9). Jesus expressed the same idea more forcefully, "Give not what is holy unto the dogs, neither cast ye your pearls before swine, lest they trample them under their feet, and then turn again and rend you" (Mt. 7:6). But I occasionally disobey these scriptural imperatives at my peril.

June 1 '17

I would like to visit Venice to see the final end product of the most commercialized and materialistic society that ever existed in the western world. It has been preserved as a vast museum. I wonder if it is the harbinger of a similar fate that awaits much of America, e.g. Las Vegas, Nevada, where I spent a few days with one of my sons.?

June 5 '17

My private philosophical business has been completed. If I wish, I can go into retirement from the business of philosophizing. No pension is required. Hopefully, the parallel lives can now converge into one.

Notebook 2

All our dignity, therefore, consists in thought. It is from that we must elevate ourselves and not from space and time, which we cannot fill. Let us work, therefore, to think well: this is the principle of morality.

Blaise Pascal, *Pensées*

INTRODUCTION

I can view my life as analogous to a trip to an unknown destination on a *diligence*[1]. Before the advent of railroads and motorized vehicles, horse-drawn carriages called 'diligences' (stage coaches in America) were the main method of long-distance travel in Europe. The trips were arduous on rocky dirt roads, dangerous because of highway bandits and involving stays in uncomfortable overnight inns. If overloaded, the diligences were

---

[1] The Portuguese writer Fernando Pessoa first created the metaphor of a *diligence* as a kind of hearse bringing a person to the land of the dead when his time on Earth was up (*Livro do Desassossego*).

subject to overturning on rough roads. This now obsolete form of travel serves as an excellent metaphor for my own life and perhaps the lives of many other individuals.

I have not intended my notebooks to depict external events that have happened during my 'journey' on the diligence. Rather I have depicted the interior events, i.e., my thoughts and feelings occurring during this period. This notebook continues the style I began with the first *Notebook of a Philosopher* (2017). Augustine wrote that there were only two things worthy of serious thought—God and the soul. The entries largely follow Augustine's advice. The rest is just wind whistling in the trees.

As I read these notebooks in their entirety, it becomes clear to me that running through them like a red thread is a record of a man's search for 'God,' however one envisions that universal, yet mysterious conception. The search has not been successful, but the desire to find Him has been so persistent that it must be meaningful in itself. Somewhere I say that my longing for God is like the needle of a compass always pointing to the north. The compass never reaches the ultimate North Pole, but the constancy of its pointing tells one something about the nature of the compass. My longing for God tells me something about my own metaphysical nature.

Why do I record these things in my little carnet, rewrite them in a more formal notebook while polishing them to the best of my ability, and then transcribe them onto a computer? It all requires considerable effort on my part. The answer is because I believe that in the process I am 'sculpting and polishing' my soul. Because in forcing myself to objectify what is inside of me, I am strengthening my soul for what I believe will be its transformation one day into a new existence. One needs a mystical consciousness to apprehend what I am writing in this Introduction. I realize that in this highly materialist, analytically-minded era, a mystical consciousness is a rarity. Yet I think the most important decision an individual must make in his life is deciding if the God conception represents gnostic *imagination* or an overarching metaphysical *reality*. No religious institution should make this decision for him.

I do not feel, as Stendhal did regarding his own *journal intime,* that I would like to throw its writer out the window. Rereading my notebooks, however, makes me realize that I am not a littérateur but rather a literary sculptor. A little new here, a little take away there. The product is always changing. There is much repetition, which I consider justified by the importance of the issues. Needless to say, absolute consistency should not be expected from me. Emerson, who was quite inconsistent himself, wrote, "Consistency is the hobgoblin of little minds," to which I heartily concur.

For any readers of this writing, I remind them it is a personal affair of mine as noted above. It is not a discursive or instructional writing. I like to have my writings put in attractive book format; this is a luxury with which I indulge myself. A reader who might like to be directed to entries best reflecting my view of the Man–God relationship could go to Oct 15, Nov. 6, Dec 31–Jan 7, May 5, and May 18.

A comment of the nineteenth century poet-novelist-philosopher Alfred de Vigny, much quoted by me regarding readers, is *a propos* here: *attrape qui peut* (catch it who can). If there be a "happy few" who catch mine, that will be fine; if there are none, that will also be fine. If there should be a few individuals who are affected by my writings, that will be their affair, not mine. More power to them.

August 20, 2017

Taking up my notebook again. I do not seem to be able to set this activity aside as I stated I would at the end of the first *Notebook of a Philosopher.*

I have needed to construct my own mental society since I have found none to which I can relate. My society is made up of great men whose writings have affected me. Their proximity to me is metaphysical in nature. I feel in touch with their spirits in a metaphysical dimension. Perhaps I affect them through my immersion in their writings. Schopenhauer envisioned a metaphysical 'Republic of Great Minds.' I have applied for citizenship in this republic.

The above thoughts require a mystical bent of mind. Reality does not fit into the neat little boxes of common sense. Uncommon sense is needed. Genuine philosophy must be metaphysics, i.e. mysticism. So it seems to me.

Aug 2 '17

"Death is the beginning of life, the beginning of a new crystallization." This statement is from the writings of the artist-philosopher, Edvard Munch, one of the greatest artists of our times. However, one must admit that what happens after corporeal death, whether the soul enters into a metaphysical dimension or is transformed into a new 'crystallization,' is a mystery not knowable by living human beings. But that *something does happen* is an absolute conviction of mine.

Nothing of real substance can be expected from anyone who believes his soul will disappear into nothingness upon his death. What would then be the point of any truly original effort? Leaving behind children, oeuvres, or monuments is no substitute for the continuation, in one form or another, of one's own unique soul. As far as those misguided individuals are concerned who have been persuaded that souls do not exist at all, the less attention paid to them, the better.

Rational arguments providing support for the soul's existence are given in my book, *Souls Exist* (2nd ed., 2013). But the real evidence stems from an individual's intensity of feeling, self-awareness, sense of uniqueness, and force of will that characterize one's soul. Scientism has displaced consciousness of the soul in favor of faith in science. Spiritual consciousness is attributed to the neurons of the brain. I would like to sell a famous bridge to anyone who believes that. Science has its place in human affairs but it has virtually destroyed the longstanding awareness of the human soul. A sad state of affairs!

Aug 22 '17

The idea I had that I could withdraw from philosophizing at a certain stage in my life was most fallacious. I find I would as soon stop breathing as stop philosophizing. Mozart's Don Giovanni said that women were as necessary for him as the air that he breathed, the food that he ate. With me, it is philosophy. The expression of my deepest thoughts, which is what philosophy is, is a need that I cannot ignore without deterioration of my soul. It is my connection to Divinity. Therefore, I must provide space and time for philosophy in my daily life—space and time to read, think, and write.

At the moment, I am dividing my reading between Nietzsche and Berdyaev. I have read everything by them before but I get new insights on rereading. They are closer in temperament and views than one might think. Zarathustra and the God-Man could be soulmates. Nietzsche is a consummate literary artist but Berdyaev is deeper. However, I admit I still have difficulties with his Christian outlook.

In his last book *The Realm of Spirit and the Realm of Caesar,* Berdyaev finally admits that Christianity has been a great failure. If he had lived longer, Berdyaev might have enlarged on this statement. The concept of 'God-Man' does not require Jesus to be the only example. Berdyaev could have brought the God-Man closer to Nietzsche's future universal Übermensch.

Meanwhile, I carry on with my double life in the terrestrial and metaphysical spheres. I feel I have no alternative. If reality is dualistic, why should not my life be the same. I am surely a *survivor* of the societal absurdities and harmful attitudes of today.

Aug 23 '17

When I look at old photographs of myself, I realize how much aging has ravaged my body. I can hardly recognize the youth I once was. Now my physical energy is easily depleted. The failings of my sense organs— sight, hearing, etc.—all confirm that I am an *old man,* whose body is gradually decaying. But—my soul is alive as ever, even more so than when I was young. My mental faculties, my emotions, my insights, my *incorrigible* will are all as strong as ever. My soul follows its own path, quite apart from my physical self. No one will ever persuade me of the incorrectness of a dualistic worldview expressing the separate natures of body and soul.

Aug 24 '17

The age-old question—why do I write? More to the point, why do I publish what I write? I don't write for money, fame, or honors since I know all too well that none of these dubious benefits will ever come my way. Yet I continue to write and go through the laborious process of publishing my writings. There seems to be in me a deep-seated imperative that commands me to write and send my writings into the world. It doesn't tell me I will obtain any rewards from this activity or even that others will read my writings. I can only imagine it must be a type of *moral imperative.* I will have to think more on this.

Aug 25 '17

My private copies of *Notebook of a Philosopher* arrived. It has an attractive yellow cover with lines suggesting a notebook. The form of the book is due to the efforts of my wife Melanie. Without her, I would have no literary 'career.' This work is a contribution to American culture—even if no one recognizes it as such.

Sept 23 '17

Another book of mine, *Philosophical Artwork II,* has just appeared on the literary scene. No sign of any interest in it. Fate has marked me to be an isolated thinker in a soulless society. Well, I have learned to love my fate. To paraphrase Samuel Johnson, I cannot aspire to praise; the most I can hope for is to avoid reproach. But I have the satisfaction of knowing I have done my duty.

Sept 26 '17

Emerson in a journal entry bemoans the uselessness of learning Greek and Latin for college students. In his wide travels among 'educated' people, he had only met three who still read Plato (he meant, of course, in the original Greek). Today the number would be zero.

As an aside, Emerson writes, "The good *Spirit of the World* never cared for colleges...and was now creating and feeding other matters at other ends of the world." I would like to know where these other ends are. That He is not at the colleges, I totally agree.

The problem is not the learning of Greek and Latin, the problem is—who is learning them? As for myself, I eternally regret not having obtained reading fluency of these languages during my school years.

I scrupulously avoid discussing my personal worldview with most people. It is an instinctive aversion on my part. It is as though I don't want to *soil* my mind by intimate contact with others. The deepest level of my soul is reserved for divine contacts, not human ones. It is only in this notebook that I can admit this fact about myself.

Emerson quotes Henry James Sr. as saying it is only as we share our existence is it divine. If this be true, I am a lost soul. But I don't believe it; it is only James' deep-seated Christianity that is speaking. I prefer Nietzsche's view to James'; in last analysis, 'sharing' is *dominating.*

Sept 29 '17

Quite disappointed in Max Scheler's, *Die Stellung des Menschen im Kosmos.* The title intrigued me, making me want to know Scheler's thoughts on the subject. But the book (in English translation) is just a medley of dilettante biology, phenomenological psychology, personal metaphysical anecdotes—all with a strong dash of Freudian theory. Scheler thinks 'man' has a special place in the cosmos, but his leading up to this opinion is quite disorganized.

Now I am reading Fritz Heinemann and hope to get a better feeling about German twentieth century philosophy.

Oct 1 '17

If I were to issue the most important commandment for individuals, it would be to become conscious of the need to develop their souls. Becoming conscious of a soul and development of it are simultaneous processes. The word for becoming conscious of one's soul is *self-consciousness.* It is telling that this word has a pejorative meaning in English.

If I were to add a second commandment, it would be to become concerned with the fate of one's own soul and work out a belief about this burning question.

All this requires a metaphysical consciousness that is sadly lacking in societies of the western world.

Oct 15 '17 (eve of my 87th birthday)

After much reflection and soul-searching, there are three items of faith to which I have committed myself:

1. I believe in the existence of my soul as a metaphysical entity.
2. I believe in the existence of a transcendental ultimate reality (God) to which my soul aspires.
3. I believe my soul will undergo a transformation upon death of my body and join God—thereby *enriching* his reality.

I will try to fully assimilate these beliefs into my soul so that they are an essential part of my existence.

I am reading Heidegger's *Introduction to Metaphysics* (1935). His mind operates on a different level than mine, making him hard for me to understand. But I find I am interested in what he has to say even if I do not understand it, something that is not the case for most books I run across. I do not presume to critique or analyze his writing.

Last week, I ordered Fritz Heinemann's *Existenz Philosophie—lebendig or tot*? Now I discover it is in my library (as an inheritance from the former Germanophil owner of the house). I even read it some years ago, making notes in the margins. This mental lapse makes me worry that age is catching up with me.

Sent out my essay, "The One Essential Thing" to two journals today—one literary, the other philosophical. I am not optimistic about the chances for acceptance. My time has not yet come for literary recognition—and probably never will.

My writings have two purposes: a principal one and a secondary one. The principal one is the development of my soul in which I have been successful. The secondary one is to make available my writings to whoever may be interested. I have done this to the best of my ability. *Attrape qui peut.*

Spent the day as security guard at a gallery in which some of my books are displayed. Observing the people passing through makes it clear to me why my books do not sell.

Oct 20 '17

Submitting my work to publishers is like buying tickets for the California lottery—the chances for success are infinitesimally small. Someone would have to be receptive to what I have to say and how

I say it—sufficiently so as to overcome my lack of academic or celebrity status. Given the current environment in America, this is a futile expectation.

Oct 23 '17

I think I am better off living in a country where I have only a rudimentary knowledge of the spoken language. Too close contact with the *hoi polloi* is not good for my soul. Better to keep a healthy distance and communicate only about essentials for living.

This obviously does not apply to reading select books where contact with profound minds in their own language is a great privilege. Right now I am deriving much pleasure from reading Fritz Heinemann in German (albeit with recourse to a dictionary).

Oct 28 '17

The first twenty years of my adult life were spent being alienated from myself. Since that time, I have become more authentically myself but have become alienated from society. I am alienated from my ancestral religion, my profession, my society, and from the literary-philosophical world to which I ought to belong. I have myself, but nothing more (excepting my devoted wife who saves me from utter isolation).

I am not sure if I should attempt to reach out to other people or whether I should strengthen my ability to be psychologically self-sufficient. Since in truth the former option does not appeal to me in any way, I must fall back on the latter for better or for worse. In the world of nature, the mountain lion is my ideal, showing that isolation is a normal possibility among animals—of which I am a representative.

Fritz Heinemann wrote that the world is not in need of existential philosophies, but does need existential philosophers—to which I concur. But none of the philosophers I know about today fall into this category.

When the antique philosopher Hegesias wanted to borrow a book from Diogenes of Sinope (founder of Cynic philosophy), the latter replied, "Poor fool that you are Hegesias, you want real figs, not artificial ones; yet you ignore real life in favor of written rules" (D.L. VI, 48).

This was true existentialism yet I am reduced to reading books like that of Diogenes Laertius. But every time I step into the world of people, my real self disappears like a puff of smoke. Such a quandary!

Nov 5 '17

Now I am immersed in Miguel de Unamuno, *Del Sentimiento Trágico de la Vida*. Unamuno's writings are very meaningful to me. The questions he considers are the ones with which I wrestle. He has said that the English translation of his book is better than the original Spanish version (but I still like to compare the two).

Unamuno stimulates me to rethink my own beliefs (reexamine may be better). What do I want from the few years left of my life? In truth, it is what I have always wanted—to *develop* myself, to develop my mind and my soul. Why is this important to me, more important than all the pleasures and diversions still available to me? There is only one answer that stands the test of my critical thinking—I am preparing to meet God and to provide him with the fullness of my soul. It is not immortality that I crave (as did Unamuno), but joining with the ultimate metaphysical reality. The society I crave is a divine society, not the one in which I am stuck in my terrestrial abode. My life has been a preparation to enter this higher society.

Unamuno would say that no matter how intensely one feels about their soul surviving biological death (as he did himself), one's reason can provide no proof. That is why he entitled his book, *The Tragic Sense of Life*. The best one can do is to think Plato's thought that belief in the soul's survival is a noble risk for the mind and worth taking. This was Pascal's idea in *Pensées*. But the possibility that there is no truth, no *reality* in these noble metaphysical ideas lends them a tragic quality—according to Unamuno. He cannot completely escape the noxious influence of 'Scientism'.

I do not feel that my soul's desire to join with God has a tragic quality. Of course, my mind is not to be completely trusted in metaphysical matters. Even more pertinent is the possibility that God may not consider me worthy of a place beside Him. But I claim only the *desire* that it will come about. If not, it was a noble desire, to paraphrase Plato. Whether desiring it will make it more likely to happen—as Unamuno implies—I cannot say. There is only so much my mind is capable of encompassing. If the desire is noble, that is enough for me. Meanwhile, I can rise above the triviality and grossness of American societal culture.

It amazes me that Miguel de Unamuno is hardly mentioned by the pundits of academic philosophy, even of existential philosophy. He is the existential thinker *par excellence*—on the level of Kierkegaard. Plus the fact of his remarkable erudition with which he quotes from half a dozen European languages, plus Greek and Latin. His problem, I suppose, with academic philosophers is that he is not analytic.

My 'desire' must have significance. Just as my body desires food or drink when I am hungry or thirsty, so my soul desires proximity to the ultimate metaphysical reality of the universe. I have not always had this desire but it is strong within me now. I cannot say it is a consciousness of 'God'; rather it is the desire to possess this reality—and be possessed by it.

Desire rather than faith is the principal feature of my own metaphysics. As I understand him, such was the metaphysics of Jacob Boehme. Immortality, with its temporal connotation, is an irrelevant concept for me.

I write down all this to become aware of my soul's desire. Otherwise, I could drown spiritually in the soul-killing materialism of the society in which I live. Now I am finished.

Addendum to above: I don't pray to God, I reflect about Him.

Nov 6 '17

I need to *schematize* my thoughts about survival of the soul so that I can retain them more clearly in my mind whenever I dip into the "storehouse of my soul."

1. My soul must survive the death of my body. For it to disappear into thin air seems absurd to me.

2. I am compelled to believe in the existence of an Ultimate Metaphysical Reality (God). No alternative seems possible to me.

3. My soul must participate in the Ultimate Metaphysical Reality. For it to float about aimlessly in some kind of metaphysical cosmic space is inconceivable to me.

These beliefs do not rise to the level of 'faith' but rather reflect my considered opinions about my soul and about God. If they are erroneous in part or in whole, at least they have been a worthy conceptual effort on my part.

Meanwhile, I must do the best I can in this life with my neurological apparatus and my emotional qualities to form my soul. To a skeptical reader, I retort, *"honi soit qui mal y pense."*

Nov 7 '17

Looking over my published and unpublished writings, I am astounded at the vast quantity of words that I have written down. There must be some significance in this fact alone.

Undated –

The older I get and the more I wander through the byways of culture, religion, and daily living, the more convinced I am of the necessity of consciousness of one's own soul and of its needs. Without this consciousness, all the paths of life inevitably lead to decadence. One must look to his own soul if he wishes to be liberated from the frenetic rat races that constitute modern societies, especially the American one.

The curse of every society is the lack of spiritual consciousness. An exclusively materialist worldview is like being a ravenous wolf always needing more flesh to feed its appetite.

Nov 9 '17

Miguel de Unamuno in *La Agonia del Christianismo* says Christianity is radical individualism. Jesus was certainly a radical individualist preaching insights that opposed the rigid doctrines of the Jewish establishment of his day. I am a radical individualist who admires Jesus as a revolutionary religious figure placing the emphasis in human life on spirituality. If no further qualification is needed, then I can regard myself as an authentic 'Christian'.

Nov 12 '17– Some Thoughts about Jesus of Nazareth

I consider it necessary to emphasize that from birth Jesus was through and through a Jew. He was circumcised at eight days of age according to Jewish law. He was raised within a Jewish family, he was deeply versed in the Hebrew Scriptures (from which he quoted often without acknowledging his source), he directed his teachings exclusively to Jews, preaching sermons in synagogues, and, most importantly, his teachings were preserved by his Jewish followers— albeit imperfectly due to the development of worship of him, second hand transmission, and translation of his Aramaic speech into Koiné Greek. It is likely that none of the actual writers of the Gospels had any direct contact with Jesus, excepting John who scholars now think was only the titular author of the gospel bearing his name. Still, without these writers, the words of Jesus would have been totally lost to history. Unfortunately, Jesus did not have a Plato (or even a Xenophon), as did Socrates, to brilliantly transmit his thoughts and personality to posterity.

According to the majority of Gospel accounts, the Jews were in awe of him and enthralled by Jesus the prophet and miracle-worker—even if the deification of him was later rejected. The

149

Jewish religious establishment, which feared Jesus and had him put to death, did not represent the feelings of the Jewish populace. Actually, they feared his impact on the people. It may be some kind of strange poetic justice that the most significant Jewish prophet since Isaiah was hijacked by a separatist movement and made into its God. But it must be admitted that Judaism has never claimed the prophet Jesus as its own—perhaps due to a reluctance to accept the testimony of Gospels written in Greek by early Christians. No other primary sources are available.

The only parts of the New Testament I find enlivening are the *sayings* of Jesus himself. They stand out in my mind. The rest of the Gospels seem to me to be composed of fantastic legends and propaganda of doctrinaire believers in the divinity of Jesus Christ. The introduction to the synoptic gospels in the scholarly Jerusalem Bible clearly states the situation: "The purposes of a written gospel are to convert, to edify, to infuse faith, to enlighten, and to defend it against its opponents." Any rearrangement of reality may be thought to be warranted in the service of these aims.

The Jesus of the Gospel attributed to John lecturing on abstruse theological and metaphysical concepts is quite a different one from that of the synoptics. It is hard for me to imagine that the Jewish Jesus formed from Hebrew Scriptures and speaking Aramaic would deliver these kinds of formal lectures to unlettered Galileans, Samaritans, or to anyone else who would listen to him. I think the

Jesus of John was largely an invention of John's circle to suit the purposes of the budding Christian churches.

All this fits into a feeling that the real historical Jesus is lost forever in the mists of antiquity. However, his astounding impact on his followers and on people throughout the ages cannot be denied.

Nov 15 '17

Unamuno is interesting to me because he is deeply involved in metaphysical thought—something that does not exist among philosophers today. His major work is virtually entirely devoted to the question of immortality of the soul. I do not think so much verbiage is necessary for the topic. Heraclitus said what needs to be said, "What awaits men at death they cannot anticipate or even imagine." Nothing more is necessary. I believe something will happen to my soul when death disconnects it from my body, but what it is I cannot know nor need to know. The belief is based on an intuition that I cannot reject.

There are more things in heaven and earth, Horatio,

than are dreamt of in your philosophy.

Hamlet, Shakespeare

Horatio was a precursor to modern analytic philosophy. The quote is only one of Shakespeare's many profundities.

Nov 16 '17 – A Mystical Vision

It has come upon me that God is the vital force within me. My body and brain are like an incubator in which he develops. The development of my own soul is a guise He assumes to further Himself. When the incubator breaks down so that it can no longer serve His needs, God spreads his cosmic wings and pff!, he is gone in a flash. Remnants of biological life may remain for a while but to no purpose.

[Reader, why are you here? This is my private domain that I carefully guard. Since you are here, tread carefully and do not disturb my world.]

Nov 17 '17

There is something deeply wrong with the medical industries of today. This is nowhere more evident than in the treatment of 'hypertension.' It is all profit oriented, leading to fallacious assumptions and assertions. After fifty years of coping with doctors' approach to my blood pressure, I know! But it is only a part of the assaults of society on my personality.

Nov 18 '17

When considering my belief in the transcendent nature of the human soul and its involvement with an ultimate reality, the question inevitably arises as to the impact of this reality on human affairs. How does it relate to the miseries that affect human beings?—war, disease, famine, violence, genocide, earthquakes, floods, fires—the list could go on and on. This question has plagued spiritually-minded philosophers throughout history.

The Biblical story of Job is a prime example of man questioning God's apparent toleration of unjust happenings. The problem was resolved by certain religious thinkers of antiquity who postulated two Gods instead of one. The arch Christian 'heresiarch' Marcion asserted the existence of two ultimate powers in the universe—the stern, cruel Jehovah of the Old Testament and the loving God-Father of Christianity. Manichaeism, a highly successful religion of late antiquity that claimed Augustine as one of its adherents for a time, spoke of the existence of 'Powers of Light' and 'Powers of Darkness.' One's body belonged to the latter, one's soul to the former. In contemporary times, the eminent philosopher Nicholas Berdyaev (a onetime guru for me) expressed a view very close to Manichaeism in *The Realm of Spirit and the Realm of Caesar.*

What shall I believe? The faith I hold that my soul exists is based on a deep and continuing intuitive feeling. My belief in its transcendent nature is similar. However, thoughts about the nature of an ultimate reality, whether unitary or dualistic, are speculative, not intuitive. They do not merit the same consideration as one's intuitive awareness of self. I do not think human beings are privy to all the secrets of the cosmos, even if they are inspired individuals like Jesus of Nazareth or Mani of Persia. The human metaphysical 'shoemaker' should stick to his last, which is his own soul. *Gnosticism* is a vice to be shunned by all serious participants in the human condition.

Nov 19 '17 – On reading Karl Jaspers
Jaspers' post World War II essays assert that the basic problem for philosophy is the conflict between freedom and tyranny (*Philosophie und Welt*). This was the great issue of his day.

Human beings do need political and economic freedom, as well as security and health. One must make his contribution to a society that provides for his physical needs. However, when these needs are met, the *real issues* of human existence emerge—What are we? What shall we do? Where are we going? These are spiritual, not earthly issues. If they are not confronted, an individual degenerates as a spiritual human being.

Nov 20 '17
Had I been born into a different society with a different culture, I might have played some role in it. As it is, I am a non-entity in the eyes of the society in which I live. This may have been a blessing for the development of my soul—the most important thing.

Nov 21 '17
The presence of a transcendental element (i.e. God) within one's soul reveals the significance of one's life. The social whirl without

is analogous to the to and fro movement of ants in their anthills. It plays a minor role in the development of the soul but is important for little else. On its own account, it should not be taken too seriously by serious individuals.

Nov 24 '17

Is the transcendental element mentioned above a 'real' presence in my soul?—or is it merely the product of a solipsistic imagination? What is 'real' becomes the real question. Is it the world without, which deep thinkers since Kant have realized bears little resemblance to one's perceptions? The world without is a mysterious world of matter and energy. Limited human beings like myself can have no inkling whatever of its basic nature or purpose. What I only really know is my interior self and its consciousness of a transcendental element within it. That is what is 'real' for me. When my soul is finally released from the constraints of its body, I may come to know more.

Nov 26 '17

From an early age, I wanted to read books that I deemed important, worth reading. I began to study Latin on my own at age 11 yrs. I was never interested in comic books or the like. Now I see these were the first signs of a drive toward *transcendence*, a desire to move beyond myself.

One seeks out God as one seeks out significant literature or art. The direction of movement toward transcendence is usually centrifugal—outward from the self. Actually, it should be centripetal—inward toward the self. The term 'God' has been so misused as to undermine its suitability to refer to a divine transcendent being. I prefer the term 'ultimate metaphysical reality' instead of God.

What is the reason or purpose of my constant searching for transcendence? Is it all meaningless? I cannot accept this thought. There must be meaning to my searching even if I am unable to discern it.

Speculation on the meaning of one's search for transcendence expresses what one *wishes* to be the case instead of what one *knows*. But what in last analysis is the difference? Ultimately one knows nothing (Socrates' assertion) but can wish for much. One becomes what one consistently wishes for. *Desire* is the basic ground of human existence, as was taught by Jacob Boehme.

If desire is the basic element of my existence, I am free to choose what I will make of myself. I can decide what I desire. If I genuinely desire to know the ultimate metaphysical reality (God), I will acquire its features. I will develop myself in that direction.

"Love of God" essentially means the desire to know God. This is a powerful drive in metaphysically minded individuals such as myself.

In last analysis, the only ultimately valid knowledge in the ordinary meaning of the term is *utilitarian* knowledge that secures one's existence in the world. The ancient sophists were well aware of this fact, which is what distinguished them from Socrates. Utilitarian knowledge has its purposes but ought not to be overvalued in the larger scheme of human existence.

If there is such a thing as a meaningful *ontology*, it must be constituted outside of the space-time continuum in which individuals live their daily lives. The hope for immortality must be abandoned in favor of the wish for eternity. If I think of 'developing' myself, it cannot be in a temporal sense even though my mind seems to be incapable of visualizing the process in any other way.

Alfred North Whitehead said the same in his books but in an unnecessarily complex manner. Unnecessary complexity is an inbred vice of philosophers.

Nov 28 '17 – Night Thoughts

Life is a metaphysical force that science has not explained and will never explain.

- The human soul is a special form of life. Human life is the highest form of life because it can evolve into a soul.

- Death ends the mystical connection of a living organism with its constituent living cells.

157

- The individual lives of cells of a living organism are dependent upon and subservient to the ruling life force of their organism. Death ends this relationship.

- The problem of the survival of the human soul is a special problem of the survival of the life force.

- There is a selective principle regulating the fate of the different varieties of the life force. The fate of the human soul is more important than that of the life of unicellular organisms.

- An Ultimate Metaphysical Reality regulates the fate of the diverse forms of life.

- A human soul possessing a higher consciousness is aware of the existence of an Ultimate Metaphysical Reality and yearns to be 'involved' with it.

- One does not know the fate of his or her soul when it is cast loose from its body but it is reasonable and *necessary* to realize that it becomes involved with the Ultimate Metaphysical Reality. Absent this realization, human life is a tissue of absurdities—as has been recognized by many thoughtful individuals.

Nov 30 '17

I think yearning to find the Ultimate Metaphysical Reality (a.k.a. God) is the only legitimate means of relating to Him. When this yearning attains to a certain level of intensity, it may be called the love of God. All other ways claimed to relate to Him are either attachments to traditional myths or are hallucinations. Religious rituals, obeying God's commands, prayers of praise or supplication—all these are at best only expressions of the yearning to find Him. One yearns to know God as an orphan yearns to know his natural family. But the God who is the Ultimate Metaphysical Reality cannot be 'known' by living human beings. One must wait until the mortal coil has been shuffled off to know Him.

The yearning to find God is a sign of elevated consciousness in an individual since it presupposes awareness of His existence. If the existence of God is denied or ignored by an individual, there is no chance of knowing him. Such individuals are 'fools' (spiritually deficient), as a Psalmist once said (Ps. 14).

All this was expressed by Seneca two millennia ago in his *Consolation* and *Epistles*, but in a more exalted manner.

Dec 2 '17

According to the New International Version of the Bible, the term 'fools' in the 14th Psalm is a translation of a Hebrew word meaning morally or spiritually deficient. Lack of consciousness of the existence of God is a spiritual deficiency. It is the condition of most 'educated' people in the present age.

Undated –

If I had been part of a circle of university intelligentsia, of which a few exist in the USA, I would not have been capable of writing the books that have made me what I am; instead, I would have spent time and energy at the conferences, congresses, seminars, and preparing lectures that are required of university intelligentsia. I would have written scholarly tomes instead of existential works. I have much preferred the rich private life I have led with my wife Melanie and the leisure to read, think, and write in my own way. Public life may feed one's ego but provides little else in my opinion.

My books have almost all been published at my own expense. In spite of the prejudices against self-publishing, I consider it to be an honest way of presenting one's writings for public scrutiny without requiring the inflated advertisements of marketing. Commercial literary life is like a book I once had in which the first few pages were enticing, but the rest of the book faded out. Something is commonly missing from the commercial literary world. It is called *honesty*. Without honesty, literary or otherwise, one's work is a fraud.

Undated – Peter Sloterdijk, *Rules for the Human Park*
Sloterdijk has provided the latest version of a utopia in which the 'shepherds' (guardians) arrange things for the best in society. He relies heavily on Plato's dialogue *Statesman* for guidance. He utilizes the age-old ideas of how to improve life on earth for

mankind. None of these have ever worked out to improve societies; beginning with Plato's ill-fated ventures into the Greek cities of Sicily and through the French Revolution, socialism, communism, anarchism, fascism—all the 'isms' that have made the life of individuals worse than before.

What is missing in Sloterdijk's book is an awareness that the human soul must undergo a metamorphosis into a new reality, a religious transformation. By religious, I mean emergence of a metaphysical consciousness. Religious symbols and dogmas have been no more successful than political utopias in changing the human soul. Regarding Christian beliefs, Christ must come down from his cross and resume his role as Jesus of Nazareth, the spiritually inspired prophet of the Jewish people. The Apostle Paul must be read out of the religious world as someone whose influence is a distraction from the development of authentic individual spirituality.

Dec 16 '17

I have completely lost interest in my literary and philosophical surroundings—such as they are. I have absorbed enough of the thoughts of others, past and present. Schopenhauer wrote somewhere that reading was thinking with another person's mind. Exposure to other minds to a certain extent is valuable for one's mental development. But I have passed the stage of profiting from such exposure. What is important for me now is to establish my own worldview and prepare myself for the transition that cannot be far away.

'God' is the ultimate reality that is impossible for me to know or even imagine. However, I firmly believe that I must do my best in this life to prepare my soul for joining this reality. It is of no further benefit to me to be exposed to the thoughts of others, either by reading or verbal interchanges. I have given up on the idea that some spiritual 'grace' will descend upon me. The preparation must happen through my own efforts. What I cannot accomplish on my own will not be accomplished.

If what I have written above is mere fantasy, then upon my death, my soul will quietly sink into oblivion, returning to the state of maximum entropy from which it began. But I do not think this will be the case.

My last readings have been from religious existential philosophers who believed in God. Lev Shestov was a Russian litterateur, Abraham Joshua Heschel a philosophical Rabbi, and Karl Jaspers a German university *Philosoph*. They all had very different approaches to the God questions. None of them, however, represented my point of view. The only philosopher who ever really touched my soul was Friedrich Nietzsche—and he went mad. I hope not to follow his example but I recognize my independent life status is becoming increasingly precarious. I'm too old, too computer illiterate, and too intellectually isolated. The United States is a strange foreign country for me. I can say no more.

Dec 17 '17

It has come to me that awareness of the spirituality of self (one's soul) must precede awareness of the Ultimate Reality called 'God'. To love God "with all thy heart, all thy mind, all thy soul, and all thy strength" as Scripture recommends, one must be conscious of his existence. Those who are not conscious of their own metaphysical souls cannot possibly be conscious of God.

The Psalmist cries, "As the deer pants for streams of water, so my soul pants for you, O God" (Ps 42). Because it is difficult to find him, people create surrogates as substitutes. The Torah, the Virgin Mary, Holy Scripture, Jesus Christ himself are all surrogates for Divinity. But the principle enunciated by Thoreau that when one is at the pearly gates, "do not speak to any of the servants, ask only for the Master himself," holds true for all spiritual encounters.

The simplest definition of 'faith' is awareness of the existence of an Ultimate Metaphysical Reality (a.k.a. God). All additions to this definition would be superfluous.

My favorite book in the Bible is *Psalms*. It is the most personal and 'existential' of all the books. If I could add to it, it would be:

Psalm 151

Blessed be the one in whom the Lord makes his presence known, i.e. possesses a metaphysical consciousness;

Blessed be the one who has this consciousness all the days of his life.

Dec 18 '17

The long history of the Catholic Church conducting its rituals in Latin (lessened lately), a language incomprehensible to most, has been imitated by academic philosophy, with its incomprehensible technical mumbo-jumbo. The philosophy of universities today requires a long period of study to be comprehensible to a reader.

Immanuel Kant, the quintessential professor of philosophy, set the example of turgid prose, which has remained the ideal of academic philosophers ever since. His few important thoughts are buried in a mass of densely stated abstractions. Gone are the days when educated readers could be enlivened by philosophy. Goethe, one of the profoundest thinkers of all times, would have nothing to do with philosophical gibberish. Ditto for Heinrich Heine, Ralph Waldo Emerson, Friedrich Nietzsche, Nicholas Berdyaev, and many other truly humanistic thinkers.

The original thinkers of the past have virtually always been independents working outside of universities. The confinement of philosophy to universities has been catastrophic for it. The breed of independent philosophers seems to have disappeared during the twentieth century in the English-language world. All that exists today is the professional gibberish of professors. Whenever I hear someone purported to be a philosopher addressed as 'professor,' I cannot help a visceral reaction of contempt. In the old wild West, a 'professor' was someone who played the piano in a whorehouse.

Dec 20 '17

I continue to be aware of really how much I yearn to find 'God'. The yearning, however, is never fulfilled. I never feel an intimate association with Him. I do not think any intimacy will occur during my lifetime; what will happen afterwards is an impenetrable mystery. But the yearning seems to be a constant feature of my life. It must have some significance. God for me is a hidden God, a *Deus absconditus*.

Had a long discussion with Fr. X. today. Even though he is a Catholic priest and I a free-thinker, we both have remarkably similar theologies. Beyond that, we both are essentially trapped; he in the grip of the Church; I in the demands of bourgeois life.

Dec 22 '17

The most important thing in the life of an individual is to prepare his soul for its transition upon death. The preparation requires exposures to and experiences of the manifold facets of the human condition. It requires absorbing their meaning into the initially undeveloped soul.

Intelligence and character play a large part in the process. During its development, one becomes conscious of his or her soul. Without this consciousness, there are major limitations on one's development. The distractions imposed by earning a living in society are too strong to be resisted without appreciation of the significance of the soul. It is revealing and ironical that the term 'self-conscious' has a pejorative connotation in the English language.

I am of the opinion that the Ultimate Metaphysical Reality (God) is in need of developed souls and the creation of a multitude of human lives is His means of insuring the emergence of a few.

Dec 26 '17

A sadness has penetrated my entire being. I can't attribute it to any event, situation, or the current holiday season. It is a deep-seated sadness verging on clinical depression. I have had this feeling before but not as severely as at this moment. Often it dissipates when my usual mundane pursuits take over my life. I don't know what will happen now.

I think this sadness stems from a *metaphysical loneliness* that affects me, a feeling that my soul is alone in the world. It has no friends, no companions, no 'soulmates.' Religiously devout individuals claim that God or Jesus fill this gap in their lives, but I do not feel the presence of God or Jesus or anything remotely resembling them. I have never felt their presence.

I will have to be patient until the sadness lifts and I can return to my worldly existence with its superficial relationships. Perhaps this recurrent feeling of sadness and loneliness will finally be ended when I leave this life and my soul—hopefully—enters into a metaphysical realm. That event is to be fervently desired.

I am told by a 'friend' that I should deal with my morbid disposition. What is there to be sad about, he asks, if one has a loving wife, financial wellbeing, intact physical and mental capacities? He dismisses the idea of a metaphysical consciousness; he is dominated by his rational materialist mind and cannot comprehend my predicament. All this only deepens my feeling of loneliness and strengthens my tendency toward misanthropy.

Ça c'est ma vie.

Dec 27 '17

Went to our secondhand bookshop in Alamos. Even in this remote little Mexican pueblo, the number of English-language books available is incredible. There are so many writers writing so much. Yet how much thinking of others can one absorb? Reading is thinking with someone else's brain (Schopenhauer). Pretty soon, the voracious reader will find himself unable to think original thoughts himself. He will only be able to pass judgment on others' writings. The whole enterprise of developing creativity in one's own soul will come to naught.

I recommend spending about 40% of one's sedentary leisure time (assuming one has true leisure time) in reading and 60% in reflection or writing. Erudition should be looked upon as a vice, not a virtue.

Roaming around Alamos on foot, I feel the pleasure of the simple life. There is not one traffic light and pedestrians outnumber motorized vehicles. People are attending to the basics of their life. I could abandon my preoccupation with writing and live here contentedly while awaiting the great transition of physical living to ???. Writing down this thought impresses it on my soul and may make its realization possible one day.

Dec 28 '17
Had a spiritually significant telephone conversation with my son. A great pleasure for me.

Dec 31 '17
On the last day of 2017, an insight came to me during the night while I was still in bed. Nighttime in bed is sacred to me; the distractions of the day are absent and my soul has the benefit of aloneness.

I came to the realization that I am alive in order to fulfill the needs of God. My soul is essential to him. The principal purpose of my life is to create a soul for his benefit. I am his workshop where he develops himself in the guise of my personality. Without my participation in this project of God, my life would be meaningless, purposeless, "a tale told by an idiot, signifying nothing." All the comings and goings of the world are merely the infrastructure of God's metaphysical project; if they do not have as their goal the creation of souls, there is no point to their existence.

At this stage in my life, other individuals or their books have little to offer me. They need to step out of the way of the movements of my soul toward the Ultimate Metaphysical Reality, which is God. My attitude toward religious institutions is unchanged; they are part of the infrastructure of God's project with individual souls, and must not stand in the way of the latter's free development. Tragically, that is usually not the case. Buddhism may be the best of the lot (as Einstein thought), but it has not been part of my formative years. Also, I believe in the essentiality of a strong personality, which Buddhism seems not to foster. The figure of Kierkegaard is more inspiring to me than all the Buddhas or all the saints of Christendom.

Now I must let this revelation ripen in my mind and assure its permanence.

January 1, 2018

'Revelation' for me does not mean a message from a distant deity, it is an awareness that has been incubating *within* me and finally emerging into my consciousness. My awareness of the immediate presence of the Ultimate Metaphysical Reality falls into the category of an internally generated revelation. I *feel* that this reality exists. No doubt many factors may be responsible for this revelation —my upbringing, my life circumstances, my experiences, my education (largely self-acquired), and so forth. But additionally, I believe that in some way my soul is part of this UMR and, as such, I can develop consciousness of what and who I am. I can't universalize this thought, I only speak for myself.

My whole interior life has trended in this direction—beginning with my adolescent interest in philosophy, then existing underground during my misguided entry into a career in academic medicine, and finally giving up a tenured professorship in order to return to independent philosophy.

Writing has in large part formed who I am at the present moment. All my vague feelings and disconnected thoughts are welded into a coherent whole for me through writing. This is the principal purpose for me to write; the question of readers is an irrelevant side issue.

Now, at 87 years of age, awaiting my soul's transition from terrestrial life, I must treat the divinity within me with proper reverence. I hope that after the transition, my soul will find its appropriate destiny. But what this may be is not for me to know now. Those who tell me that belief in an after-life is an absurdity do not believe in the existence of their own souls. They are the 'fools' referred to in Psalm 14.

Jan 3 '18

I must again confess that God is really more of an aspiration for me than an actual presence. My soul yearns toward him. I have a sense that he needs me as well. That is as much as I can say regarding my "belief in God." That is how I interpret the Scriptural injunction to "love God with all thy heart, all thy soul, and all thy strength" (Dt. 6:5-6). Jesus famously quoted this as the most important commandment, adding 'mind' to the faculties utilized in the love of God (Mk 12:30-31). This was a most important addition on his part.

Jan 7 '18

Reality is what I have been seeking ever since I threw over my academic life and published my first philosophy book entitled *Affirmation of Reality.* But 'reality' is a complex multifaceted conception. Reality for my senses is the phenomenal existence of the world. But reality for my soul exists in a metaphysical dimension, quite apart from the physical spatial world. God and my soul exist in a metaphysical 'space'. Thus, I cannot conceive of either of them existing in physical space. They have no spatial features, only qualities. I have come to think my soul has been 'thrown' into my body (shades of Heidegger!) in order to develop. When my life is over, it will return to its original metaphysical state, but in an enriched condition. The Buddhists call this state *Nirvana,* but I call it fulfillment of its destiny.

Since I am now physically old and my bodily existence is wearing thin, I have turned my attention to metaphysical existence. Is this latter a reality or merely a figment of my fevered imagination? I answer it is as much a reality as is the world of my five senses. One may believe in one as well as the other.

The time-honored concept of *faith* for me is belief in the reality of a metaphysical world. This faith comes from the depth of my inner self—perhaps it is a gift from God. Excessive attention to the perceptions of the physical world stifles my awareness of the metaphysical one, and stifles my awareness of God himself—never mind my culinary and sexual appetites!

Jan 10 '18

Whoever comes telling me about the meaning of life and says nothing about Jesus of Nazareth called the Messiah has nothing of value to tell me. Jesus shifted emphasis from the material to the spiritual aspect of the human condition—a revolutionary change for the Judaism of that time.

Miguel de Unamuno asserted that whoever looked upon the figure of Jesus with affection and respect is a Christian. If this definition holds, I am a Christian.

I have been carefully perusing the book *Athens and Jerusalem* by the Russian-Jewish philosopher Lev Shestov (Léon Chestoff). He is excessively garrulous in his writing (a trait of most philosophers), but I still feel he has something of value to teach me—an uncommon feeling for me. I haven't quite decided what that something is. He writes that 'faith' has been neglected in western spiritual development in favor of logic and rationality, but he never quite says what that faith should be. 'Faith' without the content of faith is a meaningless term. His followers need to create their own content of faith to supplement Shestov's vagueness.

Jan 13 '18

I think it important every so often to honestly examine the direction of one's life of the past and its errors. Otherwise there is no possibility of affecting one's future.

Early in my adolescence, I became aware of the pull philosophy exerted upon me. I majored in philosophy at New York University. But then, because of improper influences from my family, especially an uncle whom I will not name, I entered upon a career in medicine, even though I was totally unsuited for that profession. In the New York City of my youth, Jewish boys strove to become doctors. My parents were exhilarated when I was accepted into several medical schools. But instead of striking out on my own in philosophy, I supinely followed the expectations of my family. It was the first evidence of a certain character flaw in my nature.

A similar sign of a character flaw was marrying my first wife. I realized months before the wedding that I did not want to marry her. But because I could not bring myself to break my commitment and bring pain upon her and her family, I did not end the engagement. Even though the marriage lasted many years, I see it now as a sad mistake. I did not have the courage to do what I should have done.

When I reached my fortieth year, probably because of dissatisfaction with my entire life, I entered into a period of involvement with various other women that lasted for a decade. Since I was married, it was necessary for me to live a life of deceit. This produced constant anxiety in me and misery for my wife. No doubt this era had a permanent effect on my soul. I should have terminated my first marriage far earlier than I did. I told myself I remained in the marriage for the sake of my children but the reality was that I was afraid of my wife's rage and hysteria. It was another sign of my character flaw.

It pains me greatly now to realize how poorly I treated my parents once I left the home of my youth. Driven by my career ambitions, I lost interest in maintaining a relationship with them. The Scriptural commandment to "honor thy father and mother" was ignored by me. Now I deeply repent my ungrateful behavior, which I can only attribute to a character flaw.

As a Jew, I was heir to a three-thousand-year-old spiritual tradition. This I discarded after my Bar Mitzvah as if it were a worn-out dishrag. I saw being Jewish as an impediment with no redeeming features. It is no excuse to say I was not provided with any spiritual inspiration from my family or my Jewish experiences. I should have had sufficient wherewithal to look beyond them.

All these errors date from the first half of my life, but their influences persist up to my present state. I am not sure that repentance is of any help for my soul. What is done, is done. Yet somehow I feel relief putting down my 'sins' on paper. Perhaps a merciful providence will make allowances for my weakness.

Jan 14 '18

It comes to me that consciousness is not the only requirement for the soul to flourish; *character* and *freedom* are required as well. One must be able to do what is right in the face of adversity and the need to survive in the world. Suddenly, I fear for my own soul's fate! Is it true that fear of the Lord is the beginning of wisdom? I must be becoming wise; I am afraid—but of what? Of whom?

Jan 17 '18

Sometimes in the darkness of the night, I lie in bed awake and fully conscious, but without any feeling of my body. All my senses are quiescent; there is no input from them to my mind. I am unaware of the passage of time. It is a pleasurable state, which I often am reluctant to end.

I think this condition is akin to dying, except I can return to my terrestrial life at will. With death, there is no return; one's soul must move on—but to where? I do not know the answer but, to tell the truth, I do not wish to know prematurely.

Jan. 19 '18

Like the needle of a compass always pointing north, my mind keeps returning to thoughts of God. There must be some meaning to this phenomenon.

I realize now that my upbringing was completely devoid of any spiritual experience; i.e., devoid of awareness of any ultimate metaphysical reality. Perhaps now the long damned-up need is finally coming to light. But I want no surrogates, I want only the real thing. The only need I feel is the need to know God—and I think he wants to know me.

If one reads as I have the Book of Psalms in their entirety, it is evident that their composer(s) are overcome with the need to know God. Was this a neurotic delusion or a higher consciousness? The answer determines the course of one's life—Freud or God, spiritual nonexistence or spiritual awareness?

The best time for fruitful meditation on this subject is at night when the rest of the world is asleep and there are no distractions.

Jan 28 '18

It seems evident to me now that the closest I can come to God is to yearn for a relationship with him. The relationship does not truly exist. I have no genuine feeling of his presence. There are two possibilities to explain his absence; either the God I yearn for does not exist or the person that I am is incapable of forming a relationship with him. I am inclined to accept the latter possibility. An additional thought is that the immensity of his existence cannot have any meaningful connection to a miniscule speck like myself. This thought may account for the Christian conviction that Jesus, whom they believe to be God's presence among mankind, unreservedly loves them.

My upbringing and early adult years were singularly devoid of any spiritual experiences. My ethnic Jewish parents were completely secular. The one exception was their insistence that I undergo Bar Mitzvah, which turned out to be a spiritual zero. I spent a whole year learning to read aloud a section of the Torah in Hebrew, of which I understood not one word. After that, I wanted nothing to do with the Jewish religion.

As a young man, I was contemptuous of any type of religious practices. How can I now expect at my age to be capable of a spiritual relationship with a metaphysical deity? The precursors of such a relationship are utterly lacking in me. I have to accept this distressing reality.

In my opinion, spiritual experiences for children are just as important as proper nutrition or acquiring literacy. They form a ladder upon which an individual can climb toward deeper spirituality. In the secular society in which I grew up (and still live), I did not receive these experiences nor did I provide for them for my own children. I greatly regret all this but there is nothing to be done about it at this point in my life. What has been done cannot be reversed. My children (who are now adults) will have to fend for themselves—as I have to. Repentance for one's mistakes may feel good but it does not undo them.

Still, I would like to do what little I can to make up for my deficiencies. I need to give more thought to this subject.

Later...Since I cannot accept that the historical figure of Jesus of Nazareth (the greatest Jewish prophet) could become my savior and the excesses of Islam are repugnant to me, I must try at this late date to associate myself with my ancestral faith of Judaism. But how in a manner that is meaningful to me?

Feb 3 '18

Conversed at length yesterday with Fr. X. about my 'God' problem. He thinks my yearning is evidence of my involvement with God. Maybe he is right.

Feb 6 '18

I have settled on the attitude that my yearning for God cannot be satisfied by surrogates—whether they be rituals, prayers, the Torah, the Holy Virgin, or Jesus Christ. It must be the "Master of the House" or nothing. It is really not to be expected, however, that the one God would have features discernible by mere human beings. This was the view of the profound medieval Jewish thinker Maimonides.

Therefore, I must be satisfied with waiting until I shed the mortal coil in order to experience God more intimately. Either my soul will dissipate into the surrounding milieu, in which case I will feel no disappointment—or I will become involved with God and a whole new dimension of existence will be open to me.

Meanwhile I prepare myself for the great event. I believe this is the proper attitude for me to take. All the ways I can develop my soul are still available to me. Not a moment can be wasted as my time left in this life is short.

Faith in the existence of one's soul is necessary to develop it. "The noble (*vornehm*) soul has reverence for itself." This was Nietzsche's way of expressing this faith. One can hardly express it any better.

Feb 8 '18

I have reread my book, *Toward an Existential Philosophy of the Soul*. It is the most complete and best exposition of my views on the subject. I am no longer capable of writing such an organized discursive book and will have to be satisfied with writing fragments in my notebook as they occur to me.

Feb 18 '18

A metaphysical ultimate reality exists to which I will someday relate—that is all that is necessary to incorporate into my consciousness. But all expressions of consciousness of God, ranging from American Indian totem worship to Spinoza's "intellectual love of God" are worthwhile and meaningful in my opinion (even if I myself cannot worship surrogates). It is only disinterest or disbelief in God's existence that I think reprehensible. Religious institutions are of value insofar as they promote in some way consciousness of God. They are reprehensible, however, when they sow intolerance and bigotry. No religious institution has a monopoly on God consciousness.

It is enough for me to simply have a God consciousness. Since he does not communicate with me, I have no knowledge of his will. Nor do I have any idea of the nature of my relationship with him or what will become of my soul once I leave the terrestrial realm of existence. All I can say is that I yearn for my presence in Him. Perhaps this is some proof of his existence.

Feb 19 '18

I find myself often overwhelmingly sleepy during the day. Is this a sign of waning of my vital energies?—a harbinger of my imminent demise? Or does it only indicate boredom with my current existence? It is probably a mixture of both factors. Were it not for my deep attachment to my wife, I would find little to keep me here.

I am like a God to my three dogs. They yearn for my attention and monitor my every step. Perhaps God's feeling for me is like mine for my dogs—interest, affection, a sense of responsibility—but all at a great distance from my own existence.

Feb 21 '18

Rather than a dogmatic faith in an almighty, all pervasive deity, humanity today needs a *metaphysical consciousness centered on its own soul.* But with a metaphysical consciousness, there inevitably arises the yearning toward an ultimate metaphysical reality (i.e. God). The only effective way toward this reality, in my humble opinion, is through one's own soul.

From now on, I write G-d to refer to the deity. Spelling out his name implies a familiarity with him that is not warranted. The ancient Hebrews were aware of this and wrote YHWH.

How can I develop and maintain my metaphysical consciousness?—reading, writing, and keeping myself open for meaningful experiences. Others may have other methods.

Feb 25 '18

Faith as an unquestioning belief in some thing or some conception seems to be a need of the soul. Without faith in something, an individual desiccates, becomes skeptical of everything, finally cynical and sarcastic toward the world.

For the individual person, the problem is where to put his faith. The most common object of faith is the conception of an almighty G-d, a *religious* faith. Faith in G-d surrogates is common as it is easier to believe in visualized objects like Jesus, the Virgin Mother, various saints, and so forth than in an apophatic deity.

Other objects of faith can be holy scriptures, nature, homeland, ancestors, family, and even professions. Highly educated persons may put faith in literature or the arts. Today, many have faith in the power of science to produce a better world. None of these other objects of faith have the strength of faith centered on G-d. However, faith in G-d based solely on ancestral or scriptural traditions does not seem reliable to me as a basis for faith. One must discover and rediscover his own truths.

None of the objects of faith enumerated above have proven effective for me. The faith I have evolved—over a number of years—is faith in the potential of my own soul. I remember having quoted Nietzsche before, "the distinguished soul has reverence for itself." This maxim is burned into my mind. I call fulfillment of the potential of the soul *wisdom* (Attic *Sophia*). It is discussed in the antique 'wisdom' literature, especially in the *Book of Wisdom* included in the apocrypha of the Old Testament. Why the arrangers of the Jewish and Protestant Bibles saw fit to exclude this book from their canons, I do not know. It is included in the Roman Catholic Bible, which is how I gained access to it.

'Wisdom' for the religious writers of the Hellenistic world was understood as a form of divine grace, a gift from a beneficent Deity uniting the recipient soul to it. However, I see acquisition of wisdom as a creative activity of an *individual human being* arising from his or her own spiritual efforts. This requires for me a mix of experiences, reflections, reading, and writing. But expecting wisdom to drop into one's soul like manna from heaven is an unrealistic expectation. If the effort acts to unite me with G-d, so much the better!

Mar 3 '18

Back in Vieille Menton. The Germans have a saying, "*Glücklich wie Gott in Frankreich.*" (Blessed like God in France). The blueness and horizons of the Mediterranean Sea are good for my soul.

I have decided the Wisdom writings of the Old Testament refer to something very similar to my concept of spiritual development. However, for the Wisdom writers, 'wisdom' is an existent jewel waiting to be appropriated. For me, it is a 'metaorganic' development to be created through individual effort.

Meanwhile, although I am happy in Menton, I do not think it a suitable place for metaphysical development. It is too oriented to what Freud labeled "the pleasure principle." Much of my life, I must confess, has been directed by the pleasure principle. But not all, not all.

I am rereading *Spiritual Pathways*, a book I wrote about five years ago. I fear I have fallen off from the heights of metaphysical awareness that I reached toward the final portion of the book. It inspires me to read it now. Did I really write it?

Mar 9 '18

Exodus 33:20 relates that when Moses asked to see G-d, He replied; "You cannot see my face, for then you will surely die." I have a different take from the usual interpretation of this statement. I think it means that only after death can one 'see' the face of G-d, that only after one's soul enters into pure metaphysical being, can it experience directly the ultimate metaphysical reality that is G-d. If one tries to experience Him prematurely, he will die to the world. This thought does not appeal to me. It would be like being blinded by staring into the sun.

Mar 10 '18

I am impressed by the importance of sensual pleasures of *all* types for maintaining one's spiritual life at a high level of existence—

especially an aging body like mine. Freud knew whereof he was speaking when he viewed the pleasure principle as a fundamental aspect of human life.

Mar 13 '18 - 3:30 AM

My chronic hand tremor has almost disappeared! I attribute this welcomed event to a spiritual experience that I have just had. I leaned out my window facing the Mediterranean and heard the tides for the first time. There was no extraneous noise to divert me from hearing the sounds of the sea. In an analogous manner, I believe I have felt the influence of G-d for the first time. He seems to urge me to continue on my path of writing about the soul. Up to now, I have thought it was my own drive to do so, but now I think He has played a role.

Mar 19 '18

If my soul does not continue its existence in some way after my death, albeit unimaginable to me at the present time, then all my efforts of thought, all my writing, all my books these past thirty-five years have been exercises in futility. When I think about it, this possibility is disconcerting to me. But I have faith that it is not the case.

I felt closer to August Strindberg through reading his 'novels' than to most other writers. Perhaps some aspect of his troubled soul has found its way into mine.

I was so interested in him that I have looked into the Strindberg Society in Stockholm. My overwhelming reaction was what has all this academic hustle and bustle, all this scholarly frou-frou got to do with Strindberg? Hopefully he is in a place where he is unaware of it, or at least unaffected by it. Heaven protect any writer to whom a society has been dedicated!

Mar 20 '18

I have been thinking about my 'religious' experience of a week ago. The message I received must have bypassed the sensory pathways of my brain and gone directly into my mind (soul). This seems impossible at first glance but what is impossible in physical existence may be possible in the metaphysical domain.

Mar 21 '18

In the Byzantine world of university scholarship, inspiration has no place. The scholar has replaced the seer. Harvard professors are ranked higher than Emerson, Nietzsche, or Berdyaev. These latter merely serve as fodder for scholarly activity and acquiring tenure. Woe to the cultures dominated by scholars! They are sterile, bloodless, worthless…

Mar 25 '18

For many years, I have been advocating through my writings the importance of awareness of one's soul and its metaphysical nature. I have believed this effort on my part to be entirely self-motivated. Lately, however, a thought keeps emerging in me that this may not be true. The motivation seems to be emerging from somewhere outside of myself. Is G-d telling me what to write? I am becoming receptive to this possibility.

Literary society has been generally disinterested in what I write and at times has harshly ridiculed me for what I believe. I have learned to tolerate the disinterest and ridicule. "My kingdom is not of this world," I keep reminding myself. The kingdom is not for me to see in its entirety, even if I know it is out there.

I accept the label of 'mystic'; with all its negative connotations, it is the most appropriate term to apply to me. If one has no regard for mysticism, he will have no regard for me.

My one support is my wife Melanie. Without her, my personality might have disintegrated into a heap of ashes. I know this for a fact.

It is now one o'clock in the morning. The dark Mediterranean Sea stretches out from my window as far as I can see. I know I cannot see its vast extent. The same is true of the metaphysical world in which my soul exists. *Faith* that this world exists is the essential requirement for my wellbeing—and for the wellbeing of all mystical personalities. It is remarkable how often I fall back on sayings of Jesus of Nazareth in expressing myself (e.g., my kingdom is not of this world). How can I account for this? Perhaps a part of the soul of Jesus has made its way into mine. After all, we are related. This assuredly, however, does not make me a Christian in the worshipful sense of the term. He had human faults—as do all revolutionary figures.

In spite of their anti-religious inclinations, brilliant individuals like Heinrich Heine and August Strindberg found great solace in reading the Bible. It is the repository of the metaphysics of western civilization. I share that solace.

With respect to Strindberg, he quotes with approval his fellow countryman Swedenborg who wrote that one must maintain the faith of his ancestors. What am I to do about the 3000-year faith of my ancestors? I have broken away from it. To quote from the founder of Protestantism, "G-d help me, I can do no other." I wish Judaism well but it must do without me. Torah worship is no more acceptable to me than is Jesus worship.

In Vino Veritas. It dissolves in proper amounts the veneer of materialism encasing my soul. But too much dissolves my soul as well. Vigilance is necessary.

Mar 27 '18

Our social life is increasing in Menton. It makes me realize that social life is not very important to me; mainly, it counteracts my feelings of isolation. But, of course, I am isolated. Sociality is a frail crutch to help me get through daily life. It is the *inner* life that counts in the larger scheme of things. I think if social life does not contribute to one's inner life, it is really a waste of time. Strindberg says as much in his fine writing *Ensam, (Alone)*—not *Days of Loneliness* as the authoritative English translation is improperly titled.

I continue to be preoccupied by how one can arrive at consciousness of the presence of G-d. No rituals work for me; Grace? Hasn't happened to me. logical proofs of G-d? Not worth anything in my experience (or Kant's). Maybe I am just a bad lot that G-d prefers to ignore. But there is one thing I feel deeply—developing a consciousness of one's metaphysical self, one's soul, is the key problem of human life. It is the "one thing necessary" to adapt a thought of Kierkegaard. The alternative is to eat, drink, and make merry (fornication) and finally coming to the realization that one's life is absurd. Meanwhile one waits for the diligence to arrive at its destination where one's soul will be weighed and judged.

Mar 30 '18 – (extension of Mar 21)

Again, woe to the society dominated by professors, litterateurs, and money men! They value the superficial ornaments of society—wealth, sensation, and erudition—like painted Easter eggs.

Mar 31 '18

By one calculation, I am about 40 years old. The 'I' I am referring to is my interior self, my soul, which is the only self that has meaning for me. The calculation is based on events of about 40 years ago when, for the first time in my life, I gave precedence to my embryonic soul over all other considerations and allowed it to emerge. I left my soul-destroying career, my family life, and my home and went off to begin to live. In a manner of speaking, I was born again although not in the Christian way of understanding it. At 40 years of soul age, I am now at the height of my spiritual powers.

Unfortunately, my physical age does not match my spiritual one. Physically, I was born in 1930, which makes me now 87 years old, a very ancient man. This is how the world sees me and treats me, an unpleasant situation for me. I can only hope that my physical self lasts a few more years to allow my soul full scope for its development and expression.

A personal cosmology: After many years of meditation on the subject, I have concluded that my soul is connected to a larger reality that I call the ultimate metaphysical reality (a.k.a. G-d). How this connection exists, I would not dare to guess. But I believe that it does exist and influences me. When I die in the world, my soul will return to G-d and enrich Him with what it has made of itself during its terrestrial life. Again, I don't know the details of this enrichment but I feel it must occur.

I feel part of my soul is also coextensive with other developed souls with whom it has been my privilege to make contact, usually through their writings. Perhaps my soul will similarly enter into certain souls of those yet to emerge into this world. We would be all part of the ultimate metaphysical reality.

No one should ask me how my beliefs fit into the commonsense dimensions of time, space, and causality because I could not answer. They are an *uncommon* metaphysical sense. Nor should anyone *expect* me to explain my views, for as much as I may elevate my consciousness of the universe, it cannot fully apprehend the ultimate reality.

April 1 '18

Sin—the concept that is the real driving force of Christianity, especially of Roman Catholicism. Sin is defined as opposing G-d's will or acting against his nature. Jesus will not love you if you do not repent of your sins. But since no one really knows G-d's will or His nature, it devolves upon the Christian doctors and prelates of the Churches to define sin. Thus, sin becomes a very uncertain human concept. My definition of sin is failing to develop one's inner self to its fullest possible extent.

On Board the Diligence: A human life is like a journey on a nineteenth century diligence (called stage coach in America). There is information about the starting point but little about the details of the route to be followed or the destination. During the journey, one sees varied landscapes and stops in varied towns. There are fellow passengers with whom one shares experiences and thoughts. Periodically the diligence stops and one can descend to partake of the locale. All in all, the journey is filled with surprises and stimuli, although also with disappointments since the journey often fails to measure up to one's expectations.

However, this notebook is not a record of the external events occurring during my journey on the diligence called life. It is rather of the evolution of my soul during this journey. It is this evolution that is significant, not the mundane events of the journey that, as Thoreau wrote, are only the winds whistling in the trees. In this notebook, my mind, which is the cognitive element of the soul, is recording the *interior* events of my soul. This recording is an important feature in itself since it solidifies and strengthens the insights of my soul. Otherwise, who knows if these insights would be transitory and without significance. The record is there to be capable of reinforcing and further expanding my interior self.

But why do I allow this private affair of mine to enter into the public domain? The question is one that bedevils me to this day. I have no answer. Perhaps I do not want the answer because it would be shameful and embarrass me. Better to leave it in the realm of my unconscious mind.

April 2 '18

Why do I publish my books? Finally, I believe I have come upon an answer. It may be seen by others as mundane, something like the mountain laboring to give forth a mouse. It is quite simple; it is *pride*. Just as a woman likes to display her stylish clothing, especially if she has a slender figure, so I like to display my writings. They are the best part of me. There is nothing to be ashamed of in wanting to display the best aspect of oneself. Jesus said do not hide your light. Pride is a positive trait as long as it is not carried to excess. What if no one reads my books? I cannot help that but I know they are the best part of me and I still want to display them. Henry David Thoreau said he wrote for the same reason cocks crow lustily in the morning. My books are my way of crowing lustily!

April 3 '18

When I write quickly and the sentences flow forth effortlessly, sometimes I feel as if someone is dictating and I am just the amanuensis. Who is doing the dictating? A superior power? I would like to know but I don't expect to find out in this life. Meanwhile, I act as though I were the author.

I am drained and exhausted but I don't seem to be able to call a halt to this notebook. The one dictating keeps me at it!

April 4 '18

The level of deceit in this society is overwhelming. I am constantly barraged on my computer with 'messages' from banks, pension companies, 'health' providers, insurance companies, literary marketing companies, and much more—all ostensibly providing me with supposedly useful information, but really wanting to sell me their products. The Internet has given them access to my private mailbox. Advertising and consumerism rule the world. If I were ever to receive a genuinely important message, it might well be lost in the deluge of concealed advertising.

What will become of a society where the main criterion of its health is the Consumer Index? Formerly, it was thought that money ruled the world, but now it is just a vehicle for unlimited consumerism. Consumerism is the *fata morgana* for all levels of society. Those who have money consume extravagantly; those who do not, want money so they can consume more. The online retail companies have replaced the shopping malls as the principal agents of consumption. There is no honesty in the world of advertising since everything is directed toward promoting buying. Napoleon said England was a nation of shopkeepers thereby misjudging its capacities. Today he might say America is a nation of consumers, and perhaps correctly judging its capacities.

I am alienated from my society and mentally live outside its pale. For this reason, I have become interested in the writings of August Strindberg. He was most certainly an *aliené*.

Le culte de ce Moi s'affirme donc comme le but suprême et final de l'existence.

Strindberg, *Inferno*

It has come upon me that Strindberg was right; the development and the state of *Moi* (myself) is the supreme purpose of my existence. I can speculate about an ultimate metaphysical reality (G-d), but this is a secondary activity of my mind. I can speculate about the fate of my soul after death, but this is secondary. Faith in these secondary speculations is misplaced; it is faith in the *Moi* that is the truly meaningful one. Naturally for those who are incapable of such a faith for whatever reason, the secondary speculations will have to suffice. This is a sea change in the direction of my thinking.

What a strange labyrinth is my mind!!! But it is all I have to provide me with direction for my convictions. Without convictions, people are sterile and uninteresting creatures.

April 8 '18

There is no interest in America in my writings. Any occasional recognition is a fluke and tends to obscure the reality. Although I make sporadic efforts to reach readers, I know in my heart there is no public out there for my work. An occasional individual, but no public. My writing is entirely justified by the needs of my soul. But that is more than enough justification.

For reasons other than lack of personal recognition, I have come to believe American society is in an advanced state of cultural decay. If my books were to sell to any significant extent, I would have to look upon myself and my work with great suspicion. I do not want to be popular in a decadent society. I am quite satisfied— even proud—with my isolation as a writer.

In tandem with my literary isolation, I try not to be exposed to the national or world 'news.' Much of it depresses or even frightens me. I know that the filter of journalism greatly distorts the reality of current events. Why do I need to agitate myself through exposure to it? Thoreau commented once that he never read anything in a newspaper worth knowing. (I would add the Internet to this). Hyperbole perhaps, but it expresses my state of mind regarding the 'news.'

I don't talk about my personal affairs in this notebook. It is not a gossip-mongering vehicle; it is a means for recording and altering my interior life. I mean to keep it this way as long as the productivity (dictation?) continues. When it stops, these notebook entries will stop.

April 12 '18

When I closely consider the world I live in, I become anxious and depressed. It is not that my personal circumstances are poor; I recognize that I live a privileged life. But I feel that I am living on the edge of a precipice that could collapse at any time. How my society can survive the twin ills of uncontrolled consumerism and galloping technology is beyond me. On top of all this, there is the population explosion in undeveloped areas of the world and vast migrations of peoples seeking a 'better' life (more consumption). It is too much for any society to bear. Unless there arises a metaphysical dimension in human existence, there is nothing left for us other than being doomed to an unsustainable future.

It is likely that I will pass on before the precipice collapses. It is little consolation, however, to think that *"après moi, le déluge."* I do believe in a transcendental supreme being but none of the contemporary western religions give me any solace. The Torah worship of Judaism, the Jesus idolatry of Christianity, the mindless fanaticism of Islam—none of these hold any attraction for me and all are inadequate for the problems of today. The Old Testament prophets are again needed to wake the world up. But who would listen to them?

April 13 '18

August Strindberg in his novel *Kloster* wrote as a side comment that a writer is nothing in himself, but is only what others think of his talent. This is pretty much what the literati think today although they are usually not as frank as Strindberg in expressing their opinion. Strindberg, however, was only thinking of writers who write for a public as he had to make his living from writing. Strindberg was right if one accepts that motivation as the only one. But a writer is also a human being with a soul. If he writes to develop and strengthen his soul, he only needs himself as a reader. Strindberg did not have this conception of writing, perhaps because he was always in need of money. He prostituted his life for his literary career and one cannot admire him for that.

Ideally, attracting other readers would be desirable in order to establish one's place in society. But what if one lives in a society in an advanced state of cultural decadence? Then attracting a public would be a sign of one's own decadence—a condition that does not appeal to me at all.

April 14 '18

A nighttime tale: Once there was a community of human beings living in a clearing on a river bank. It was surrounded by impenetrable forests in all directions. The community drew its sustenance from the fast-flowing river but could not travel on it. The current was too strong to go upstream and there were impassible waterfalls downstream. The people called their river the *Chronos*.

The people of the community had no idea where the river came from or where it went. From time to time, the vicissitudes of life carried people over the waterfalls but then they never returned. Their leaders invented fanciful ideas to explain the origin and destination of the river, but they had no relation to reality. It was only when developed individuals died and their souls floated over the forests in their migration upward did they learn about the origin of the river from snow-covered mountains and its destination into a vast ocean. But these souls could never return to the community to communicate what they had learned.

April 15 '18

The Ultimate Metaphysical Reality (a.k.a. G-d) is lord of the metaphysical kingdom existing *outside* the space-time continuum of the physical universe. This latter with its iron principle of sufficient reason and its cruelties of life seems to be ruled by a Prince of Darkness (a.k.a. Satan). Whoever does not recognize this duality of existence is either ignorant or a fool.

I don't write for a public, I don't even write for myself; I write for the Ultimate Metaphysical Reality who is G-d. I hope he is pleased with my efforts. We need each other. If some think these thoughts verge on madness, they are right. Madness is departure from the world of men. I have lived long enough in the world of men.

I, Richard Schain, may be the most important existential philosopher since Kierkegaard. The fact that no one recognizes me as such is no objection to the validity of this thought. Recognition by society is not required for metaphysical truth. My *alter ego*, Leon Landesman is a worthy successor to Zarathustra. I cry happily in the wilderness, Holy! Holy! Holy!

The image of the mad Nietzsche looms up before me. I don't want to inherit his fate as a helpless shell of a human being. There is no alternative for me but to bear up under the burden of a degenerating society and tread the path I have marked out for myself.

April 20 '18

Confession: Whoever reads this notebook might think I am a spiritual idealist, a model of metaphysical faith, a spotless advocate of the primacy of soul. Nothing could be further from the truth. In fact, it would be the opposite of the truth. I am a repository of all kinds of amoral desires that I have chosen to ignore for this notebook. But they are there and they contaminate my soul. They belong to the terrestrial realm that I have previously mentioned. I cannot bring myself to be specific other than to say they are sexual and violent in nature.

When I wrote earlier that I have nothing to confess, I was referring to my actions—not my feelings or my thoughts. But these latter are integral aspects of my soul and therefore I am a prime example of a sinner and debauchée. I can fully understand how the concept of original sin arose since I feel myself to fall into that category.

It seems to me that my case is not unique. The two-thousand-year-old history of Christianity is permeated with references to the sinfulness of human beings. They are prevalent in mind as well as in deed. Jesus said there were none that were good and he advocated tearing out one's eye if it had led to sinful thoughts. Aside from the fact that both my eyes would have to be torn out to save me from sin, it shows how Jesus viewed mankind. Today one sees obsessions with sex and violence everywhere, but tearing out eyes is not a practical solution. I can easily understand the Islamic practice of veiling woman (even if I do not agree with it). One can go on to note that numerous Catholic priests have abused young boys; the number who have desired to do so but resisted the temptation must be much greater. There are none who are good. Freud joined Jesus in this belief.

However, my business is with myself, not with the society around me. I can control my actions; I can only repress my unsavory feelings and thoughts. They are still there, exerting their baneful effects upon my soul. I can repent but I do not believe Jesus or anyone else will save me, so repentance is of uncertain value. All I can do is hope for the best from an unknown future.

April 22 '18

Reading Antonin Artaud's *Van Gogh, Le Suicidé de la Société*. Artaud wrote it while confined to an asylum. It is interesting that the term *aliénation* in French has a double meaning, referring to madness as well as alienation in the English sense of exclusion from something. This double meaning does not exist in modern English. But it is an appropriate one since being 'alienated' from society predisposes one to madness. Nietzsche is the prime example in philosophy.

In his listing of *aliénés*, Artaud left out Gauguin and Strindberg, both of whom qualify for both meanings.

April 23 '18

From whence comes this drive of mine to *live*? As I grow older, I become more aware of it. I don't know the answer but I am sure it has a metaphysical origin. Artaud wrote that one must distinguish between living (*vivre*) and existing (*exister*); the latter being purely a biological affair. He had insights that come with madness—insights that are hard to come by for we sane mortals.

April 29 '18

Small talk in the social whirl would be justifiable if there were individuals out there worth my getting to know. But that is a debatable proposition. It is like cracking open a thousand oysters to find a pearl. Unfortunately, I no longer have the wherewithal to crack open so many oysters for the sake of one pearl.

I often feel like a character from a Joseph Conrad novel—stranded on a remote South Sea location or the like. Society has passed me by. I live in my own world. Conrad knew about isolation from society. I am a thinker without auditors, a writer without readers, a littérateur without contemporary journals. So I have constructed a society consisting of my thoughts, my journals, and my own books. In my opinion, they are superior to the society that has passed me by. Entering into that society would be the ruin of me.

April 30 '18

The only evidence I have that G-d exists is my *longing* to be part of Him. I use the term G-d without really knowing what it means. I feel there is something outside of me toward which my soul longs but I have no idea what it is or anything about its nature. It is like the magnetic attraction of a compass pointer toward an unseen North Pole. I designate it as G-d for the sake of tradition and the likelihood that those who coined the term felt as I do now. I could easily elaborate 'longing' into loving with all my heart, soul, mind, and strength. But I think longing is a more exact description of my feeling.

Beyond the above, one basis I have for hoping my soul will survive the death of my body is that it might become part of the greater metaphysical reality that the concept of G-d implies. His kingdom is not of this world. However, this is clearly speculative on my part.

More than ever, I am convinced that an amoral force is in charge of our familiar terrestrial world. G-d's kingdom consists of the metaphysical world; thus, reality has to exist as a basic dualism. This idea is certainly not original on my part; it was the essence of Manichaeism, a belief system cruelly persecuted for many centuries by the Catholic Church. Another piece of evidence that Satan has been active in institutional Christianity.

May 5 '18

I have written a book entitled *Souls Exist.* But what is the point of souls existing if there is no reason for their existence other than merely existing? No point at all; one may save himself a great deal of trouble if he has no concern for the state of his soul. One need not bother with learning, thinking, writing, experiencing, seeking wisdom, *creating,* and only do what is necessary for survival and pleasure. One then just needs to eat, drink, and engage in all the forms of making merry. Biological and social instincts lead men and women to act in ways that are more than mere merry-making, but these instincts have nothing to do with one's soul.

The single essential reason for not limiting one's life to the instincts mentioned above is a *longing* to be with G-d. But G-d wants developed souls, not merry-makers or do-gooders. If there is no G-d, there is only merry-making, acquisitiveness, and doing good. None of these lead to the Kingdom of God. And Culture with a capital C has been a great failure in providing a substitute for the Deity.

The Bible naively commands one to help widows, the fatherless, and the needy. But what if widows are miserly tyrants and the fatherless are psychopathic rogues? What if the needy are lazy and deceitful? Help for them will only accentuate their character faults. Beware of being a do-gooder to others! Developing one's own soul is the most reliable form of doing good.

Human beings sooner or later, to a greater or lesser degree, long for their souls to be accepted by the Ultimate Metaphysical Reality named G-d. The developed soul is one's ticket for entry into his Kingdom. For the fools who say in their hearts, "There is no G-d," there is no spiritual salvation—as said a Psalmist eons ago (Ps 14).

According to Jewish, Christian, and Muslim doctrine, the Word of G-d is revealed in their Holy Scriptures. Unshakable faith in this doctrine is thought to be the highest form of Godliness. If this is so, then the fanatical Islamists of today are the highest form of humanity. If G-d really told Abraham to kill his son Isaac, why could He not tell a pious Muslim to blow up a market place filled with infidels and apostates? The legend that G-d changed his mind at the last minute with Abraham is beside the point and probably apocryphal.

In fact, there is no such thing as Holy Scriptures. It is high time for religious individuals to recognize they are only writings of human beings being paraded as such and, consequently, "Holy Scriptures" exhibit all the stupidities and shortcomings as well as the spiritual heights of human beings. Furthermore, the concept of "divinely inspired" Holy Scripture puts a brake upon the metaphysical creativity of contemporary human beings.

May 7 '18 – A Note on the Muslim World
The high Arab civilization of the Baghdad caliphate of a thousand years ago was destroyed by invasions of barbarian Mongol hordes—just as the high Arab civilization of the caliphate in Iberia was destroyed by ruthless intolerant Christians. These were tragedies for world civilization that led to the intellectual decay of Muslim societies and their predilection to mindless religious fanaticism.

May 8 '18 – *Nota bene*
During the Vedic era in India 3000 years ago when the stages of a man's life were conceived by Hindu sages, the normal life span of a person was considered to be 100 years. Thus the four stages of life were divided into 25-year periods. According to my World Almanac, the average life span of a man in India today is 67 years. In Pakistan, in which was located the center of Vedic civilization,

the figure is 63 years. In America, it is 76 years and going down. The sages probably did not consider infant mortality but still…!

May 9 '18 – The Logic of My Faith

1. *Being conscious of an invisible interior self, known as my soul, I have come to realize that it exists as a* metaphysical reality.

2. My soul *intuits* a greater metaphysical reality than itself and longs to be accepted into it.

3. The consequence of these thoughts is that I have *faith* that there exists a *metaphysical reality greater than myself* within the cosmos.

4. This metaphysical reality within the cosmos is named God in English. Its dimensions were referred to as the Kingdom of God (or Heaven) by the historical Jesus of Nazareth.

5. Metaphysical reality does not appear to encompass physical reality. The latter has its own invariant, nonspiritual laws ('Kingdom of Satan').

6. Ultimately, this Manichaean duality ought to be transformed into a unity. But knowledge of how and when this transformation might occur is beyond mortal ken.

May 17 '18

Have been reading Thomas Merton's *Asian Journals*, a collection of his thoughts written shortly before his mysterious death in Thailand, age 55 yrs. Merton was a profound metaphysical thinker. He was committed to the idea of the soul as an aspect of God (Atman = Brahman). As befits a good Christian, he sensed the emergence of a universal consciousness ('communion') based on universal love, which monastic movements ought to lead. But profoundly metaphysical individuals are notoriously bad prophets. Jesus preached the immanence of Apocalypse, which has not happened in 2000 years. Nor is there any evidence that Merton's universal consciousness is coming about, unless one imagines that the universal materialism based on gadgetry that has spread over the world is a form of universal consciousness. Metaphysical fulfillment for individuals will not come about *horizontally*, i.e. through greater involvement with other people; it will come about *vertically* through a deepening of the souls of individuals. Preaching the advent of spiritual universality, the religious expression of globalism, is the most recent version of supposedly divine revelation. It is not happening, it likely will not happen.

May 18 '18 – Fate of the Soul

In spite of my injunction against metaphysical speculations, I have indulged myself in some speculation about the fate of the soul. Spiritualization during one's lifetime may determine whether on death one's soul gains entry to the 'kingdom of heaven', i.e., the metaphysical universe. (I have written much on spiritualization; it is not, in my judgment, merely meditating within a solitary space or engaging in pious exhortations toward universal love.) If entry to the kingdom does not happen, what then? The Vedic philosophers developed the concept of *reincarnation*—passage of the soul into a new living being with new opportunity for 'spiritualization'. This has become a fixture of Eastern religions. Why not? One must imagine like Jesus, "What is impossible for man is possible for G-d" (Lk. 18:27). It is certainly superior to the Christian concept of hell, which has frightened so many people in the past and done much to undermine Christian beliefs.

I differ from the Vedanta view of an infinite 'Brahman' by imagining that the spiritualized human soul can *add something of value* to it. If 'G-d' is infinite and unalterable, then the human condition with all its struggles has no meaning (some have sincerely thought this). However, one can imagine that G-d *benefits* from spiritualized souls. It would be like a new condiment added to a metaphysical cosmic stew (admittedly a crude analogy). One's sense of individual importance is preserved. This humanistic cosmology is within the bounds of reason and is gratifying to me, although no details about it can possibly be envisioned by the human mind.

Where will my own soul go on death of my body?—to G-d or to another living creature? It could be that the latter will be my soul's fate.

May 20 '18

The concept of a ubiquitous *Holy Spirit* describes how I best sense G-d. The other two members of the Trinity, God the Almighty Father and the deified suffering Jesus, have no real meaning for me. My soul is that part of the Holy Spirit developing within my living condition. When I die, I can hope it will return from whence it came, but in a state that adds something worthwhile to its origin.

May 22 '18

Basically, I am a child of my spiritless times. A materialist mentality was stamped upon my mind at a young age. I think much of the energy for my writing stems from the desire to escape this doleful situation. Complete escape may never be possible.

Notebook 3

Man's consciousness of himself as the center of the world, bearing within himself the secret of the world. and rising above all things of the world, is a prerequisite of all philosophy, without it one could not dare to philosophize.

Nicholas Berdyaev, *Meaning of the Creative Act*

July 12, 2018 – An Imperfect G-d

G-d is not perfect; the idea of a perfect G-d merely demeans and lessens the importance of individual human beings whom, I believe, represent G-d developing himself. One's soul refers to G-d working to enlarge his metaphysical self. Thus, to love G-d and to love oneself are one and the same thing.

What does this mean, 'G-d developing himself'? I imagine it to mean 'creating his consciousness.' Spiritual development for human beings is strengthening character, experiencing the world, engaging in relationships, learning, creating—above all, enlarging consciousness. These are the routes to creating a soul worthy of G-d.

In my own case, what does all this mean? I must adapt to my situation—87 years of age, married, limited capacity to function in the modern robotic world. Vital energy diminishing. What must I do? What I have always done for 40 years—objectivize my inner state through writing. In this way, I can develop my soul—and develop G-d. I live. (Living means developing one's soul; ignoring it is merely existing.)

July 14 '18 – G-d Needs Souls

The most important realization—G-d (the ultimate metaphysical reality) develops Himself by means of human souls. When these no longer serve His purpose, humankind will disappear and some new means for furthering G-d's development will emerge; either on this planet or elsewhere. This may be already occurring, as the signs of spiritual decay multiply and as the cult of Christ the Savior weakens Christians. But this prospect does not concern my own life.

I suggest that immortality signifies the incorporation of one's soul into the ultimate metaphysical reality (a.k.a. YHWH, God, Dieu, Dios, Gott, Brahman, etc.).

All one's experiences, all relationships, all learning, all creativity ultimately merge into the common pathway of forming a profound spiritual consciousness. 'G-d' develops himself by incorporating spiritually developed souls into his own being. This I hope will be the fate of my own soul.

The consequence of this realization is that I become aware my life must be devoted to G-d. I had never realized this, thinking I only had the desire to develop myself, but now I am aware it is G-d who is being developed. My existence is inextricably bound to His. I don't think I have fully yet assimilated the import of this realization.

July 15 '18

I ask myself: Richard, why are you writing out all these outlandish ideas? Is this just diverting yourself with the products of your feverish mind? In a former era, you might have been burned on a stake for expressing them, but now in a more tolerant one, you will be just ignored.

I answer: There must be a reason for my existence as an expressive human being. Or am I just a toy soldier, wound up by a frivolous creator so as to lurch about on the pavement of the world until the winding energy is exhausted? Am I just an absurd thing in an absurd universe? My mind rejects these thoughts. I have too much self-respect to accept them. G-d developing Himself through the development of my soul is the best explanation I have for my being alive. If it is an incorrect one, it is a noble belief worth maintaining (as Socrates maintained regarding his own worldview). I refuse to think of myself as a toy soldier lurching about for the pleasure of a frivolous G-d. Regarding the dogmas of Judeo-Christianity—toy soldiers, such as are devout Jews and Christians, cannot be images of their creator.

The quality of human beings that resemble their creator is the will to creative activity. Who knows how this quality arises in infinitesimally small human beings? If you do not develop this quality or abandon it, you become merely a toy soldier in the service of some other.

Awareness of one's connection to the ultimate metaphysical reality (or whatever name one prefers) is a necessary antidote to the banalities of a materialist society. Without this awareness, one's life is superficial, trivial, and finally meaningless. It becomes merely existing instead of living a truly human life.

July 16 '18

There is really nothing surprising about my assertion that G-d develops Himself through the development of human souls. If there is truth to the ancient Vedantic doctrine that "Atman [soul] is Brahman [G-d]," a concept long espoused by profound Hindu thinkers, then it naturally follows that what happens to a human soul happens to G-d. The 17th century German Catholic mystic Angelus Silesius wrote that if he were to die, God would immediately expire. Hyperbole, no doubt, but containing more than a shred of reality. Nicholai Berdyaev, a great spiritual philosopher of the 20th century, used this thought as the epigram of his signature book entitled *Meaning of the Creative Act.*

Original metaphysical thinkers have long known there is a close connection between the human soul and an Ultimate Metaphysical Reality, often termed Divinity. The main problem of the Abrahamic monotheisms (Judaism, Christianity, Islam) is their conception of Divinity as an all-powerful, all-knowing, perfect ruler of the universe who expects his human subjects to carry out his will. Aside from such a servile view of human beings, it is impossible for them to determine what that 'will' is. There is too great a gap in their conditions. Besides, the multiplicity of religions and sects all have different opinions on the subject.

My intuition of Divinity is that of a continually developing metaphysical reality who capitalizes on the ability of living human beings to utilize their lives to develop a deepened consciousness. One might say that Brahman enlarges himself through Atman. Even if Divinity (G-d) is the creator of everything within the universe, it is no objection against his need for developed souls. As an admittedly weak analogy, I create my philosophical writings, yet I learn from them as well. I need them for my spiritual growth.

The Divine Creator may grow through the growth of his creations. If this is no longer possible with human beings (due to the spiritual deterioration of the humanity), he will create a new race of living beings through which he can grow. Nietzsche was incorrect in asserting that God died from his grief over mankind. Mankind may die but G-d won't. But G-d must develop Himself.

Perhaps I have not adequately stated my conception of a developing Deity. My mind and its language have their limitations. My linguistic ability is not overly strong. But I have a powerful intuition that something like what I have described reflects reality.

July 17 '18

The traditional Christian view of the human condition is that the body is an obstacle to spiritual development at its highest level. However, I see my body as the necessary vehicle for this development to occur. How could I spiritualize myself without the experiences that my body affords? These range from simple vision or hearing to erotic fulfillment, from manual record keeping to profound literary creativity. A broad physical connection to the material world is what enables me to discover spirituality.

Charles Dickens' book, *A Christmas Carol*, literarily depicts the situation. The disembodied spirit of Scrooge's deceased partner Marley bemoans his helplessness and urges Scrooge to improve his condition while he is still living. The details of Marley's advice need not be taken at face value. The main point is that the living human condition, i.e. embodiment, is necessary for spiritual fulfillment of a soul.

Of course, those who do not think there is a posthumous existence for souls, or even that souls exist, will not concern themselves with the message of *A Christmas Carol*. But the abandoned and too often abused concepts of heaven and hell still have their significance. Those who have no concern for the fate of their souls and have no awareness of the meaning of eternity may be in for a rude awakening.

July 18 '18 – Bourgeois Existence

The problem of reconciling my spiritual focus with my bourgeois existence is often too much for me. I do not have enough strength to always deal with the tension between the two extremes. "No man can serve two masters...ye cannot serve both God and Mammon" (Mt. 6:24). The Christian solution of 'love' (*agape*) seems childish and is of no value to me. The only legitimate object of love is 'G-d,' difficult as this may be, and diverting this emotion to another human being may be considered sacrilegious. 'Loving' other human beings leads to no end of troubles and more often than not harms the love object. This is one area where Jesus gave bad advice.

Regarding serving two masters, when in competition with the ultimate metaphysical reality, Mammon usually wins out.

July 21 '18

The twentieth century Hindu philosopher Sri Aurobindo utilized his high intellect formed by an English education and immersion in Vedantic philosophy to produce a remarkable book, *The Life Divine*.

217

The work is mind boggling to me. It may take me years to assimilate the thoughts in it. One thing is clear to me—Vedantic 'intuitive knowledge starting with the Upanishads three millennia ago up to Aurobindo today is as real as any type of scientific knowledge— perhaps more so.

July 22 '18

It is beyond me how one can imagine that a human fetus is capable of spiritual development. It has no more soul than an unfertilized ovum in a woman's ovary. It has no connection with the world necessary for such development. Once the fetus enters into the outside world as a newborn, the play of stimuli upon it initiates development of a soul. But this is a slow laborious process and many individuals hardly engage in it at all.

I have no idea of the nature of the spark in individuals that enables some to proceed further than others in developing spiritual consciousness. Some mysteries are not available to human understanding. Similarly, the fate of a soul after death is not available to the human mind (in spite of the story of *A Christmas Carol*). One can only guess at the possibilities. Efforts to remedy this lack through speculative excesses are doomed to failure.

A corollary of these thoughts is that aborting pregnancy in women is not immoral. A fetus is not a spiritual human being. It has no 'right to life' in human society any more than a centipede has.

But interfering in the decision for abortion by a pregnant woman in my judgment is absolutely immoral.

July 23 '18

After reading Ralph Waldo Emerson's essays for the umpteenth time, I am convinced that he was one of the great spiritual philosophers of all time—comparable to Plato, Nietzsche, and Nikolai Berdyaev. In the history of the profound metaphysical thought of India, he rivals the anonymous authors of the Upanishads.

Yet today in America, his place is limited to the history of early American belles-lettres. Academic philosophy has completely ignored him, since he did not conform to the analytic style of writing required in Academia. Even the contemporary 'Emerson' society, dominated by academics, refers to him as an 'author,' not as a philosopher. (Emerson himself wrote the spirit of philosophy had long since departed from universities.) Like the Upanishads, his writing was intuitive and propositional, rather than analytic.

However, while the Upanishads form the foundation of Hindu philosophy, Emerson is without influence on university philosophy in America—or in Europe either. If he is occasionally mentioned in a philosophy textbook, it is as a mystical thinker. Mystics are beneath contempt for analytic philosophy. Emerson had attended Harvard Divinity School and was an ordained minister. However, his free-thinking spirit required him to abandon Christian dogmas. Today, Christian seminaries regard him in much the same way as does academia; someone who is not worthy of notice by devout Christians.

All this only confirms my opinion of Emerson as "The Philosopher," superseding Plato. His concepts of the 'Over-Soul,' of 'Transcendentalism', and of the potential of the human spiritual condition were far ahead of his times—and even more so for ours.

July 25 '18

A friend of mine (Fr. S. J.) is entranced with the French writer Léon Bloy who made a religion of poverty, suffering, and hatred of the bourgeoisie. Periodically, the French intelligentsia become interested in him. However, to me, he represents a *schnorrer*, in the exquisite Yiddish sense of the term. He is aggressive, critical, and without shame over his humiliating dependency on others. Apparently, he continually dunned friends and family for handouts.

Bloy engaged in massive rationalization in books such as *Désespéré* (e.g., suffering and poverty are noble) and in intellectual hyperbole regarding bourgeois society (e.g., bourgeois are all horribly low creatures). He should have read *The Anarchist Banker* of Fernando Pessoa (unfortunately not published in his lifetime).

July 26 '18

Like Jesus, I have come to think very highly of the Deuteronomic commandment, "Thou shall love the Lord thy God with all thy heart, all thy soul, and all thy strength" (Deut. 6:5). But I would like to make a slight alteration to this commandment: "Thou shall love the G-d in yourself with all…etc. etc." In my opinion, this is a necessary modification.

Besides the Lord, I love my library. I don't know how I would manage without it. It keeps me connected to most of everything that is worthwhile in humankind.

July 27 '18

I have become aware of my growing interest in and identification with the personality of Jesus of Nazareth. First of all, we are kinsmen; both Jews, an important racial factor. Then, Jesus was much more concerned with the spiritual element of religion rather than the ritualistic one—as am I. Both of us arose from total obscurity; neither of us had any credentials or authority in our areas of expression.

Most significant of all, however, is that he was totally rejected by the religious establishment of his day—to the point where the leaders of Judaism plotted his death. I am rejected by the literary establishment of my day, although no one is plotting my death; I am merely ignored, shut up in a closet of literary and intellectual isolation.

Jesus said prior to his arrest that if he must drink the cup his Father had prepared for him, he would do so. Shall I not do the same from a cup that is far less bitter, even in certain ways enlivening?

July 29 '18

About forty years ago, I became disillusioned with my career in academic medicine. I no longer had the heart to apply for grants, generate research, or publish my findings. It all seemed pointless, even worse, largely self-serving. As a colleague of mine commented when I revealed my feelings to him, the fire had gone out in my belly.

Now I have much the same feelings about philosophy. I no longer am consumed by the wish to present my thoughts to the world. Perhaps it is because, by and large, the world has not been interested in my thoughts. Whatever the reason, the fire has gone out in my belly. I often think of Nietzsche's fate and how a pile of ashes replaced the fire in his belly. It was the same with Aquinas toward the end of his short life.

I would like to complete the projects I have begun. I am not one to leave things hanging. But their outcome is of little interest to me and I tire quickly.

The desire to express myself in this notebook is still with me. But that is as far as my ambition goes. I prefer to attend to my own soul and fill its needs.

July 31 '18

I have never been successful when professional or societal responsibilities have been foisted upon me. Perhaps it is because I have never seriously taken the details of responsibilities that I had lightly accepted. The societies I have lived in have never fully gained my allegiance. My mind was always existing on a different plane of reality. Consequently, I was not thought of highly as a professional person, a 'professor.'

Last night I had a most disconcerting dream. I dreamt I became fully aware of the feelings of my academic colleagues about me. It was not a pretty dream. They were all contemptuous of me, thinking I was a less than mediocre worker. They did not know how I could have reached the position that I occupied. After waking up, it took me a long time to recover my equanimity.

I believe my societal maladaptation is the result of a deep alienation of myself from the society I live in. But I needed to make money. Like the anarchist banker of Fernando Pessoa, I knew I never could be truly free if I had no money. So, I made money. Was my alienated state of mind proper considering my compromises with society? Is it still proper? I do not know the answer, but one thing I do know—I could not have acted otherwise. For what was at stake was the well-being of my persona. From the beginning of my life, I have felt that I was different from others and have felt the need to preserve my individuality. But I have not thought to universalize my state of mind. Others have their own needs.

Aug 3 '18

There is a vast gulf between myself and university academic philosophers. They do not recognize any significance to my writings. On the other hand, I regard them as 'zombie' philosophers, as the talking dead as far as philosophy is concerned. My experiences with the self-serving, narrow-minded cliques in academia have led me to this attitude. In philosophy, there is no point of communication between my existential expression—real philosophy in my opinion—and the analytic mental activity in vogue in university philosophy.

Beyond academia, there is really no defined audience for my work in America—or perhaps anywhere. I have known this for a long time. It has taken a long time for this awareness to be hammered into my consciousness. My audience is my own self—or occasionally as a fluke with some similarly eccentric individual. But I think a more important audience than myself cannot be found elsewhere. My writings represent the movement of my soul toward a higher level of consciousness. Without my writing, this would not occur. I yearn to be a part of the highest form of consciousness—the ultimate metaphysical reality that is the groundwork of everything.

I am a mystical philosopher.

Aug 6 '18

I have come to the opinion that the ultimate metaphysical reality consists of a desiring consciousness—will and consciousness are fused together; will always desiring to enlarge and deepen its consciousness. The vastness of the cosmic drama may, through some humanly inconceivable, unimaginable way, represent the movements of the ultimate metaphysical reality toward a cosmic consciousness, with its intensification in selected individual living, thinking, feeling human beings. This is the meaning of 'Atman=Brahman' asserted in certain of the Upanishads. I hope to be one of these human beings.

Beyond all this my mind is unable to go, except to say that, for those capable of it, obtaining entry into the metaphorical "Kingdom of God," which essentially represents a cosmic consciousness, should supersede all earthly pleasures.

Aug 24 '18

For almost forty years now, I have been carrying out my self-imposed role as an independent philosopher. I have studiously avoided contact with academia because, as I have said before, I regard philosophy in American universities to be moribund. The analytic obsession has thoroughly devitalized it.

There may be other independent philosophers in the USA sharing my viewpoints but I have no means of contacting them. So essentially, I am on my own as a philosopher. I think it is better for me this way. The books I have written over the years are like plants I have put in the earth for the sheer pleasure of the planting. If many readers should gain pleasure from them, it will be surprising to me, since the market-oriented 'literary' industry in America does not foster interest in independent philosophy.

Meanwhile, I feel my assumed vocation benefits my entire being; I am preparing my soul for what may come after death. Plato wrote somewhere that philosophy is a preparation for death—a statement with which I heartily concur. I can think of no better way to spend my life.

Sept 1 '18

Heinrich Heine during the last few years of his life said he confined his reading to the *Bible* because he claimed it contained all that was necessary for him in his readings. I feel similarly about a few other books besides the Bible. There are two of them I can mention; the first is the *Meditations* of Marcus Aurelius. One can dip into it anywhere and draw up pearls of wisdom. I don't agree with everything Marcus says but his breadth of view and modest style are uplifting for me to read. Recently, this sentence was meaningful to me; "Away with the thirst for books" (ii, 3). It may seem contradictory to quote this from a book, but Marcus' sentence is 'books' in the plural. One or two books are allowed.

Another is the works of Nietzsche to which I continually return. The only English translations I read are those of Walter Kaufmann who has an empathy for Nietzsche that is lacking in most scholarly translators. I adapt to Nietzsche's exaggerations, hyperbole, and self-contradictions that are to be attributed to his *Übermütigkeit,* a trait commonly found in high-spirited thinkers.

I read Nietzsche for the unmatched stimulation of his thoughts. Many critics have felt his only virtue is his unique prose style but I value the 'content' of his writing most of all.

Reading too many books is the dominant vice of scholars and intellectuals. It interferes with one's own spiritual development. The only value in reading books, speaking spiritually, is to reinforce one's own insights and intuitions. If this does not occur or the insights or intuitions do not exist, the reading is a waste of time.

Writing, however, is another matter. Writing out one's insights and intuitions gives them a permanence and a stability they would otherwise not have. Writing has made me what I am; if I had not written and established my writings in a stable form, I would now be a lesser person. My soul would be unexpanded.

All this is unrelated to others reading my work. The benefit to me is entirely within my own self. It was the same with Marcus. His Meditations were by and for himself. They were written without title; they were his unadorned reflections. The 'title' is a later addition.

Sept 11 '18 – My Vision

The ultimate goal of Vedanta Hinduism and other Indian religions is sinking spiritually into a final state of 'bliss' within the Godhead (Brahman). Christianity preaches belief in the Lord Jesus Christ for one's salvation. These goals do not inspire me. I need a purpose to my spiritual being that gives something more to my life. I have to *accomplish* something unique to myself. I feel God is imperfect and needs my contribution to Him. This feeling keeps welling up inside of me.

God may have created the entire universe and set it all in motion but something is lacking in it—and in Him, since the universe is an extension of His being. To my mind, this something is *consciousness*. He has created human beings to provide Him with the consciousness he lacks and needs. I think this is what Jesus may have unconsciously implied when he said "My Father and I are one" (John 10:30), even though it got him into trouble. He was too strong and expansive a personality to be content with merely following his Father's orders. He brought a new consciousness to Divinity. Every individual human soul has the potential, *the duty*, to add to God's consciousness. It is my duty to develop my consciousness and thereby provide to God the tools to be a little more perfect.

Consciousness of what one may ask? Consciousness of all that was, is, and can be, I answer. A mystical consciousness that transcends time and space. A consciousness may persist only a brief time in the mind but the changes it imposes on one's soul—and what it adds to Divinity—are forever. It is an ambitious undertaking! Writing down my thoughts helps me with this task.

I have written what I think and what I know. *Honi soit qui mal y pense.*

Sept 23 '18 – Goal of *Homo sapiens*

In looking over the books I have written over the past 36 years, I feel the need once again to summarize my point of view, to identify the *essence* of my philosophy.

I believe the primary goal of *Homo sapiens* is to develop his or her spiritual nature, that is to say his or her *soul.* The goal is not to create wealth, to support a family, to be a professional success, or to stand up for a religion, a country, or a race. These can be secondary goals, but all in the service of the primary one, to develop one's soul. An individual has to become conscious of what it means to develop the soul. One's life is a success only to the degree that his soul is developed.

Vedanta philosophers and 'existential' Jewish or Christian theologians say identifying with the ultimate metaphysical reality (G-d) is the goal of human life. I think this is a presumptuous expectation. One may yearn for the best of reasons to merge with God, but to imagine this has truly happened is sheer hubris. The yearning ought to be more than enough for any right-minded person! The actual fulfillment of this yearning is beyond human purview.

Oct 9 '18 – Metaphysical desire

Like travel and socialization, reading is valuable when one is expanding his cultural horizons. However, at my stage of life, reading is a vice and a deterrent to my inner development (staring at a computer screen is an even worse vice, but I have that under

229

control). Thinking and writing for myself is what is best for me now although I am done with writing for publication. The only reading I intend to do at this time in my life is for relaxation—like Agatha Christie novels or *Le Figaro.*

One might say I am looking for G-d. I don't want to sit in a forest and meditate as did the ancient Indian sages. Where I live, the climate is not right for that anyway. I am not interested in classical Yoga because while I am alive, I don't want my mind to just tightly concentrate within; I want it to *soar aloft* to the maximum extent possible for me. I need the use of all my senses for that. What I really want is to find the ultimate metaphysical reality in the universe; not to love it or obey its commands (of which no one is cognizant) but to discover it, to try to approach it, to come as close as possible to realizing *Atman=Brahman* through the unique *activity* of the spirit within me. This is a tall order and I am not sure I can ever achieve it. But I will make the attempt. Could madness be the solution?—as it was for Nietzsche with his own problems. No, I can't stand being stared at!

Oct 10 '18 – The Creative Impulse

There is general agreement among spiritually enlightened individuals that the search for G-d must begin within one's own soul. The human soul is the most advanced manifestation of G-d (although not necessarily the last). Where do I find G-d within my soul? After much reflection on this subject, I have come to believe it is in my *creative impulse*; creativity is the principal focus of G-d's being and so its existence in myself must be where G-d is to be found. This was Berdyaev's view except that he was greatly distracted by his Christianity.

'Satan' (a term not to be taken literally) makes his appearance among human beings by deluding the creative person that his creations must be approved of by society. This is the feeling that most often undermines and perverts the work of creative individuals. Money is most often the sign of societal approval, but there are others such as academic recognition or public acclaim. Most of these latter, however, also usually lead to money.

G-d does not seek approval for his creations; He decides for himself whether they are 'good.' (His judgment about the human race probably remains undecided.) Therefore, I have trained myself to make my own decisions about my creative work. They stand on their own, for better or for worse. They reflect my own *consciousness of existence*, which, in my opinion, is also G-d's ultimate expression of Himself.

If Nietzsche had had more of a metaphysical consciousness, he might not have felt the need to descend into madness (an idea I have developed in an essay entitled 'Nietzsche's Will to Madness').

All this at the end of my ninth decade of existence, indicating how slow my spiritual development has been.

Oct 13 '18 – Cliques and Societies

Controlling cliques in the form of exclusive societies or organizations are the ruination of human progress, whether the progress be in the form of ideas or activities. There are religious cliques, professional cliques, academic cliques, political cliques, workers cliques, and others I may have overlooked. They are always ultimately in the service of the power needs of their members, never for the public at large. Cliques act to impede individual creativity, which is the spearhead of progress. It would be much better to allow many weeds to grow for the sake of occasional flowers. When nothing is allowed to grow spontaneously outside a controlling clique, the human race ossifies and degenerates.

Oct 17 '18 – G-d's Tool

In the past, I have felt that writing developed myself and enhanced my consciousness of the metaphysical basis of the universe in which I lived. Now I think that it is 'G-d' who is being developed and whose consciousness is being extended. I am G-d's tool for developing Himself.

I have left 'culture' behind. The only important thing is to do G-d's work of self-development. I will never reach the point where I can say as Jesus did: "I and my Father, we are one" (Jn 10:30). But I hope to be making progress.

The key is becoming *fully* aware of the metaphysical nature of the human reality—and of all reality.

Oct 29 '18 – Reading My Own Books

I find it rewarding to read my own books; more so than most other things I read. The 'me' that reads my books is different than the 'me' that has written them. When I read my own books, I can absorb their meaning in a way that doesn't occur when I am writing them. Moreover, reading books I have written many years ago is like reading works of a different person. The feeling is quite an interesting one.

Reading again *The Gnostic Gospels* by Elaine Pagels. I read it over 20 years ago but it is more meaningful to me now. The book is a wonderfully written account of the first centuries of Christianity, contrasting the orthodox Catholic church doctrines with that of the Gnostic attitudes of that era. There is no doubt which one I would have subscribed to if I lived at that time – it would have been the Gnostic religious philosophy that denied dogmatic doctrines, downplayed rituals, and rejected clerical hierarchies. It was individual *spirituality* that was the most important element in their religious practices. However, the Catholic Church Fathers deemed them heretical and expelled them from the Christian churches.

Nov 1 '18

My essay *Nietzsche's Will to Madness* was rejected by the scholarly Journal of Nietzsche Studies. This confirms for me that my mental world is far removed from academia. I would deteriorate quickly trying to play the role of scholar.

Nov 2 '18 – Gresham's Law

Mankind is moving in two different directions: development of spiritual individuality and the mechanization of its life. These are opposing trends; the dominance of one or the other will determine the nature of future human society. My preference is of course for the former, but looking at the world objectively, one must admit the latter is winning out. It is confirmation of Gresham's Law of economics that bad money drives out good as applied to the whole of human existence. Depressing, but there seems to be nothing that can be done to change the situation except to look to development of one's own soul.

Nov 4 '18 – Metaphysical Uncertainty

Lately, I have felt on and off depressed. Why? I find it hard to explain—my life circumstances do not admit any cause for depression. Is it my 'literary' situation? (My books do not sell.) My age? My infirmities? My life's end approaching? Perhaps it is the metaphysical awareness that a transcendental God, if he should exist, has no contact with me. Perhaps it is all of the above.

I have recently been reading *The Gnostic Religions* by Hans Jonas, especially its epilogue, 'Gnosticism, Existentialism and Nihilism. Perhaps I fear that down deep, I am a nihilist. Nihilism is a bad state to be in; it may have led to Nietzsche's breakdown...well, it does me good to bring out these thoughts.

I think what is necessary for me is to adapt to *metaphysical uncertainty*. We poor limited human beings are not privy to the ultimate depths of the universe. (Pascal wrote eloquently on this subject in *Pensées #72.)* That's just the reality. One does not *know* what is outside of one's self. There is no *gnosis*, there is only *speculation* regarding ultimate metaphysical realities. A transcendental philosophy not centered in the philosopher's own soul is mere intellectual amusement—useful perhaps for the careers of academics or for the influence of the clergy but of little meaning for the independent thinker.

Nov 5'18

'Scholarship' has descended like a dense gray fog over the intellectual life of western societies, which today is dominated by universities. Scholarship has its place in learning but it inhibits creative thought. The requirements of analytic scholarship are directly antithetical to creativity. It is all due to the academic guilds in universities suppressing independent free thinking. A person who has made his mark as a scholar may think he is capable of independent thought but his mind has been formed in the scholar's mold. The truly creative thinkers of yesteryear—Herder, Fichte, Rousseau, Kierkegaard, Nietzsche, Berdyaev, and many others— would have little chance of being valued by contemporary universities if they were alive today. They would have to find some form of celebrity status in order to be noticed. Upon academia belongs the curse uttered by Jesus, "Woe to you who are versed in the law; because you took away the key of 'knowledge' [*gnosis*]; you yourselves did not enter and those entering, you hindered" (Lk. 11:52).

What is a scholar but someone who expends his energies on studying the accomplishments of individuals of the past. His focus is on looking backward, not forward. He exhibits an ingrained skepticism about contemporary creativity and, unconsciously perhaps, does not want to attribute much value to it. The Alexandrian culture during the Hellenistic era was a culture of scholars; nothing of enduring value came out of it. Future observers—should there be any—may say the same of American culture.

Nov 6 '18

The 'liberal' left-wing mentality of the Democratic party has adopted the universalist Christian morality without subscribing to Christian faith. Thus, there is no foundation for their moral beliefs and they easily descend into self-serving hypocrisy with no respect for individual values. But this seems to be the future for America. I have my own morality based on my own beliefs that alienates me from the direction of the society around me.

Nov 8 '18 – A Metaphysical Consciousness

I have published many books on metaphysical matters (principally the soul) over a long period of time. None of them have received any attention from the literary world in the U.S. Most literary people would regard me as a pathetic figure—a prolific writer without readers who continues to publish without the slightest sign of literary success. Only the fact that I have an independent income has allowed me to continue on my isolated path. Most writers are not so fortunate, although some would say my financial independence has led me down a path of folly.

However, I do not consider my activity as a writer to be folly. *My writing has made me what I am today.* My writing has deepened and strengthened my soul. There is nothing else I could have done of equal value for me. What do I care about acquiring unknown readers? What do I care about societal plaudits—or their lack?— from academic or literary critics. None of that amounts to anything of substance in my life—except to feed my ego, which is something of dubious value.

Developing my soul (i.e. interior self) is of the greatest importance to me. By doing so, I feel a 'transcendental' awareness entering into it. The transcendental element of my soul permits me to dismiss the trivialities of societal success. They are of no consequence in a larger scheme of things. Success to me is developing a soul with firm metaphysical awareness. Some would say I am really referring to an awareness of 'G-d' but I do not wish to go so far. No almighty G-d has made himself known to me so I cannot include him in my own scheme of things.

Now I know that all of the above could be construed as the rationalizations of a failed writer. One needs a broad *metaphysical consciousness* to appreciate my perspective. This is all too rare in academic and literary circles. That is just the way things are in America today.

What is my conception of 'transcendental awareness'? First of all, it is the basic Kantian 'transcendental aesthetic, the awareness of space and time originating from one's own mind. But beyond that, it is the awareness of a transcendental 'force,' a *Logos* existing throughout the cosmos that affects everything. The force of gravity is a physical expression of this force, but there is a metaphysical expression as well, affecting human souls. One can name the *Logos* 'G-d'; however, this is just a question of semantics.

Nov 10 '18 – My Fate

At 88 years of age, my proper task is to put the finishing touches on my life. I have done what I can to make something of my soul. I am proud of what I have made of it, intellectually and spiritually—even morally, although I can see some disputing this last claim. Most of the vitality of my past life is exhausted, but enough remains to complete the task. In certain ways, I am a perfectionist and do not like to leave anything undone.

As far as my literary work is concerned, it seems likely to me that posterity will accord me no more recognition than I have received during my lifetime. Not for me will be posthumous fame that was accorded to a few icons of world literature (e.g. Poe, Kierkegaard, Nietzsche, Pessoa). Far more likely is that I will join the ranks of the vast number of "unsung Miltons" who have disappeared into societal oblivion. It does me good to clearly state this reality.

I know no more about the fate of my soul than I knew when I started writing on this topic almost forty years ago. I speculate but I don't *know*. It is quite obvious that this is how it should be for mentally limited human beings like myself. The one thing of which I am certain is that *my soul exists*, albeit I do not know what will ultimately become of it.

There are a few loose ends of my writings that I would like to tie up before I pass on. Mainly, a collection of essays that I believe to be worthwhile and deserving to appear in print. In particular, my essay *Nietzsche's Will to Madness* must see the light of day [later - published in *The Agonist*]. I will keep writing in this notebook. Then *finis.*

Nov 20'18 – Teleology

It seems evident to me that there is a *teleological* basis for the development of my body, neuromuscular system, and especially my brain. They permit me to survive and cope with my environment—

often a hostile one. The Darwinian explanation seems adequate. But beyond survival, they make possible the development of my *soul*, something unrelated to physical survival. I need to hear, see, feel, *think*, and freely move about in order to acquire the experiences necessary for my spiritual development.

Teleology has been said to be the unacknowledged mistress of scientific physiology. I personally have no problem acknowledging it since I cannot imagine any other basis for my existence on this earth. My soul is going somewhere, even if I have no knowledge of where that somewhere is. It is unlikely that it has anything to do with the space-time continuum in which I lead my daily life. Some mysterious force is forever making me push on with my self-development, even at my advanced age.

Why is it that I prefer turn of the nineteenth century literature to the twentieth century versions? George Gissing, José Rodó, William James, Miguel de Unamuno, Somerset Maugham, August Strindberg, Jack London, F.C.S. Schiller, D. H. Lawrence, to name a few from widely disparate fields, are infinitely more interesting to me than those of a century later—I cannot remember any names from the latter, which in itself is significant. In my judgment, creative writing in the English language world is rapidly degenerating through vile sex, lurid violence, crass voyeurism, or scholarly jargons. At best, the mentality of the feuilleton is dominant. There is not the great sweep of thought of former times. It's really a shame.

Nov 27 '18 – 'Gardening'

My own published books have been my private garden. I have carefully nurtured them individually through the years until each one blossomed in its own right over a period of time. Now they have faded and sit silently on my library shelves. One day they will all turn to dust. But like the effect of any garden upon the gardener, they have greatly enriched my life and made me a better person through their cultivation. What more than becoming a better person could one ask from any vocation? Certainly not corrosive fame or filthy lucre!

The lucky few who have had the privilege of visiting my garden will have derived pleasure from the experience. They too may have had their lives enriched.

Nov 28 '18 – Spirituality

The realization has come to me that I live in an essentially pagan society. The Christian element in it views spirituality through the lenses of morality and Christian dogmas, which I consider fallacious and based upon pagan attitudes rather than spiritual ones. Jesus preached giving to the poor as a way of escaping materialism, not as a means of socialist leveling. His followers misread his purposes. In this concept, he was preceded by some three centuries by the Cynic philosopher Crates who distributed his wealth among his fellow citizens, not for morality's sake, but because his own life was more tranquil and fulfilling when devoid of excessive material goods.

Pagan societies are materialist in nature and their worship is of material objects. Scientism as a means of progress is a pagan ideology. As far as western religions are concerned, the ritualism of Judaism, the icon worship of Catholicism, and the Jesus idolatry of Protestantism are forms of paganism. Genuine spirituality requires a *metaphysical consciousness*. Without this last, a spiritual nature is not possible. God is *spirit*, not love, morality, or piety. These are my convictions and that is why I am so intellectually isolated from American culture.

All three synoptic Gospels relate Jesus as saying only God is 'good' (*agathos*) and disclaiming that he himself was good. This seems to me to clearly eliminate the idea that he was God come to Earth for the purpose of redeeming mankind. Jesus was human and like all humans, he exhibited his share of human failings, albeit possessing a unique spiritual consciousness.

Looking at the evolution of western societies, I notice that as the mentality of scientism has taken possession of these societies (led by America), spirituality has concomitantly diminished. The phenomenon of a Jesus of Nazareth (or Crates, Savonarola, Spinoza, or even Emerson) affecting society is impossible today. There has been great progress in technology, morality, and scholarship, but not in spirituality. All western utopias have failed. Seers like Hölderlin,

Thoreau, Nietzsche, and Gissing die young or go mad. If God is Spirit as the gospel of John asserts, and as I believe, then western civilization is not only not progressing but is degenerating rapidly.

Dec 2 '18 – Hasidic Wisdom

According to Rabbi Michel of Zlotchov, an Hasidic master (Kushner, *Kabbalah*), an individual person is like a drop of water that continuously wants to fall back into the 'ocean' (*Ayn Sof*) from whence it came. When that occurs, the individual is one with the waters of the ocean and is no longer yearning and restless. I think, however, that this drop may contain a 'metaphysical consciousness' needed by the ocean. It is not merely a return, but an enrichment of the oceanic water. Thus, the development of a metaphysical consciousness is the purpose of the human condition, leading to fulfillment of the 'ultimate metaphysical reality,' however one names it

(G-d, Jehovah, Brahman, Allah, Manitou, etc.).

Without this kind of mystical inclination, human beings are indeed poor creatures.

Dec 12 '18 – Metaphysical Rambling

I have been browsing through widely disparate and dense discussions about metaphysical matters. These books are:

Sri Aurobindo – *The Life Divine*

Martin Buber – *The Hasidic Message*

RICHARD SCHAIN

Paul Tillich – *Systematic Theology*

Georges Bataille – *The Interior Experience*

Exposure to the Vedanta world of Aurobindo is like being overwhelmed by a metaphysical Tsunami. The others are similar, only somewhat less intense.

After trying to digest all these bookish experiences, I come away with the same views I had before, only with more awareness of the astonishing fertility of the human mind regarding metaphysical thought. The writers I have mentioned above have their own unique viewpoints on the human condition. Following these readings, I feel compelled to review and simplify my own metaphysical worldview.

Essentially, I am still persuaded of the *perennial triune nature of human reality*: the metaphysical soul within; the material world without (nature, cosmos); and 'G-d', the ultimate metaphysical and material force-reality. My thoughts on these subjects may vary from year to year, but the triune categorization remains. Some of the polarities are: immortality vs extinction of the soul, contemplation vs experience (action), involvement in society vs contempt of it, significance of human life vs its meaninglessness, yearning for 'G-d' vs rejection of such yearning. There may be others. But there are certain convictions that are constant—my soul exists as a metaphysical reality, there is a dominant world out there as a material reality, there is an 'Ultimate Reality' with which my soul has a connection (a crucial one for myself as well as Itself).

There! I have said it all—again. May the Power that must exist have a benevolent view towards me.

Dec 26 '18 – Shriveling of the Self

I have been laid low these past two weeks with a virulent chest cold—what the Mexicans call *catarro*. At my age, it could be dangerous. Lots of coughing and phlegm. But now I am recovering. It has reminded me of my mortality—as if I needed reminders. No energy, no writing.

Yesterday I felt well enough to attend one of the 'grand affairs' that affluent expats like to give during the holiday season. It was an unwise decision. As Melanie and I entered the large reception area, suddenly there appeared over 100 people standing about with glasses of spirits or wine, little plates of tidbits, all apparently happily chatting with each other about the usual expat topics—home repairs, travel to the border, shopping in the Mercado, exchange rates, problems with help, etc., etc. Just as suddenly, I froze as if I had been abruptly thrust into a cold-water bathtub. My inner self shriveled up like a flower exposed to a harsh winter wind. I can't function any longer with small talk; my psyche just won't perform. The mask I used to don is no longer available to me. No doubt it is another capacity I have lost due to aging. I am reduced to retreating to a hidden corner of the scene where no one will make demands on my personality. It is a humiliating experience not to be repeated.

January 11, 2019 – Sri Aurobindo

I have been spending the last few weeks reading and rereading chapters from *The Life Divine* of Sri Aurobindo. His writings touch me deeply because he provides an intuitive yet intellectual foundation for my own thoughts about the Soul, the Ultimate Metaphysical Reality (G-d), and their relationship. Aurobindo never questions the *reality* of his metaphysical concepts—which are mine also. These are what is real to him—a refreshing attitude for the materialist society in which I live.

Aurobindo was a genius in metaphysical thought. But I think, like most geniuses, he overextends himself. He developed an outline of a spiritual Utopia that seems to me to be fruitless—like all previous Utopias. He does better when he sticks to discussing the attainment of spirituality by individuals. Nevertheless, his writings are *inspirational*. I don't know of any recent philosophical works that approach Aurobindo in insight into the present human condition and its need for spiritual development.

Like most philosophers, Aurobindo is often verbose and repetitive in his writing. He seems to derive pleasure from demonstrating his mastery of the English language. His virtues, however, far outweigh his faults. He has things to say that are important for all thoughtful human beings. And he knows better than anyone how to reveal the limitations of the materialist mindset. Reading him is a great comfort for me and an inspirational experience.

Jan 13 '19 – Forgotten Notes

Notes written last year that I have discovered:

- Origins—undifferentiated energy, Absolute Divinity, the 'big bang'
- Development of cosmos with its laws
- Evolution of life, humanity, human spirituality
- Physical body and brain are produced by life force and spirit.
- The Absolute Divinity becomes more 'absolute' through the spirituality of humans.

These few phrases express what Sri Aurobindo elaborates in a thousand pages.

Jan 18 '19 – End of an Involvement

My involvement with Sri Aurobindo is coming to an end. I stand by everything I have written about him, but I am aware of an increasing discomfort, irritation, and even depression after I read chapters from *The Life Divine*. Putting it bluntly in the vernacular, I feel he is too big for his britches, his mind goes beyond the possible extent of human knowledge. Of course, he is only following in the footsteps of the forest sages of India who created Vedanta Hinduism three millennia ago. But what was permissible for them at the dawn of philosophy is not permissible in the 20th century C.E. Aurobindo should have confined his brilliant mind to the *human* spiritual condition and left Brahman to Hindu tradition.

I stick by what has been written earlier; the human soul must have a 'connection' to an ultimate metaphysical reality, but what that connection is, is beyond human ken. Postpone the idea that 'Atman is Brahman'! That concept undermines the human need to develop his own soul.

I received today a book manuscript by G.K (*Philosophizer's Bible).* Dipping into it reminds me of Nietzsche's *Ecce Homo*, but is even more 'liberated' than that book. G.K. claims to have been 'born again.' Perhaps it is so.

Basta for tonight.

Jan 19 '19 – Awareness of the Soul

Last night I realized that in the forty years I have been reflecting on G-d (the Absolute, the Ineffable, Brahman) and yearning to find Him, my knowledge of Him is no better than it was forty years ago. He is just a concept in my mind, nothing more. I have never had any direct experience of Him. Much as I have tried through deep meditation and Yogic exercises to find G-d meaningfully, I have never been successful. It has all been a waste of my precious mental energy. I know there are those who claim a link of some sort with G-d, a consciousness of His presence. More power to them! Perhaps I am not worthy of His attention. It is possible, but in my heart I don't believe it. I really think there is just no route to connect with Divinity within the limited conditions of human life.

It is quite different with the awareness of my soul. I have during forty years increased my intuitive certainty that *I am* a soul, that I am a spiritual entity. I have labored to develop this entity, this *moi*, this *yo*, this *Ich* as long as I can remember. In fact, it has become the overriding purpose of my conscious existence. I believe there is a cosmic purpose to the development of my soul even if I don't know what it may be. Many of my writings explain how I have worked toward this goal. Perhaps on my demise I will be rewarded for my efforts. I know this confession will open me up to ridicule and sarcasm should it ever come into public view (a most unlikely possibility). However, I do not care about the cynicism of limited materialist-minded critics.

Jan 26 '19 – 'Knowing' G-d

I have decided that if someone does not have some level of spiritual awareness, some kind of yearning toward the 'Beyond,' it is too difficult for me to maintain a significant personal relationship. We can 'get along,' be neighborly, have occasional superficial conversations, but not a significant personal relationship. I just cannot maintain an interest.

In spite of what I have formerly said about Aurobindo, I seem not to tire of reading from him. The combination of western intellectuality and a consistent spiritual high-mindedness is good for my soul. Like Emerson, he appears to think any human being is capable of attaining to the highest form of spiritual consciousness. Perhaps he is right in so thinking, but that has not been my experience. No doubt his British education (St. Paul's, Cambridge) accounts for his remarkable mastery of the English language.

It would not surprise me if one day a new religion would emerge based on the writings of Sri Aurobindo. I would probably not be a member since I cannot subscribe to any system of belief that might try to direct my mental freedom.

I may wish to know 'G-d' but I can never really know Him—just as I cannot learn all languages that are worthy of learning or experience all places in the world that are worthy of experiencing. I must accept my limitations. My own small piece of existence is as much as my mind can know. Christian Grace or Hindu (or Buddhist) enlightenment, for whatever reason, has not come down to me. Whether it truly does to anyone in this Age of Human Communication is not for me to judge.

My adorable cat Ruby views me as her God—although she requires utter independence. She often wants to be as close to me as possible, nestling against me and seeking out my caresses. But she has no idea, can have no conception of the breadth and depth of my existence. So it must be with my awareness of 'G-d.'

Jan 28 '19 – Modernized Vedanta

Aurobindo has created a modernized expanded version of Vedanta thought that I find absorbing. I would like one day to visit the Aurobindo center in Pondicherry, but this may be now beyond me. Meanwhile, his writing enriches my mind. His metaphysics is inspirational. I view Sri Aurobindo as *the* modern Hindu Scholastic, the Thomas Aquinas of Vedanta, but superior to Aquinas in literary virtuosity as he was the fortunate recipient of the best of British education. Furthermore, he is not burdened by viewing myths as reality as is the case with Christianity and Judaism.

Jan 31 '19 – *Ultimate Divine Reality*

Aurobindo has developed a rational comprehensive scheme in *The Life Divine* of the totality of 'Existence' and the human place within it. How much of it corresponds to reality I don't know, but it is a remarkable intellectual achievement. My mind may not be large enough to absorb his vision. I have constructed a much simpler scheme in the form of a metaphor. The Ultimate Divine Reality is a kind of giant cosmic *'Amoeba'* with innumerable tiny pseudopods (developing human souls) radiating out from its body. The pseudopods are "consciousness pods" that eventually return to the body of the Amoeba, nourishing it spiritually. Then, when biological life leaves the individual pod, its soul enriches Divinity. There is no need for transmigration of souls since empty pods will be absorbed back into the body of the Divine Amoeba as well as those bursting with spiritual nourishment. Admittedly a crude analogy, relying on spatial and temporal imagery that may not apply to an Ultimate Metaphysical Reality, but one that is based on my intuitions and which provides purpose to my life.

Feb 2 '19 – Planes of Existence

I have no desire to enter into other *planes* of spiritual existence while I still possess my vitality and ability to enrich my soul through terrestrial life experiences and learning. Time enough after I die to pass into higher planes. It seems unnatural to me to try to train myself to move out of the terrestrial plane while I am still in this life. All these years and energies devoted to extreme forms of Yoga or suchlike meditations are not for me. I don't think the obsession with Yoga has been beneficial to the civilization of India.

Feb 5 '19 – Superiority of Vedanta

Unlike the Abrahamic religions, the Vedanta element of Hinduism has not incorporated legends and myths as dogmas within its religious thought. Consequently, it is far ahead of western religion in the depth of its theology and its eschatology. It is only *tradition* that the Judeo-Christian-Moslem religions have going for them. This thought should be further developed but someone else will have to do it.

At 88 years of age, after a 23-year career in medical academia and then 37 years of philosophical thinking, reading, and writing, I am ready to withdraw to a life of a non-ascetic, itinerant, western-style 'sannyasin' seeking spiritual inner peace within myself. I will try to fend off physical decrepitude. The spirit of Sri Aurobindo can be my companion.

Mar 1 '19 – Differences from Aurobindo

I have significant differences from Sri Aurobindo. Some of these are:

1. Mind and Soul are not different entities. They are part of the same mental-spiritual Self (Atman).
2. Maturation, not evolution, is the appointed end of the individual Self. Maturation occurs during the life span of an individual. Rebirth of a 'soul' is a fiction to be discarded.
3. The 'soul' (self) does not merely rejoin the Absolute (Brahman), it *enriches* it. If the whole saga of the soul is only to rejoin its origin, what was the point of it? None at all.
4. The Absolute (G-d) is not perfect, but needs enrichment.
5. "Atman=Brahman" is a misleading expression. A better one would be, 'Atman is a part of Brahman' or 'Atman belongs to Brahman.' Best of all is the expression of Jesus, "God is within you,"—i.e., Brahman can be found within the Self.

To say it once more—since I have disdain for the culture of my American society, there is no reason to expect that society to have any regard for me. It does not. Instead of societal acclaim, I have my involvement with an Ultimate Metaphysical Reality. I much prefer it to involvement with societal circles.

The best time for my soul is when I am in my bed enveloped by the blackness of the night. Then there are no material distractions. My *consciousness* reigns supreme. But if my whole life were spent in this way?—I would have nothing to be conscious about!

Mar 10 '19 – in Menton

Perhaps it was unfortunate that my physical appetites during my early life were too great to permit me to devote myself unreservedly to my metaphysical needs. I was no Thoreau who had no interest in women and became a vegetarian. Consequently, my spiritual development has not been what it could have been. Biological pressures have been too strong in my life. *Tant pis*!

At this stage of my life, I have no desire to be a philosophical systematizer. There have been enough of these in the past to satisfy those with a yearning for systems in philosophy. I prefer to express myself *organically*—the way thoughts emerge in my mind. But I have a horror of becoming *garrulous*.

Living in France for extended time periods has made me realize that the French way of life is the epitome of materialist culture. Food, clothing, women, manners, intellectuality are unsurpassed anywhere else. Somerset Maugham in his wonderful novel *The Razor's Edge* was right in having a character state that the only place for a 'civilized' person to live was Paris. Consequently, however, the French intellectual has no spiritual sense or respect for spirituality. It is no way of life for me.

Why did so many artists and writers in past times leave their homeland to go to Paris? What was special about Paris? It has a bad climate, too many people, difficulty in earning a living. I think the draw was *escape* from the pressures, habits, distractions of their own life, and the mystique of a marvelous Paris. They thought they could find their own souls in the City of Light. Unfortunately, if this were once true, it is no longer the case. Today, Paris is just an elitist, style-dominated, clique-ridden museum living on its past glories. It is no place for an original creative life. Give me a place in Italy any time! I like *Mentone* because it is so Italianate and the beauties of the Mediterranean and Maritime Alps cannot be ruined. Unfortunately, my Italian is non-existent and I must struggle to express myself in 'Franglish.'

Mar 11 '19 – Metaphysical Needs
Would it have been better for my life if I had not had my own means and had been forced to direct my writing to a public instead of toward my own needs? I might have then had a connection to my society, although my metaphysical needs would have surely suffered. In retrospect, I am glad to have been able to attend to my

own needs instead of those of society. Metaphysical needs are more important than material or psychological ones.

I am more like Henry David Thoreau who attended to his own needs than Ralph Waldo Emerson who grew to attend to society's needs. It was a fluke of fate that Thoreau received posthumous recognition. I am sure I will not.

I have assiduously tried to find some clear evidence or signs that there is an Ultimate Metaphysical Reality with whom I am involved. But I can find none. What I have is *faith* that It exists and I am involved with It. That is my faith; I have had it for years. It must be based on a deep intuition, the basis of which has not been vouchsafed to me to understand. I cannot answer anything about Its nature or its will because I do not have answers. I only know my faith.

Mar 12 '19 – What is Faith?

What is faith? In my judgment, the significant element is not belief *per se* but what is believed. Faith is an intuition, a feeling, a belief that something is absolutely so without any concrete evidence. However, for me the belief must meet the test of my intellectual conscience. Belief in Santa Claus or the good fairy does not pass the test. Nor does the faith in Jesus Christ as savior of my soul.

The nature of a faith must be sufficiently broad to allow varied interpretations of it. For example, a faith that G-d exists can allow for a concept of G-d as a judgmental Lord, a benevolent father, an ultimate metaphysical reality (my view), or even a vague pantheistic entity. In my case, the main feature of my intuition is that I am in some way intimately *involved* with G-d.

Why should I believe this? Here is the crucial question. Can I discover the basis of this intuition? Or is it just a feeling welling up inside of me without a discernable cause? This seems to be the case. Thus, it qualifies as a "revelation" from outside of myself, something I have denied ever having in the past. However, it is a revelation that differs from just awareness of G-d's presence, it is a revelation of my involvement with G-d.

I regard any extensive analysis of G-d's nature, one's soul, or their interactions as essentially imaginative rather than intuitional. Aquinas, Spinoza, Tillich, Aurobindo are for me writers of dreams or speculations. There is no *truth* for me in their writings. Only Berdyaev remained 'faithful' to the idea of an apophatic G-d. That is why I accord him high honors as a philosopher.

Mar 13 '19 – Consciousness of Reality

I shall for once depart from my principle of holding to the apophatic nature of Deity and assert its central feature is *consciousness of reality*. I can't support this assertion with any arguments except that I feel strongly it is so. The central feature of a human soul is consciousness—this I know from my own personal experience. Here is the key to the involvement of a soul with G-d.

Consciousness is the apex of existence of living creatures and the common denominator between G-d and man. To those including myself who wish to develop their souls and find G-d, I say "Cultivate consciousness of reality. G-d is in need of your consciousness." I don't think I can ever improve on this guideline in my search for enlightenment.

Mar 14 '19

"|*Dieu parle, il faut qu'on lui réponde*" (Alfred de Musset). But he hasn't spoken to me.

March 18 '19 – The Human Soul

The question of the human soul has been the most important issue throughout virtually all recorded history. It is only in the past two centuries in Europe and European-origin societies that 'scientism' has delegated it to a meaningless question. It has been replaced by materialist values in the form of societal status, object acquisition, and sex. Over all this, money rules.

There can be no doubt that human beings have certain needs that are physically and psychologically unrelated to spiritual (i.e. soul) existence. Among these are the sexual drive, the need for societal status, the need for personal and family security, the feeling of perpetuating oneself through children, the need for emotional attachments. Some would add the need to find G-d, but I regard this as a manifestation of concern with one's soul. One must come to terms with these various needs while maintaining the most important focus on the development of the soul. In human affairs, consciousness of one's soul has a determining effect on one's behavior.

Unfortunately, today the term 'soul' has no currency in intellectual materialist circles. There is the feeling that the concept is a myth, a superstition, a 'ghost in the machine'; there is no belief in the reality of its existence. It is my opinion that lack of consciousness of the reality of the soul ultimately renders societies untenable. It seems that the Abrahamic religions (Judaism. Christianity, Islam) have failed in their duty to maintain focus on the soul in their adherents. Only the various forms of Hindu Vedanta traditions with their metaphysical depth have succeeded in this role. But India today is going the route of western materialist societies. Too bad for the world!

The beauty of the Mediterranean Sea on a bright sunny day is beyond the imagination of those who have never seen it. If only Dostoevsky had been right in saying that beauty would save the world. But the beauty of the Mediterranean has not saved the Riviera from the worst excesses of over-development and profiteering. Sad to see.

Mar 20 '19 – Sudden Insight

The *soul* is a form of *spiritualized* life, it is a special form of life, it is its highest manifestation. Life itself must be a *metaphysical* phenomenon. Scientists have described life in the minutest detail but cannot really comprehend it or explain why it should continuously occur violating the second law of thermodynamics.

Individual human life begins when a male spermatozoon enters into a female ovum. Physical development then occurs as a result of the metaphysical life force exerting its predestined actions. Brain development similarly occurs as a result of life's force. The questions of exactly how metaphysical life appears, stimulating the formation of an individual physical body and brain and transforming itself into a developed soul are eternal mysteries that science will never solve. It is enough for the individual to be conscious of these processes and act to promote the soul's development.

Upon death, the physical body and brain decay and return to the dust from which they were formed. The developed soul, however, returns to *enrich* the Ultimate Metaphysical Reality (G-d) out of which it originally arose. 'Nirvana' must be more than mere reabsorption of a soul into an Absolute; it must serve to enrich the Absolute as a consequence of its development within human life. (Rebirth or transmigration of undeveloped souls is postulated by Indian religious traditions but I think it unlikely.)

Mar 21 '19 – Meaning of Life

I don't attempt to explain the origin of life on Earth billions of years ago or how the complex structure of the executive brain conducts the work of the metaphysical soul. This would be like an oyster sitting on a shallow ocean bed trying to explain the worldwide movements of all the oceans of the world. There is no need for me— or anyone else—to attempt to do so. What is important for me is to be conscious of the meaning of my life and the need to form my soul. A certain amount of knowledge about human physiology and of human history is valuable and adds to consciousness of the world. But to overdo efforts in this direction is to miss the metaphysical goal of one's existence—development of one's soul. This failure is the consequence of the pathological scientism that is current today.

In the bourgeois type of society in which I live, *money* makes one free (Pessoa, *The Anarchist Banker*). I have no compunctions about the fact that I have amassed some money. It has freed me to develop myself. I see no virtue in existing in poverty and expending one's energies in surviving it. I have not fallen victim to the obsession with mere wealth or object acquisition and hope that when I die, my money will have been utilized in a worthwhile manner—or left to support the one near and dear to me.

Mar 23 '19 – Christianity – Sophistry of The Bhagavad-Gita

Christianity has amassed a vast reservoir of spiritual knowledge and spiritual depth throughout its two millennia of existence. It is high time that it abandon its childish legends and dogmas about Jesus Christ and recognize Jesus of Nazareth for whom he was—a great spiritual teacher of the Jewish people. "Christianity devoid of Christology"—that is my prescription for western spiritual development.

The immense sophistry of the Bhagavad-Gita, the Bible of Hindu India, may be the reason why India has been decaying for so many centuries. The sophisms urging Arjuna to war against his kinsmen and teachers are embedded in a metaphysics derived from earlier Upanishads. But the 'Gita' is a purely didactic work while the Upanishads are largely personal revelations in nature representing the insights of their originators. It is hard not to think that Arjuna was a far nobler figure than Krishna even if he is said to have fallen victim to the latter's sophistical arguments.

Mar 25 '19 – A Better Scheme of Things

During almost forty years of unscholarly but nevertheless meaningful writing and publishing philosophy (at my own expense), I have never been noticed by either the academic or literary 'intelligentsia' of my country. I have been often told that I write well; thus, my utter isolation cannot be attributed to poor writing skills. Rather, I believe, it is due to 1) a total lack of interest today in the metaphysical subjects on which I write, and 2) to an absence of institutional affiliations or clique memberships on my part. The intrinsic significance of my writings is not enough to offset the isolation occasioned by these two factors, especially in a market-obsessed literary industry.

What to do in the twilight of my life? Perhaps I should look upon myself as a tragic figure and bask in that feeling. But I do not feel tragic. I see myself as destined by an immutable fate to live outside my society's literary circles. I prefer to *love my fate* as Nietzsche ordained for lonely figures like himself. *Amor fati*—that is the proper attitude to be cultivated.

In a better and higher scheme of things, my fate may well be preferable to that of the circus creatures of the American literary establishment.

Mar 26 '19 – Herd Mentality

"Herd" mentality is a constant feature of the human psyche. Whether one aspires to be a leader, a follower, or a participating member, it is a herd mentality that dominates the mind of most human beings. Genuine individuality is rare. Most people are desirous of being part of some herd. But real spiritual development—the proper goal of Homo sapiens—stems from the individual, not the herd. And human beings have, first and foremost, a responsibility for their own spiritual development.

Associations, societies, communities, cliques, etc. are all means for gratifying an atavistic herd instinct. The current enthusiasm over "intersubjectivity" espoused by intellectuals is a more subtle means to the same end. I believe, however, that human individuals should live psychologically more like mountain lions than like wolves—the latter live in packs but the former maintain their unique individual independence. Right now, it seems that Homo sapiens are like lemmings madly rushing into a sea that drowns them. G-d may have given up on us—as the American poet Robinson Jeffers suggested many moons ago.

Mar 27 '19 – Metaphysics of Consciousness

I read today about some 'neuroscientist' studying the mechanism of consciousness in the brain. Even though I once could have been considered a neuroscientist, I didn't understand much of the esoteric terminology. But the basic approach was clear: changes in brain electrical activity were correlated with changes in consciousness, thus giving insight into how consciousness arises. There was no consideration of the possibility—the likelihood in my judgment— that it is consciousness that *causes* brain activity, thus preparing one to be able to act on his consciousness. The brain is the master *executive* organ of a human being. Even more unjustified is the idea that if an area of the brain is damaged, the resulting alteration of consciousness indicates the origin of consciousness in it. It is like saying if the legs of a person are broken and he cannot walk, the origin of the act of walking is in the legs. The legs are the executive organs for walking but not their origin.

As long as the metaphysical nature of Homo sapiens is ignored or denied, this kind of unproductive (and costly) folderol will continue to go on. "The proper study of Mankind is man," the Poet wrote. Not his physical brain.

Mar 28 '19—Morning in Menton

Looking at the great red ball that is the sun rising over the vastness of the Mediterranean Sea, I am reminded of my inexpressible smallness as a human individual. Only my soul justifies any concern with my existence. Rejection of its reality would reject my significance. These thoughts would sooner or later disappear from my consciousness if I did not write them down. What does this signify? It signifies that the act of writing seems to be necessary to establish my metaphysical existence. It has made me what I am today.

At 88 years of age, there are likely to be no more bends ahead of my terrestrial road. I begin to visualize its termination. I can only hope I have done my duty as a human being endowed with a potential for metaphysical development.

The terrestrial world will continue to exist without me.

Mar 31 '19 – Night Fears and Tight Corners
Sometimes when I am in a state of semi-wakefulness at night, there come upon me, suddenly, dreadful fears. If there are no metaphysical realities in which I participate, then my writing life has been meaningless. The only spirits of significance are those that one drinks. I am assailed by the feeling that all my years of philosophical activity about metaphysical matters and the state of the soul are all mere illusions without any basis in reality. Perhaps the only *real* reality is the concrete material world, the world of the here and now, the *mondain* societal world all around me. These are the realities; the others are my fantasies. My fear is I have wasted forty years of my life on metaphysical fantasies.

The undeniable fact is that I have no assurance that the metaphysical world my mind has visualized is a real one. I only have my intuitions, my revelations, and my desires. Somewhere in one of Plato's dialogues, Socrates, after describing his belief about the fate of the soul, says he cannot be certain of the absolute truth of his belief, but *it is a noble belief,* one worth maintaining. If pressed, that is how I feel about my own metaphysical beliefs. They are beliefs worth having and I intend to stick to them. Perhaps they come under the category of *faith*, which according to Christian scripture is the belief in things unseen. All the Christian legends and myths in my judgment are unconscious allegories meant to promote metaphysical faith. Without metaphysical faith, one's soul cannot flourish.

I have been interested in many religions, many philosophies, many profound thinkers during the course of my philosophical activity. However, I have never confined myself to a tight little corner with any of them. Commitment to the ideas of others, living or dead, is not my way. Even more, I do not subscribe to esoteric academic fads that I consider without meaning for my own persona. My philosophical efforts are centered around my own soul. At times, I have wondered if someone could accuse me of spiritual narcissism and this may well be true. But I consider it necessary in view of the spiritual desert in which I live. If all this leads to night fears, so be it. I am willing to tolerate them.

May the Cosmic Power that must exist look favorably upon my soul.

April 24 '19 – "The Will to Believe"

Finally, I must decide whether the development of my soul is enough in itself for a fulfilling life or whether some kind of external accomplishment is required for me to feel successful. If the latter is the case, my life has been a failure. Which is it to be—success or failure? No further procrastination can be allowed to me.

I assert that a *reverence* for my soul, a faith in its *importance*, is what I need to be 'successful.' *Faith* is what I need; the kind of faith described in the scriptural 'Letter to the Hebrews' but with a different content… I *will* find that faith! I *will* not be a person of little faith! I *will* have faith in myself as soul. If I have this faith, then

I am a successful person. Not just thinking or feeling, but *willing* is the secret to a spiritually-based 'successful' life. It is debasing to a developing individual to have to accept childish religious dogmas, or to passively wait for a revelation or epiphany (rarely, if ever, appearing) in order to acquire a spiritual faith. The *will* to spiritual development is an unrecognized human reality, yet it is the key to genuine success in life. (The intellectual philosopher William James respected and wrote about the 'Will to Believe' even if he did not have it himself.) This *will* stems from deep within an individual—from his mysterious innermost being. Indian Vedanta philosophy refers to this inner self as *Atman,* which it sees as coextensive with *Brahman* (the Christian Kingdom of God). Validation by one's society has nothing to do with the issue. A lifelong dependence on societal crutches and connections means one's life has not been fulfilled. Today, this attitude is politically incorrect but I believe it is in accord with the highest element of the human condition.

Do I have that degree of will? I have achieved material independence but have I reached the equally important psychological independence? Time may tell—although I do not have a great deal of time left to me to make a success of my life in these terms. Writing these lines to myself teaches me and strengthens my will. I have come to believe one must *create* his own spiritual reality through a spiritually-inclined will. Intellectuality is only a tool and not an end in itself. The current state of affairs in 'developed' civilizations reveals the fate of a purely materialist intellectuality. I have no more interest in becoming such an 'intellectual' than in becoming a religious fanatic.

I believe my admittedly limited desire to communicate with others through my publications is based upon a selfless altruism, not upon any concealed need for societal status and certainly not for more money than I already have. All that I have to give to unknown others are my thoughts expressed in a clear and cogent manner. These I would like to provide to spiritually-inclined individuals who are interested and might be responsive to them.

May 7 '19 – "Me, I Put My Guts on the Table" (Céline)

In spite of my past reluctance to admit any kind of *knowability* about the ultimate metaphysical reality called G-d, I now have a powerful inward sense that my thoughts promote his *consciousness*. G-d must be more than Christian love, he must be all forms of consciousness. He must expand his consciousness since from his consciousness comes his creative power. He desires human meta-physical expression that becomes part of himself. It may be that my "guts on the table" is really God developing his consciousness. If this idea seems absurd and indicative of megalomania, it may nevertheless contain the truth. I stand by my intuition. Yet the desire for approval by a market-obsessed cliquish literary industry lingers within my soul and, like a deep-rooted weed, is difficult to expurgate completely. Nevertheless, I work at its expurgation.

I fear physical decrepitude is gaining ground upon me. May I become a worthy representative of God before my earthly end.

The other day I worshipped at the altar of Aphrodite. It was an enthralling, rejuvenating, even exalting experience. The altar must be sweet, fresh, and welcoming. Without this worship, I might lapse into a permanent misanthropy.

May 22 '19 – An Abbreviated Summing Up

I have probably written and published more during my writing era than I should have; thus, I feel the need to emphasize the important metaphysical ideas that I have come to believe. For the better part of my writing career, I concentrated on establishing the *reality* of my soul; an idea that has been in poor repute during the age of scientism. Immersion in the writings of Nikolai Berdyaev did much to strengthen this belief. My book *Souls Exist* established to my own satisfaction the basis for my conviction. I don't feel the need to repeat what is in that book and its sequel, *Toward an Existential Philosophy of the Soul.*

For many years, I thought that was as far as I could go in my metaphysical investigations. The idea of God was relegated to a speculative position since I had no basis for accepting that ancient concept. 'God' had never communicated with me directly nor were the traditional religious teachings about him persuasive to my mind.

In recent years, however, my thoughts on the subject of G-d have changed. Not that he has 'spoken' to me, but I have discovered in myself a *yearning* toward an Ultimate Metaphysical Reality. I have no problem in calling this ultimate reality 'G-d'. At times, this yearning is so intense that it verges into a visceral feeling that such an ultimate metaphysical reality must exist. Furthermore, I have come to take seriously Aristotle's thoughts on the subject. I cannot escape believing that there must be a 'first cause' for the universe in all its dimensions, metaphysical as well as physical. This first cause would be G-d and if someone were to ask me now if I believe in G-d, I would have to answer in the affirmative.

Most recently, an intuition has developed within me that I have a closeness with G-d, even more, that he needs my consciousness. I can't defend this intuition with any objective facts but I feel that it has significance and it is growing in clarity. This feeling is not far removed from ideas expressed in the twentieth century books of the Jewish philosopher Abraham Joshua Heschel (and the Catholic Angelus Silesius long before him).

I think these thoughts may be my final philosophical position. It does me much good to write them out. As far as the religions of the world are concerned, I have never been able to take seriously their legends and rituals. I know they are "the metaphysics of the people," but I need a different route to metaphysical belief. If some reader should find some common ground with my beliefs, I would be pleased. If not, not. If all my writings were to be

271

incinerated in one vast pyre of my books, I would not be unduly distressed. They have served their main purpose for me. It is important that I keep this reality in mind.

Needless to say, I have not found any interest in my writings in the American literary industry, nor have I been inclined to seek out a market on my own. My situation as a writer in the literary world can be regarded as the epitome of 'anti-success.' As a consequence, I feel my personality has developed fruitfully in an inward manner, which is not often the case with 'successful' writers. I am grateful for having had the freedom to develop myself through my writings for these many years.

And once again to those with an analytic, materialist, society-fixated disposition: *Honi Soit qui Mal y Pense*.

Notebook 4

He who floats with the current, who does not guide himself by higher principles, who has no ideal, no convictions, is a mere article of the world's furniture, a puppet instead of a living independent being, an echo and not a voice. Whoever has no interior life is the slave of his surroundings, as the barometer is the obedient servant of the quiet air and the weathercock the humble servant of the air in movement.

Henri-Frédéric Amiel, *Journal Intime*

Metaphysical Night Thoughts: These thoughts represent the evolution of my personal metaphysics well after the termination of my formal publication works. Yet I believe it may contain the most profound of my writings in its later sections. In this era of spiritual disinterest, parading under the guise of religious 'toleration,' I can express my metaphysical beliefs freely without fear. I have done so once again in these night thoughts. Consistency must not be expected and repetition forgiven, as is the case with all creative writing.

On the small possibility that readers besides myself may come upon these pages (I am the main reader of my own writings so as to fully assimilate what I have written), I beg him or her to consider them in the context of my past philosophical writings on the soul, especially the book *Souls Exist* 2nd ed. (2013).

August 18, 2019

"Hear O Mankind, the Lord thy God is manifold and everywhere." Polytheism (imagination) is for children, monotheism (autocracy) is for adolescents, pantheism (intellectuality) is for Spinozists, but *panentheism* (God everywhere as *the soul* of the universe) is for spiritually developed minds. After the intuition of a universal metaphysical divinity comes the intuition of the potential divinity of the human soul.

Aug 19 '19 – "Workplace of the Lord"

The individual human ego, usually oblivious of its role in the cosmic drama, is the driving force toward development of consciousness of divinity. It needs training to perform its appointed task. However, denigration of the ego because of ignorant misdirection, throws out the baby with the bathwater. Spiritual *egoism*, i.e. reverence for one's soul, is the central feature of the developed human mind. Spiritual egoism to my mind is a *holy* phenomenon.

Jesus of Nazareth was primarily a teacher of Israel and thought 'teaching' (continuously and variably repeating his message) would accomplish his goals. He didn't seem to realize that one's 'persona' is the only effective teacher. Later, serious followers of his realized this and developed the concept of the Holy Spirit acting through the self. By then, Christianity had become an idol-worshipping religion, with 'Jesus the Christ' the idol. The 'self' became denigrated.

The human soul is the workplace of an incomplete Lord striving to develop a higher consciousness for Itself. When the 'material' of the workplace is exhausted, souls are 'recycled' within the being of the Lord. How do I *know* all this? I don't know it, I only 'suspect' it. Suspicions are worth asserting even if they do not rise to the same level of knowledge as intuitions or factual information. Metaphysical matters cannot be known, they can only be suspected or, at best, intuited.

Aug 20 '19 – My book *Interior Lights*
I have been rereading *Interior Lights*, published by me seven years ago. It is one of my best books, perhaps the best. During this time, I have been unjustly ignoring it due to my own absurd fault. Six years ago I took the stupid step of purchasing a review for it. I should have known better. As I might have expected, the anonymous reviewer must have been a hidebound academic who had no empathy for my writing and was irritated by its style and substance. He wrote a

negative review, concluding with the opinion (expressed sarcastically) that it never should have been published. But the real absurdity was the impact his review had upon me. I was crushed, embarrassed, and unable to open or even mention the book until the present time. Now I know better. I should have expected nothing less from an anonymous academic reviewer. Now I can appreciate the writing and thank a kind fate that has allowed me to live long enough to make good in my mind my former pusillanimity. What a fool I was!

Melanie and I are thinking about relocating to a smaller, more accessible home. Then what will I do with my library of at least a thousand books? It is painful to me to think about it. My library is the record of my life.

It is getting more difficult for me to keep old age at bay. There is my defective hearing, defective vision, a hernia, my worsening hand tremor, my poor balance due to the vertigo attacks. So far, I soldier on with the aid of my devoted wife. But how long can this go on? My mind remains intact although the energy for expression is slipping. At some point, I must call it quits.

Yet I may have one more geographic life in my quiver!! I won't reject it, I will try to welcome it.

(later) rejuvenated by worshipping at the shrine of Aphrodite!

Aug 28 '19

There is a force within me constantly striving to strengthen my spiritual being. I think that this force is coextensive in some way with the ultimate metaphysical reality (Divinity). On what do I base this belief? On an intuition that it is the way things are in the metaphysical universe. It is fruitless to attempt to comprehend the details of the connection of one's own spiritual being with that of Divinity. Enough to intuit (divine?) their involvement with each other without resorting to meaningless speculation, imagination, or self-serving commands falsely attributed to G-d.

G-d lives and grows through my soul's activity!

Sept 1 '19 – "A Voice Crying in the Wilderness"

When I reread my books, I feel like "a voice crying in the wilderness"—except I am not proclaiming the way of the Lord, I am merely asserting my belief in the reality of my soul and its connection to G-d. Unlike the voice of John the Baptist, however, there is no evidence that anyone has heard my voice. It has not emerged from the wilderness.

I do not think the Hollywood ending of the Christian cult will ever apply to me. Nor would I want it to, given the spiritually degenerate state of my society. I know my fate; it is to disappear from this world without leaving a trace. My books will be recycled into from whence their paper came. But the metaphysical world is another matter. I have high hopes for my soul's existence there.

Sept 2 '19

Now that I have stopped writing except for sporadic entries in this notebook, I notice an element of boredom entering into my life. I am often sleepy for no reason. The saying comes to my mind, from where I don't remember, "Woe to him who abandons the passions of his society." Is my life becoming woeful? Perhaps it is so. Yet there is still some vitality in my aging corpus. What to do? I must think carefully and deeply on this question.

Sept 3 '19

It occurs to me that I am living on experiences of my past life. It is time for me to acquire some new meaningful ones. At my age, these are hard to come by. But I must make the effort. Live the life you have until you die.

Sept 13 '19 – Hindu Scriptures

I have long been Intrigued by the ancient Hindu scriptures. Their main message as far as I can tell is to *reach* Divinity (Brahman) in oneself. However, I feel the emphasis should be on *developing* spirituality within the self. Brahman needs the development that individual souls can provide. Thus, a *purpose* is given to human life. Brahman is not 'perfect'; He needs *augmentation of his reality*.

That is my intuitive view. I have said it before.

Oct 18 '19 – Augmenting Divinity

Have been thinking rather than writing this past month. The principle idea I emphasize to myself is the obligation to *augment* the being of Divinity (God, Brahman, Ultimate Metaphysical Reality) through developing my own soul. This follows naturally from the recurrent intuition of spiritually-minded individuals that the human soul is a part of Divinity. But the soul must be developed.

I have finally accepted the fact that I do not belong in any organized church or fellowship. Places of religious worship are essentially social institutions and I cannot develop my spirituality through social institutions. I am an *independent* in every sense of the word. I have found inspiration in written words, not in social interactions or listening to sermons.

What is important to me as the essence of spirituality is consciousness of my spiritual significance and its contribution to Divinity.

Again, I firmly resist the temptation to speculate on exactly how I might augment the being of Divinity. It is enough for me to intuit that it can occur. Virtually all the spiritually-minded philosophers I read have used their imagination to supplement their intuition. It is impossible to distinguish imagination from intuition in Christian faith-based dogmas. These are grave problems in my opinion and undermines spiritual reliability. Human individuals are limited in the ability to develop a detailed consciousness of cosmic realities—material or spiritual.

Oct 21 '19 – A Transcendental Consciousness

Another way of expressing the principal responsibility of human beings is the need to develop a *transcendental* consciousness and follow wherever this may lead. Neglect of this responsibility, for whatever reason, is the ultimate sin toward the self. The assumption that there is a G-d somewhere in the cosmos who knows all and can tell human beings what to think and how to behave is erroneous. A spiritual individual is like a pioneer in a vast wilderness who must establish his own worldview and way of life.

"Purity of heart is to will one thing." Kierkegaard's spiritual genius perceived this truth even if the 'one thing' he asserted was a bit wide of the mark.

Contemporary 'culture' with its unrestrained materialism is the main hindrance today to spiritual development of an individual.

Oct 22 '19 – Becoming Spiritual

To say it again, even more concisely, the one thing needful is to become spiritual. It needs saying many times to counteract the crushing robotization of current life. As far as I can tell, it is the same everywhere on this overburdened planet.

To yearn for a God to befriend one (never mind J.C.), is to evade one's responsibility. It leads to a false spirituality based upon an imaginary companion. If there is a 'compassionate' God in the cosmos, He probably could not concern himself with all the specks of yearning dust. Even if he did, he would not be the pompous Judeo-Christian Jehovah, but something more akin to Spinoza's pantheistic God or to the Hindu Brahman. These latter, however, cannot be anthropomorphized.

"Become spiritual"—that is the alpha and omega of the human condition—at least of my condition. God needs my spiritual consciousness. Modern spirituality represents the transition of rational physical creatures to intuitive metaphysical creatures; creatures that intuit and express instead of measure and explain— just as an earlier transition was from instinctive creatures to rational ones. This is sarcastically expressed by Mephistopheles in Goethe's Faust. 1st Act, Part II:

> Now I recognize the learned master!
> What you can't touch is of no consequence,
> What you can't hold, has no meaning,
> What you can't calculate, can't be true,
> What you can't weigh, has no weight for you,
> What you can't 'coin', that, you think, is worthless.

(My translation)

The worst error is to confuse spirituality with morality. Morality may be an element within spirituality but it is not the most important one and the dimensions of one's wide ego must be respected.

Oct 23 '19

Definition of 'spiritual'—concerned with the state of the inner, metaphysical self, the 'soul'. A spiritual person has reverence for his soul and seeks to enhance and preserve it. In so doing, I believe, he can *augment* God's being.

Oct 24 '19 – Development of Self

Today, all the progress of so-called spiritual thought is directed toward relationships with others rather than individual development. The latter is regarded suspiciously as 'egotism,' the ultimate sin. In a recent colloquium on the Russian philosopher Nicholas Berdyaev, a prominent contemporary philosopher and cleric asserted that "man only arrives at his [true] self through relations with others." Martin Buber's famous book *I and Thou* (Ich und Du—the English translation gives an unjustified archaic quality to it) provided a powerful intellectual basis for this concept. However, in the present age with trivialization of conversation, self-serving socializations, and dominance of electronic talk, I–Thou relationships are hard to come by. Professional relationships are primarily means for career development. Church activities, in my experience, are forms of socialization and not of spiritual enhancement. Thus, one is necessarily thrown back alone into his inner self for meaningful spiritual development.

The Scriptural injunction, "Love thy neighbor as thyself," has to do with morality, compassionate behavior that is far removed from the spiritual "I–Thou" relationship. This is made clear by Jesus' 'Golden Rule' asserted in the Sermon on the Mount, "So in everything, do unto others what you would have them do unto you, for this is all the Law and the Prophets" (Matthew 7:12). Jesus himself did not seem to have any significant spiritual relationships; his role with his disciples and other followers was that of a teacher and leader.

It is my considered opinion that the development of self is a solitary activity, far removed from the usual madding crowds. If an individual arrives at one genuine I–Thou relationship in this life, he or she is fortunate indeed.

Oct 25 '19 – Dualism

I do not agree with the sharp tripartite division of human beings into body, soul, and metaphysically deeper spirit. To my mind, human spirituality derives from activity, both on a physical and psychical level. I don't believe spirituality is a gift from G-d that descends on special individuals. Nor do I think it is only reached through trance-like yogic states. The individual soul and the transcendental spirit are a continuum—and perhaps including the physical body as well. However, given the state of affairs in the world today, *dualism* is a necessary corrective to the overwhelming materialist mentality that rules everywhere.

I write all this not to influence my society, which I have learned to be an impossible expectation, but to clarify for myself what I believe.

Oct 27 '19 – Intuiting vs Imagining

'Metaphysics' falls into two categories:

1) A spiritual subject *intuiting* metaphysical reality, and

2) A thinking subject *imagining* metaphysical possibility.

The task of a critically significant philosophy is to distinguish between these two categories of thought. In my opinion, most religious beliefs fall into the second category. Intuiting metaphysical reality is a lifelong task undertaken by very few individuals.

Oct 30 '19 – The Good Fight

It is crystal clear to me that I am profoundly out of touch with the prevailing culture. After forty years of writing philosophy, I cannot say there has been one iota of interest in my writings in the culture world—other than my ventures into Nietzsche studies, which do not reflect my own philosophical thought. I believe in independent development; the watchword today is 'interdependence.' I believe in the reality of the soul; today the world is committed to an electronic type of society where AI and its derivatives are reigning supreme. Academic, celebrity, and literary cliques rule literature. There is no place for me.

Nor do I have any illusions of posthumous 'success.' The after-death notoriety of a Kierkegaard, a Nietzsche, a Pessoa will not come my way. So be it. I have led a full life and expressed myself fully within it. That is more than most can say. I have fought the good fight as I have seen fit to fight it. Soon I must lay down all my arms and commend my soul to an unknown fate, hoping fate will deal kindly with it.

Nov 4 '19 – Divinity Can Wait

I believe the development of consciousness is the essence and driving force of the human condition. "All men by nature desire to know" is how Aristotle began the *Metaphysics*. Consciousness means 'knowing'. Animals have the same sensations and activity that have humans, some even more intensely, but they have only the rudiments of consciousness. It is only humans who can develop their consciousness to higher levels of understanding and wisdom.

According to Eastern spiritual lore, consciousness of the identity of the human and divine spirit is the final goal of human development. However, I think this is very rarely—perhaps never—completely accomplished; nor can it be in my opinion, since I think *the purpose of the development of individual human beings is to augment, enrich, or further develop the divine spirit, not merely to fuse with it.*

Individualized life is a learning experience for human beings of all ages and circumstances, for the callow youth as well as the aging octogenarian. The more individuals live their own lives, the more they can develop their consciousness. As long as one is alive, one should not abandon experiential living for any reason whatever, including temporarily experiencing divinity. The ego is the necessary feature for living fully. "Live 'til you die!" is my motto. Divinity can wait.

Nov 27 '19 – Metaphysical Existence

All the great metaphysically-minded philosophers from Plato to Paul Tillich have believed that the ultimate goal of an individual can only be fulfilled through a spiritual connection with Divinity. The same is true of the Vedanta and Buddhist thinkers of India. St. Augustine asserted that the only real questions for philosophy were the soul and God. He might have added, 'and how the former finds fulfillment through the latter.' Divinity is always envisioned as an 'entity' (with the exception of Spinoza), albeit infinite in all possible properties and powers. They have based their opinions on the ever present 'yearning' of thoughtful individuals to find something fulfilling beyond earthly satisfactions, something more than the day to day pleasures and pains of societal living. This yearning has been interpreted as a desire to 'find G-d'.

I have certainly felt this yearning and have recorded it in my writings. But now, the feeling has come upon me that I am not yearning for connection to a putative divinity, but rather I yearn to enter into a *metaphysical dimension* of existence beyond the material dimension in which I now live. I sense that the 'goal' of spiritual development is to enter this dimension; physical life may only be the breeding ground for growth of the soul. Perhaps the chief creator and inhabitant of the metaphysical dimension is the Judeo-Christian Jehovah, but the important thing for my soul is to gain access to this dimension. If Jehovah and I communicate and we share our spiritual beings with each other, that is all to the good. If some would like to label the metaphysical dimension of existence as Heaven and set up criteria for entrance, I would have no objection—as long as I and others like me were not excluded.

I believe I enter into the metaphysical dimension briefly at certain times when I am able to disconnect from the surrounding physical world. Periods of meditation, especially when lying awake at night, are times when this seems to occur. But these are brief and always terminated by either sleep or interruptions from the surroundings. I like to think that death will afford me the opportunity to permanently pass over into metaphysical existence. This may be wishful thinking but something within me says there is truth in it. Just as ages ago certain animals left their watery milieu for the completely different world of life on land, so certain human beings are destined to leave the physical world for existence in a metaphysical one. The analogy is not perfect but there are many similarities.

My intuition may not solve the great perennial problems of cosmology or theology, but then again there is no reason why my limited being should be capable of solving them. I am content to merely be aware of their nature and adjust my terrestrial way of life accordingly.

Dec 1 '19 – Metaphysical Existence (cont'd)

I have allowed myself to wonder what metaphysical existence might be like. Doubtless the familiar time and space categories of terrestrial existence by which one experiences the universe will no longer be in force. This can be a frightening thought. But the best comment on the subject is that of Heraclitus, which I have often reread and reflected on: "What awaits human beings at death they do not anticipate nor even imagine" (Fragment LXXXIV). It is foolish to expect otherwise. One can only await the great event of passing with hope.

Devout Christians and Jews will think what is missing from these reflections is G-d. That is undoubtedly true, but it is because He has never directly communicated with me nor have I been aware of His influence. I can't trust second hand messages from so-called authorities on these important matters. Consequently, I must create my own worldview without His help. What faith I have is based on a sense of my own intellectual and spiritual powers.

It must be admitted that I cannot exclude the possibility of an unnoticed influence upon me by an all-powerful G-d.

Kierkegaard says G-d is present in the world 'incognito'. If this be the case, He is well disguised since I have no awareness of His presence. So-called 'Grace' (which may be just a pervasive delusion of Christianity) has not descended upon me. Therefore, I cannot ascribe any aspect of my consciousness or will to Him. My intellectual conscience forbids it.

Dec 5 '19 – Immortality

The thought has again forcefully come to me that the essential thing in human life may be not just to 'find' Divinity or to merely love and obey it like a child to a parent, but to so significantly live that upon one's passage through death, one's soul may be integrated within it—thereby *augmenting* its reality. This then will constitute a meaningful immortality and it assigns great importance to human life. While some may dismiss these thoughts as merely imaginative mysticism, they are no more so than the belief in a supreme almighty God that is a heritage of most advanced civilizations!

January 3, 2020 – The Most Important Thing

With his usual ability to penetrate to the heart of things, Jesus said that the most important commandment of the Hebrew Law is to love God with all one's mind, heart, soul, and strength. However, in order to love 'God' (i.e. a metaphysical Divinity) to this degree, one must become *conscious* of his existence. Thus, becoming conscious of God's existence is a crucial factor in the life of Homo sapiens. How to accomplish this task is a perennial problem for man and is especially acute in materialist societies such as now exist in developed countries of the world.

How does one become conscious of the existence of a metaphysical Divinity? Historically, there have been two main routes—revelation from above and personal meditation. Religious traditions can provide a foundation for God consciousness but without individual effort are of lesser value, often only resulting in superficial ritualistic practices and Pharisaism. Education is valuable in broadening one's horizons, but commonly ends in mere erudition, which is unrelated to G-d consciousness.

Genuine revelation in contemporary societies is very rare today to the point of disappearance of the phenomenon, probably due to dominance of the materialist-scientific worldview. So, one is only left with the necessity for spiritual meditation to become conscious of G-d. This is the message of Hindu Vedanta teaching whose influence ought to become more widespread in the western World. Meditation requires much mental effort, with which I have been wrestling for many years. But for me, the goal of meditation is entry of myself into a metaphysical dimension of being, not personal oblivion or loss of self in 'Nirvana'.

My view about Christianity is that the metaphysically lazy concept of salvation through 'accepting' the Lord Jesus Christ as one's Savior, so prevalent now in Protestant Christianity, has served its historical purpose to promote spiritual awareness and needs to be abandoned in order for individuals to obtain a deeper and more profound spiritual consciousness. Neither the practice of Christian (or Jewish) religious commandments serve to achieve this end. There is no suitable substitute for an individual's personal search for the metaphysical dimension. A clue to finding it is the significant statement attributed to Jesus that "the Kingdom of God is within you" (Lk. 17:21).

Jan 4 '20

Continuing on the thought of the last sentence of the previous entry: if the Kingdom of God is within the individual, the obligation to develop a God consciousness is closely related to the dictum of the Delphic Oracle—"Know Yourself." This maxim was a main principle of Socrates as related by both Plato and Xenophon. Thus, the statement of Jesus about the 'location' of the Kingdom of God can be reconciled with antique Greek wisdom. The truth of the human condition is the same everywhere and at all times, either potentially or actually.

Jan 7 '20 – My Sin

I have been daily reading the Bible—both Testaments and the Wisdom books. The Gospels say John the Baptist was "a voice in the wilderness crying, 'Repent your sins!'" What have I to repent? I follow my conscience; not the primitive ethics of the Pentateuch or the exaggerated injunctions of the Sermon on the Mount. I have never thought I had anything to repent about but now I know I do. My 'sin' is that I have not been sufficiently conscious of the *metaphysical dimension* of human existence, a grave fault in human beings. Now I will try to repent that fault by striving to be cognizant of it and act accordingly. Mere intellectual belief is not enough.

"The fear of the Lord is the beginning of Wisdom" (Ecclesiasticus 39). I would replace the words 'fear of the Lord' with 'consciousness of metaphysical reality.'

The 'Law' of the Hebrew Scriptures is a human product, not a divine one, and should be treated as such—as are the sayings of Jesus of Nazareth. But as human spiritual expressions, they are worthy of respect and consideration without requiring obedience.

"Yes, the heavens are as high above earth

As my thoughts are above your ways,

My thoughts above your thoughts."

G-d speaking to man in Isaiah 55:9

Jan 9 '20 – The Kingdom of Heaven

How does one arrive at consciousness of the metaphysical dimension or in Jesus' terms the Kingdom of Heaven? I have meditated much on this question. I do not believe it appears suddenly, like a bolt of lightning out of the blue. It requires sustained effort on the part of the spiritual seeker. These are some paths I have found that lead to a metaphysical consciousness:

- Study of the Scriptures of historically significant religions: the Judeo-Christian Old and New Testaments, the Upanishads, the Bhagavad-Gita, Buddhist tracts
- Study of existential philosophers: e.g. Kierkegaard, Berdyaev, Tillich
- Philosophically knowledgeable reflections on the meaning of existence
- Techniques of deep meditation (e.g. Yoga)
- Acts directed toward Divinity; deeds, rituals, sacrifices (*Mitzvot* in Judaism)
- Meaningful experiences: creative activity, *significant* human interactions, travels in nature and cultures
- Prayers of gratitude and praise of the metaphysical Kingdom
- Writing out one's insights and understanding (most important for me)
- Finding the leisure to engage in all of the above things

None of the above are adequate alone; all require a sincere seeking spirit.

Jan 12 '20 – Loss of Capacity to be aware of Metaphysical Reality
It is well known that a lifelong dependence on a single language greatly reduces ability to learn a new language. Similarly, I believe, lifelong dominance of a scientific mindset results in loss of the ability of an individual to be aware of metaphysical reality, i.e. the

Kingdom of Heaven in Gospel terms (synonymous with the term Kingdom of God).

Logical Positivism has been the philosophical movement underpinning a scientific mindset (scientism). It is based on the principles of objective observation, analytic thinking, and verifiability of conclusions. Metaphysics is ruled out of court as founded on emotionality and superstition. In recent years, logical positivism has been downgraded in academic philosophy but still reigns supreme in the worldview of 'advanced' civilizations. This is because the modern worldview does not depend on the abstractions of academic philosophy, but rather on the remarkable successes of 'scientism' in controlling nature, empowering societies, and advancing the physical welfare of populations in innumerable ways.

All this, however, has been done at a cost to the spiritual welfare of individuals. The capacity to enter upon metaphysical reality has been lost. Christianity emphasizes love of one's fellow man because the capacity for love of God has been lost among Christians. G-d-consciousness is only possible on intellectual terms, not directly as one spirit searching for a higher one. When Spinoza advocated the "intellectual love of G-d," he perceived the coming dominance of scientism. He saw no other possibility to develop a G-d-consciousness.

This is all entirely noticeable in myself. I can mainly envision metaphysical consciousness in intellectual terms. In my opinion, this is quite inferior to an intuitional consciousness but it is the best I can do with my history and at my stage in life. I believe my soul has been scarred by its development in a world dominated by scientism. I think I might have become a spiritually better person in a different world. However, I try to make the best of my circumstances.

Jan 14 '20 – Philosophical Mind Storming

Significant spiritual developments in the western world:

- Hebrew prophets (ending with J.C.)
- Ancient Greek philosophers
- Scholastic thinkers (Christian)
- German mystics
- American transcendentalists
- Pre-revolution Russian intelligentsia (e.g. N. Berdyaev)

Nothing new for over a century. Spiritual expression has been inhibited since the dominance of scientism and logical positivism in societal cultures. What is new now is the computer age with accompanying digitalization of human activity in 'advanced' societies.

The concept of Robinson Jeffers that the human race represents a failed experiment of God seems to best fit the current situation as I see it.

Jan 18 '20 -- Technology run amok

The novel by the Portuguese writer Eça de Queiroz entitled *The City and the Mountains* (published posthumously in 1901) depicts in a satirical vein the dominance of the philosophy of logical positivism in fin-de-siècle Paris. The profusion of gadgetry and technology thought to represent scientific 'progress' and purporting to improve 'civilized' life destroys the well-being of the protagonist Jacinto. Eça attributes Jacinto's predicament to the absurd technological civilization of large cities, exemplified by Paris. Today, however, there is no escape anywhere in 'developed' nations, city or country, from the evils of profit-oriented technology run amok.

Feb 11 '20 – My Worldview

My mind is gradually settling on a 'worldview'. It is a trinitarian concept of the cosmos, except my trinity is myself, Divinity, and the universe without. My task is to integrate these three elements into one reality. Divinity emerges in me and I in It. Divinity *needs* me and I need It for mutual fulfillment. G-d is the soul of the universe and, therefore I in a certain sense am that also. 'Loving G-d' is the same as loving myself.

The task is to convert these mental concepts into a unitary personal reality. Here Hindu Vedanta is far ahead of Christianity or Judaism in accomplishing this task.

Needless to say, my vision of Divinity is as an 'Ultimate Metaphysical Being', not the Lord of Judeo-Christendom. This assertion could be set forth in much greater detail one day.

Feb 24 '20 – "Better Late than Never"

After a long period of worrying and brooding over various aspects of my life, I have succeeding in bringing into consciousness the most important thing—my 'relationship' with Divinity. By Divinity, I do not mean an all-powerful, judgmental Jehovah, but rather an ultimate metaphysical reality that I am sure exists. I must maintain my focus on this aspect of my life. The first thing necessary is to become *conscious* of Divinity; more than consciousness may come later.

Furthermore, the awareness has come to me that Divinity exists within myself as Jesus is said to have asserted in the Gospel of Luke. There is a part of me that coexists intimately within it and a part that is just an aging human being. When I arrive at consciousness of my condition, I believe the reality of the Divinity is *augmented* ('augmented' is an especially valuable word in the English language).

There are multiple aspects to my human condition: an animal nature, a marital role, an American, a Jew, a member of worldwide humanity. All these roles must be attended to in due measure. But the primary, most important need of mine is to develop a relationship with the ultimate metaphysical reality I call Divinity.

This must be paramount. Otherwise, I would remain in a restless, irritable, unhappy, and unfulfilled state. (I now prefer the term 'Divinity' to that of 'God' because there are too many unfortunate associations with the latter term. However, in my writings, the words are used interchangeably.}

It is amazing to me that I have only fully arrived at this insight when approaching the ninetieth year of my life. Others have arrived at it far earlier. But I have always known I am slow to mature. Better late than never!

I have not found that participation in church or synagogue activities has led me to Divinity. The main emphasis in them has been on rituals, sermons, and social 'do-gooding', which do not engage my interest. Religious organizations for me are agents for fellowship, not for experiencing the metaphysical dimension of existence, never mind participating in the nature of Divinity.

The thoughts I have expressed above have often been put forth as *speculations* in my past writings. It has taken a long time for them to mature in my mind, to be *assimilated* into my soul so that they are now firm intuitions instead of speculative suggestions. I have no idea how or why this has happened. Some process must have been at work within the recesses of my soul to make me conscious of my participation in Divinity. Perhaps unbeknownst to me, 'G-d' was at work. Whatever the reason, I am grateful to have finally realized this essential thing in my life.

It matters little what others may think of my personal metaphysics. I live in a place and at a time where 'blasphemy' is not punished but only ignored—or ridiculed. However, in my opinion, most people in America today, especially scholarly-minded ones, are starved for G-d. I pity them even if they reject my pity and think poorly of me.

"*Honi soit qui mal y pense.*"

Perhaps it is too much to say I have been 'born again' (albeit with lapses), but I notice a certain resemblance between my new self and evangelical Christians who claim to have been born again through accepting their Lord Jesus Christ. Our theologies are quite different yet this may not be so important. The main thing is a turning toward an awareness of a metaphysical Divinity, however one conceives of Its nature.

Feb 26 '20 – The Need for Spirituality

I do not feel a compulsion to force my thoughts and insights upon others. I have often had the suspicion that imparting one's strongly held views to other people is a subtle means of dominating them. Nietzsche thought Christianity to be the most powerful tool for dominating minds of the people. It is enough for me to develop my own interior self without attempting to develop those of others.

Writing is the most effective means I have found for developing myself. Writing out my thoughts and feelings enhances greatly their value for me. They are then available for my study and reflection. If others find them of interest, I do not mind but such occurrences are entirely superfluous. Basically, I have come to the realization that I seek to be incorporated into Divinity. This is the alpha and omega of my spiritual life.

For me, spirituality is the continuous effort to arrive at consciousness of an Ultimate Metaphysical Reality, aka G-d. The Psalms of Hebrew Scripture are the most potent testimonial of this effort. I read them often. I feel the outside world is trying to destroy me just as the Psalmists felt, albeit spiritually rather than physically. We communicate over almost three millennia of history.

In referring to the souls of the virtuous, the apocryphal Book of Wisdom, composed by an Alexandrian Jew, says:

God has put them to the test

and proved them to be worthy to be with Him.

I sometimes feel I am putting God to the test. A blasphemous thought worthy of Lucifer!

Someone may think I have missed my vocation by not entering into a monastic life. However, my individuality and animal appetites were always too strong to permit such a step—and still are. One must be realistic about one's capacities.

Prolonged meditation has been a great benefit to me. Then I feel I am leaving the corpse called my body to enter into a better metaphysical existence. It is at once both exhilarating and frightening. Sometimes, I fear not being able to return to the terrestrial world since I am not done yet with the world I live in.

Feb 28 '20 – Intellectual Consciousness and Intellectual Love

It is not easy to make the transition from terrestrial to metaphysical existence. Praying is not enough. Circumstances must be favorable. Undisturbed solitude and concentration are required. One's stars must be in the proper alignment. Materialist-minded skeptics may smile and think all this is illusion and self-deception. They belong to the same category as those Eastern thinkers who believe the entire physical world perceived by the senses is illusory. One is as rigidly narrow-minded as the other. A thoughtful human being must trust his intuitions. Otherwise, it is easy to fall into the slough of cynicism and contempt.

Meanwhile, the *intellectual consciousness* of the existence of an Ultimate Metaphysical Reality carries an individual a long way toward spiritual fulfillment. One may add that the *intellectual love* of G-d (after Spinoza) also suffices.

Feb 29 '20 (Leap Year) – Why Night Thoughts

Daylight is the enemy of metaphysical awareness. It is only when physiological sight is suppressed by darkness that metaphysical sight is possible. 'Outsight' blocks out 'insight', just as solar vision prevents lunar vision. Night thoughts are the most profound of all.

In tenebris, veritas. Then the question arises as to why I should be so desirous of metaphysical insight when it may be only fully possible after the 'mortal coil' has been shed. I suppose it is because my restless nature is always ahead of itself.

The chief antique exponent of metaphysical philosophy, Plotinus, said he only glimpsed the metaphysical universe four times in his life. That should give one pause for expecting to do so antemortem. And few people have the spiritual depth of Plotinus. Like Jesus, Plotinus did not see fit to convert his insights into discursive writings, which were great losses for their posterity. Like the case of Jesus, modernity is dependent on the listeners of these great men to transmit their thoughts.

If these superior minds did not write out their insights, I ask myself often why should I feel the need to do so? One reason is that they had listeners, whereas in my solitary state I do not. Another is that modern technology makes it possible to do so in a convenient manner. There is no laborious struggle with parchment or papyrus. I believe myself to be fortunate to have modern tools for writing available to me. Most importantly, when these insights fade in my mind, as they inevitably must in the midst of earthly distractions, my writings remind me of them.

Darkness does not only create the possibility of revealing the metaphysical universe, it also can reveal the yearnings of raw animality under the civilized veneer, e.g. uninhibited sexuality, uncontrolled aggression, surges of rage, and so forth. Fear and paranoia may emerge. All this is the very antithesis of metaphysical awareness but may be necessary for it—in a Heraclitean sense of the unity of opposites. In my case, I think only death will curb the fierce yearnings of my animality.

How to *act* on yearnings is another matter entirely. This is a question of one's philosophy of life, attitude toward societal mores, and the courage of one's convictions.

Mar 10 '20 – Eschatology of the Soul

A summing-up of the development of my thoughts over many years about the destiny of the soul. It is *speculation* since I have no way of truly *knowing* its exact fate. But I have the feeling that something resembling my speculations will come to pass for myself—and for all other human beings. The worst idea a person can have is that there is no ultimate metaphysical destiny in store for his metaphysical soul. A yet worse idea is that souls do not exist at all (see *Souls Exist*, 2nd ed., 2013).

I conceive that following my death, my soul will return to the Universal Soul (aka God) from whence it came. It will contain the metaphysical qualities that it developed during the experiences of biological, interpersonal, and societal existence. These qualities are manifold, but the soul is unitary, and its fate on returning to God will depend on the amalgam of these qualities. If God deems my

303

soul worthy, it will be incorporated into His nature. If not, it will be discarded among the vast trash pile of unworthy souls. (A shorthand for these fates are the terms 'heaven' and 'hell.') God needs worthy souls. He needs them to augment His own nature, to provide it with more depth and breath. The attraction between man and God is a reciprocal one.

What are the qualities that form the worthy soul? They are familiar to all thoughtful individuals: wisdom, insight, vision, honor, kindness, self-awareness, self-respect, character, vitality, creativity, boldness, determination, endurance, modesty, spiritual consciousness—especially this last one. Others may come to one's mind. The unitary soul, however, is an amalgam of all the qualities—or lack of them—that will determine its final destiny and relationship to the Universal Soul.

All this, as I have said, is speculative, subject to the limitations of my mind and my language. However, there is a fine line between speculation, which is the product of one's imagination, and intuition, which is insight into reality. I like to think that my speculations about the destiny of the soul are more intuition than imagination.

> Remember him [G-d] ... before the dust returns to the
> ground it came from,
> And the spirit returns to G-d who gave it.
>
> Eccl. 12:6-7

April 7 '20 – In the Midst of the 'Raging' Pandemic

It would be easy for some observer to conclude that my life has been an abject failure. An early academic career in medicine came to naught. Forty years as an independent philosopher ended without any discernable impact on my society. No roots formed anywhere, no contributions to society of any type. Genuine friends none, only acquaintances. The only evident bright light is my devoted wife, whose devotion, however, may be misplaced. One might say I have meaninglessly taken up space on this already crowded planet for nigh on ninety years. Perhaps it would be desirable for the pandemic virus to carry me away without further ado.

Can there be another point of view about my life other than a totally failed one? I believe that there is one possible. It is that I have developed and maintained a *spiritual integrity*, while surrounded by a decadent and corrupt society—a modern-day Roman Empire in its last convulsions. I do not want to actively participate in that society. It is spiritually rotted-out. The only positive thing I can say is that it can serve as a proving ground for one's personal development. I have the intuition that in developing my spiritual integrity, I am making a contribution to a larger metaphysical reality whose dimensions I only dimly perceive. That is the promised land of the human condition. I will stand by this intuition to my dying day.

My response to a skeptical, cynical society that disapproves of me is always: "*Honi soit qui mal y pense.*"

Meanwhile, I try to meet my obligations and enjoy my little pleasures without concerning myself too much about the big picture. Life must go on!

April 15 '20 – A Rewarding Study

I am studying these Night Thoughts and also my book *Concluding Metaphysical Perambulations*. The purpose? To expand my mind into metaphysical awareness. I know of no better way to accomplish this task. Metaphysical awareness means preparing myself for what is to come; namely, Judgment Day, where the decision will be made of the fate of my soul—divinity or oblivion! To become conscious of metaphysical existence is to prepare for divinity.

One must not expect the gratifications of metaphysical existence to be the same as those of biological existence. They are different—more rarified, elevating the soul into a higher level of being. Antemortem, they can only be a taste of what might come. They act to release the soul from the tyranny and miseries of the world. Giving up its transitory pleasures is a small price to pay.

April 18 '20 – Sri Aurobindo

Rereading *The Life Divine* of Aurobindo. His is a far higher level of insight and integration of matter and spirit. Next to him, I feel like a child embarking on halting steps toward enlightenment. Yet I still have my own vision of spiritual fulfillment. I try not to be intimidated by Aurobindo's relentless intellectuality. Like

Nietzsche, he is someone who must be gotten through and mastered. His vast creative consciousness is an *original, new addition* to the All, the One, Brahman, God—even if he might not have accepted this thought during his lifetime.

April 24 '20 – Confession of Faith

Entering my final years and having done all that was possible for me to do given my capacities and character, I need to fall back on a *faith* to sustain me. Nietzsche said faith was cowardice, but I don't agree; faith in my judgment is a necessary part of the human condition. Every individual must find his own proper faith concordant with his experiences, his mind, and his soul. Mine is that there must be a transcendent all-encompassing Divinity (God) existing within and without the universe. I aspire to be part of this Divinity, although an infinitesimally small part. More specifically, I believe the development of my consciousness *augments* His nature. Thus, it is incumbent upon me to develop my *consciousness* in all possible ways and to the maximum extent possible. Unconsciously, I have tried to do this throughout most of my life by act and thought—albeit without awareness of a hidden metaphysical motive.

This is the faith that now sustains me and seems to propel me toward new levels of understanding; even at my advanced age.

April 25 '20 – Teleology

What is the point of aligning one's infinitesimal self with an already perfect Deity? If nothing can be added to him, it is all an exercise in meaninglessness. If there is no final *teleology* in the universe, but only a static perfection, there is no point in exercising one's own mind over the larger cosmic questions. One should confine his concerns to the problems of human—and personal—survival, meaningless though they may be.

But my mind forbids this worldview.

Hindu Vedanta philosophy deals with the problem with the concept of Deity's *lila* (delight, joy). The Infinite 'delights' in experiencing its multitudinous forms, mainly human beings. Teleology is dispensed with. A rank anthropomorphism if I've ever seen one! On the other hand, teleology (purposefulness) is essential in the metaphysical phenomenon called life. Why should it not be part of the condition of Deity?

April 26 '20 – In the Midst of the 'Raging' Pandemic (cont'd)

The annual death rate from all causes in the US is close to 3 million according to the World Almanac. If it were not for these deaths, the country would soon be crushed by the burden of the elderly and infirm. The addition of 50 thousand, 100 thousand, or even much more to this death rate would be minor. In fact, since the great majority of Covid-19 deaths are in the elderly and infirm who may soon die, the increase would be even less. Yet the media and the leaders of the country show no compunction in virtually destroying the financial status and well-being of all the people (but not that of the politicians and health savants) in trying to control the epidemic.

What is the reason for this apparently irrational behavior. In my judgement, it is the worship of raw individual life no matter what its condition, fostered by Judeo-Christian 'ethics', and furthered by the absence of a metaphysical consciousness in the population. What is to be done? I have no idea.

April 27 '20 – Céline's *Voyage au bout de la nuit*

I should have read this book many years ago. I was put off by Céline's reputation as an anti-Semite and pro-Nazi. I have not read his anti-Semitic pamphlets of the 1930s, but if he was anti-Semitic, he was also anti-France, anti-the French, anti-war, contemptuous of African blacks, anti-science, anti-bourgeois life, and any other antis one can think of. Regarding his Nazi connections, while he was friendly with notorious French collaborators, Nazi officialdom did not want much to do with him. They recognized his mentality was quite different from theirs. (It was the same with the Nazi attitude toward Nietzsche.)

Céline's black pessimism is as relevant for consideration today as it was in his time. It is known that *Voyage* served as a model for Henry Miller who raised Céline's crude sexuality into an art form. So what is one to say about his bleak outlook on life? In my view, it is an extreme example of the attitude of an honest no-nonsense thoughtful person without a shred of metaphysical consciousness. Céline is so anxious not to accept prevalent illusions that he refuses to be open to metaphysical intuitions. If all metaphysics is illusory, perhaps he is right about human life on this planet. The issue deserves serious thought.

A principal character in *Voyage* who expresses Céline's ideas pushed to their limit is Léon Robinson. Robinson is not a French name. Had Céline read Robinson Jeffers who expresses similar ideas about human society in his poetry? (Or was Jeffers influenced by Céline?) Their lives coincided throughout two World Wars. One can only speculate.

May 1 '20 – Finale

The thought of Céline occurs to me that everything in time becomes spoiled. It could be the same with the expression of my *Notebook*. So I will end it here.

Notebook 5

Recognize your place; let the living live; and you, gather together your thoughts; leave behind you a legacy of feelings and ideas; you will be most useful so.

Henri-Frédéric Amiel, *Le Journal Intime*

July 16, 2020 – "Live 'til you die"

I take up my notebook again since there are a few more things I have to say. "Live 'til you die" is still my maxim and, for me, writing is living. One truth has forcefully crystallized in my mind. It is that I must not generalize from myself to anyone else. The insights I have obtained for my own life are only applicable to myself. The rest of the world has its own truths, which are not for me to judge. The materialist worldview may be suitable today for everyone else—with only rare exceptions. My writings are not relevant to virtually all of my contemporaries. Valuation of a higher consciousness does not exist for them. My thoughts are not their thoughts.

Therefore, as I have emphasized many times, *I write for myself alone*. If some few individuals should benefit from my writings, I would not be displeased. If not, I am still greatly pleased to have written them.

In spite of primitive medical care, many of the philosophers of classical Greece lived well into their eighties, even nineties. The record of longevity is held by Democritus of Abdera, who is said by Diogenes Laertius to have lived to 109 years of age. Very few died before seventy. (Aristotle who died at 62 is an exception, perhaps because of his tight mental mindset!) Identifying with the antique philosophers makes me feel more 'normal' as I approach 90 years of age. I don't wonder so much why I am living so long.

Melanie and I are considering relocating to Charleston. The independent spirit that has characterized the city in the past—especially during the succession—has always appealed to me. Now, there may be more Yankees than Southerners in the city, but something of the old 'rebellious' spirit might remain. If the move comes to pass, I will find out. Meanwhile, the Charleston 'mystique' still attracts me.

July 19 '20 – US elections – a very personal view
The United States will have an election in four months that will determine its future. On one side is President Trump who would no

doubt like to reign as an emperor but cannot because the organization of the United States government does not give absolute power to the president. On the other is a pack of unscrupulous socialist-minded populists and their media cohorts. They hate Trump and want to bring him down at all costs. They care little about maintaining the unique traditions of America. Their appeal is largely to 'liberal' and cultural dregs of the country. Given a choice between 'Emperor' Trump and rule of the unprincipled populists, I choose the former. At least Trump has the well-being of a freedom-loving nation at heart—even if his personal qualities leave much to be desired.

If Trump loses the election, it will mean the dregs have won. Then poor America; it may go the way of Argentina, Mexico, Greece, Lebanon, Venezuela, and other failing nations.

July 26 '20 – Simba

Our Rhodesian Ridgeback dog Simba died unexpectedly two days ago. He was 12 years old and had been a loyal devoted friend to us for all those years. He was the epitome of a 'good old dog.'

The loss is very painful; a gaping hole has been opened in our lives. I have always thought dogs were the most faithful friends of all— more so than family or human friends. Simba exemplified this thought. Time is said to heal all grief; but meanwhile a pall has settled over our lives.

Aug 2 '20 – *Senancour*

It is four months that I am living in isolation in our eyrie in the high grasslands of far southeastern Arizona. The pandemic seems to be raging on in the world but we have been unaffected. It is lonely at times, but a major benefit for me is I don't have to force myself to relate to visitors with whom I have little in common.

I don't write (other than this notebook) and have returned to reading. Étienne de Senancour (French writer of the early nineteenth century) is my focus at the present time. I feel a strong kinship with him in spite of the distance in time, space, and culture that separates us. He understood the real reason for creative writing is to establish one's own persona. *Obermann* is his most powerful book. When I read this 'novel', I am privileged to gain access to the soul of a highly intelligent, deeply sensitive individual. Senancour was the first modern existential writer. He wrote *Obermann* during the Napoleonic era when the mentality of 'empire' dominated political and cultural life of France—an individual's soul counted for little. Such is the case today in America; except today it is called globalization and multiculturalism. France was the superpower then; now it is America.

My health is becoming precarious—as befits someone who is approaching ninety years of age.

Aug 4 '20 – A Metaphysical Task

I have counted 20 books published by myself in the past 40 years. A few have received some recognition, most have not. These are minor details of little importance to me—what is important is that my metaphysical interior self (my soul) has emerged as a consequence of my writing activity. *Writing has made me what I am today.* It has been the principal mission of my life to which I have devoted these 40 years. No level of 'artificial intelligence' could have accomplished this task because the task was a metaphysical, not a physical one. As far as I can tell, computer scientists today do not take the reality of this distinction seriously. This failure may doom our computer civilization since *Homo sapiens* is at heart a metaphysical creature. If he does not develop his 'spirit', he deteriorates. This is my firm conviction.

Artificial Intelligence represents the ultimate accomplishment of modern technological man—*Homo faber.* However, I believe the final goal of the human condition should be the establishment of a higher consciousness or 'wisdom', thus confirming him as *Homo sapiens.* This was always the view of philosophers throughout the world until the advent of modern technology and its seductive promise of mastery of nature and everything else.

Aug 5 '20 – Archeological Man versus Metaphysical Man – A Mini Essay

Archeological man, according to the archeologists, dates back some millions of years ago. He is taxonomically defined mostly by his physical characteristics like skull size, facial bones, skeletal density, etc., as well as by his 'intelligence.' The taxonomy label given to the latest form of archeological man, *Homo sapiens*, is a misnomer because nothing in the evidence about him indicates prevailing 'sapient' qualities, i.e., wise, sagacious, spiritually insightful, possessing 'wisdom' as the term was understood in antiquity. There is little about his history that suggests wisdom could be possible for more than a very few exceptional individuals. Intelligence is not equivalent to sapience. The label *Homo faber* has been recently thought by certain philosophers to be a more accurate description of the special mental status of this latest form of man. The term means 'tool-making' man,' a capacity that has elevated him far above the lower animals from which he arose, according to evolutionary theory.

For a long time, the acquisition of tools was a slow process but during the relatively recent period of recorded 'civilization' (five to six thousand years), their development has increased exponentially, giving *Homo sapiens* an unparalleled mastery over nature and often over other men. The more sophisticated term 'technology' has replaced the older simpler concept of tool-making, but both expressions apply to essentially the same phenomenon, development of techniques to increase the power of human beings. The most recent 'tool,' 'Artificial Intelligence' (AI), promises to provide push-button control over all aspects of human activity.

Along with man as *Homo faber* and his dominating drives, but slowly and perhaps much later, there appeared a different set of qualities, which might be dubbed 'metaphysical' ones. First and foremost, these include a 'higher consciousness' of oneself and an awareness of a metaphysical dimension of existence. Other descriptive terms are spirituality, depth, and wisdom. These terms are harder to define as befits metaphysical descriptors. The term *'Homo sapiens'* is more appropriately applied to metaphysical man.

Homo sapiens does not replace *Homo faber,* but rather is superimposed upon him. And this erratically, often not at all. There is not a total 'transfiguration' but an 'addition' to the existent human condition. When the process reaches a certain point, the individual can be said to be a 'spiritual' person, i.e., he or she possesses a soul with its transcendental qualities. The insight of the Vedanta sages of ancient India might then come close to applying: "Atman (Soul) equals Brahman (God)." This expression, however, hardly does justice to the original intuitions of the Indian wise men. Metaphysical insights are basically ineffable even though philosophers constantly labor to express them.

One may wonder if there is a 'purpose' to the phenomenon of Man? The Hebrew Bible says Man was created by God in His image to people the Earth, to subdue and rule over all the creatures

317

in it (Gen. 1:26-28). This he has certainly done. Man as *Homo faber* has dominated the entire planet and everything on it to an inordinate extent. But what is the purpose of *Homo sapiens* or metaphysical man? He does not dominate anything, does not preserve human life, does not engage in procreation, does not advance the power of the species. The mandate of Scripture does not seem to apply to him.

I submit that metaphysical man is the 'workplace' of the Ultimate Metaphysical Reality called God in the Judeo-Christian world. An analysis of whether or not such a 'reality' truly exists is beyond the scope of this essay; however, this writer has come to believe a UMR exists everywhere and through the development of a spiritual consciousness in human individuals, it *augments* its own being. More than this cannot be said without drifting into unproductive speculation. If this seems to be a totally improbable, if not blasphemous idea, it is because it runs counter to the prevailing religious view of a God perfect and all-powerful in every way. But a creative God may be in the process of 'creating' Himself, just as the entire universe and everything in it is being 'created.' If this be so, He must need to augment Himself and has created Man for that purpose. One can then modify the Vedantic insight to say "Atman augments Brahman," or, in more familiar terms to western readers, a spiritually developed mind of an individual augments the Divinity. Here is an optimistic belief that enhances the human condition!

Sept 11 '20 – Being Overwhelmed

I feel I am being overwhelmed by the torrents of advertising, information, digitalization, automation, news reports, and more that is constantly bombarding me. Gradually, they are trying to change me into a mere processing machine. What will become of the essential me, my soul? I do not know. Perhaps it is time for me to pass on from this hollow society before the process is too advanced.

Sept 27 '20 – Sri Aurobindo

Having immersed myself in *The Life Divine* by Sri Aurobindo for the past two weeks, I have concluded that he developed his life in a spiritually oriented society totally alien to me. His book interests me but, in last analysis, I cannot believe it is relevant for me. An inscrutable fate has thrown my soul into a completely materialist society and it is within this society that I must play out my life. I have developed myself in it and have come to the tentative belief that this 'terrestrial' development has meaning for the Ultimate Transcendental Reality.

I have grown to maturity in western civilization, not India; this circumstance has permanently marked my soul.

Sept 28 '20 – Barbarization of Society

Finished reading J. Huizinga's *In the Shadow of Tomorrow*. Written in 1936, J.H. describes in great detail the spiritual 'barbarization' of western societies. Today, this process has accelerated exponentially.

Huizinga knew nothing of addiction to television screens, hand-held computers for communicating, digitalization of most human intercourse. The world has gone far down the road that he could only begin to envision.

But of solutions, Huizinga has little to offer other than opining that societies need to be "permeated again with spirit." He briefly mentions Christian faith as an answer but does not pursue this questionable solution. At the end of his book, Huizinga bravely asserts he has faith in youth, an even more dubious solution. One has the feeling the mountain has labored, and come forth with a few mice.

However, the book is of value as a description of the spiritual deterioration of western societies at an earlier stage.

Oct 2 '20 – The Poet Keats

A quote from a letter of John Keats has come to my attention. "This world is the vale of soul-making." A remarkable thought from a doomed individual still in his twenties.

Oct 7 '20 – Presidential Election

In the midst of the American presidential election contest. The American people love a public contest and that is what the media provide them. But in-depth substantive discussions—none. The comment of Heraclitus about the exile of his countryman

Hermodorus says it all for America: "The best man among them is ostracized and driven out of Ephesus."

Oct 24 '20 – Sri Aurobindo

I have come to the opinion that Sri Aurobindo is a titanic figure ('Asura' in Sanskrit) in metaphysical thought. Titanic figures are extremely interesting and have much to offer, but cannot be blindly followed. Much of what SA writes is profound and poetical, yet questionably representative of human reality. He may be regarded as a 'metaphysical fanatic'. Yet I am oddly attracted to his thought, although a final judgment is yet to come. There are similarities between his God-centered philosophy and orthodox Judaism.

Nov 13 '20 – The Metaphysical Universe

Sri Aurobindo—he was an explorer of a vast new metaphysical universe. The question is whether this universe is real or imaginary, in other words, existent outside Aurobindo's mind or not. In any case, one's soul during life should not be the burier of the terrestrial world but rather be its supervisor. The metaphysical universe, whether real or imaginary, seems a poor place compared to the dazzling world external to the self. Exile to a metaphysical universe might be like living on the moon.

Metaphysics ought to be the crown of one's life, not its substitute. SA has as the epigraph of his book, *The Synthesis of Yoga*, "Life is Yoga." After ploughing through the book, although he plays lip service to terrestrial living, I believe he really thinks, "Yoga is life." I cannot adopt his worldview.

Nov 16 '20 – Purpose of Publication

I have published numerous books and pamphlets during the years I have engaged in independent philosophy. None of these are an 'opus magnum' as the term is generally understood; rather they show the progress of my thought during this period. They represent 'me' and are not oriented toward literary markets. Since in America today, the literary industry is exclusively oriented to large public markets (with the exception of some specialist fields), it is not surprising my writings have received no recognition or popularity. This is as it should be; if my work were popular, I would be concerned about its seriousness.

Although I did not have this idea originally, in retrospect it is clear to me that I write in order to develop myself. As I have said somewhere else, "my writings have made me what I am." This is far more important to me than popularity.

Nov 29 '20 (Alamos) – Ennui

'Ennui'—the principal problem of my life at present. De Vigny in his 'Journal' says it is the main problem of human life. At 90 years of age, I may have said everything I am capable of saying. Can anything new emerge from my aged brain? But somewhere I have read that it is a disgrace for the mind to wear out before the body. I ought not to let that happen.

Returning to Alamos is like stepping back in time. There are no new experiences here to stimulate me. I am looking forward to one last chapter of my life.

Whatever happens, I must maintain my individuality and strength of mind to the end.

Nov 30 '20 – Significant Experiences

More and more, I am persuaded of the importance of 'significant' experiences. They may be in the form of reading, travel, relationships, or accomplishments. But they must be significant, enlivening, life changing. A special reading can alter one's mind. Man does not develop his soul in a closet. This principle applies at every age from one year to 100.

"Away with the thirst for books!" Marcus Aurelius wrote in his very personal journal. Reading books can become a vice as is the case with every human activity. Schopenhauer said that reading is thinking with another person's brain. It is useful as a training exercise but carried to excess is counter-productive. Ultimately, one must develop his own 'Weltanschauung' and not depend on that of others.

At 90 years of age, I feel people look upon me as a museum piece and do not take my thoughts seriously. I don't like the feeling but I suppose it's inevitable in America with its youth culture.

Fr. X. says I am too 'sensual' to be intimate with God. What a joke!! But he had the right idea that my mind is clogged up with extraneous stimuli. They come from too much reading.

Dec 1 '20 – *Siddhartha*
I think *Siddhartha* is the greatest of Hesse's novels. It is the most interesting, most profound, most 'apropos' of the human condition—certainly, of my condition. The fundamental issues of life are faced in it. I am rereading it in Spanish since that is the only version I have here in Alamos. But I derive more from it now because I must read it slowly. It is not a work to be scanned like a trashy novel.

Jesus said do not cast your pearls in front of swine because they will trample on them and then turn and rend you (Mt 7:6.). This is a lesson I must learn once and for all (written on the occasion of an offensive note sent to me by a recipient of one of my books).

Dec 8 '20 – Life's Sunset
In the sunset of my life, I must adapt my attitudes accordingly. My physical self is no longer capable of supporting demanding new

experiences. My vision permits reading for only brief time periods. Memory is not what it used to be. My sense of balance is diminished and I must use a cane at night. The course of nature is inexorable; one cannot fight it forever.

Finished reading *Siddhartha*. Although I still think it is Hesse's profoundest book, I am not in accord with his final solution for the principal character—abandonment of his personal ego and losing himself in the consciousness of a universal unity. I was made to be an individual with my own unique personality, consciousness, and thoughts. These I intend to preserve until the end of my days on Earth. I believe this is what Divinity expects of me.

Dec 12 '20

My capacities for engaging in the business of societal living are waning. I need help for many things I used to do effortlessly. I don't think my mind is fading, except for my memory for names, which has always been a problem for me. An acquaintance has said she noticed when elderly people reach 90 years of age. they begin to fail. This seems to be true of me physically. No point complaining about it, but I do wonder how much time is left for me? I don't fear death at all, but I hate to leave Melanie alone. (She may, however, do very well without me.)

Dec 19 '20 – The 'Jew'

I thought I had seen the last of the 'Jew' label long ago, but that seems not to be the case. Someone who I thought was a friend has written a nasty critique of my writings, calling me "a peculiar type of Jewish psychic." Well, as a child I had to contend with being contemptuously called "Jew boy" (and even worse) and now as an old man, the 'Jew' label appears again. Sad, it's like the mark of Cain.

The new moderator of the Nicholas Berdyaev discussion group has taken a lively interest in my writings. It is interesting how little his praise affects me. I am amused, but nothing more. Anyway, I'm sure it is just a flash in the pan and will soon peter out. I don't have any celebrity or academic status to maintain his interest.

I've tried once again to enter into the thought of Aurobindo but cannot sustain the concentration necessary. It seems to me as if he were living in a different world and writing about a different species of human being. There is now virtually no point of contact between him and myself. (Formerly I was able to bridge the gap to some degree.)

In my waning years, I would like to retreat to some semi-isolated place near an ocean. However, I don't think this will be possible.

Dec 20 '20 – Alpha and Omega of Spirituality

"Love the Lord thy God with all thy soul, all thy heart, all thy mind, all thy strength" (Dt. 6:5, Lk. 10:27). This is the be all and end all of spirituality, the alpha and omega of self-development. It is the highest achievement of a metaphysical mind. All the rest is utilitarian activity or mere housekeeping.

It says somewhere in Scripture that the appointed time of one's life is seventy years—eighty if one is exceptionally strong. It says nothing about ninety years. I feel the ability of my decaying body to support life is fast coming to an end. What will become of my soul?—dissipation into the ether or movement into a metaphysical dimension of being? Neither possibility is a terrible outcome although I would prefer the latter. Divinity will take what is important from it for Its own purposes.

Dec 21 '20 – Love of God

Nietzsche wrote that "faith is cowardice"; probably he was referring to Judeo-Christian faith. I say that religious faith is hiding one's soul in a closet, straight-jacketing the mind. It has occurred to me that when one 'loves' God, one really loves the idea or awareness of the existence of God, not God Himself, who is impossible for a human being to know. The Absolute, by definition, is beyond the scope of the human mind. Even if he should 'communicate' with individuals—apparently not uncommon in the Biblical eras—this is not the same as 'knowing.'

The way to manifest one's 'love' of God, in my opinion, is to develop one's own soul, one's spiritual consciousness. How does one develop the soul? Through meaningful experiences—reading, relationships, reflection, experiences of the world. All these acts to enhance one's spiritual consciousness. Powerful events such as combat or imprisonment can be soul-forming. I have discussed soul formation in my books *Souls Exist* and *Toward an Existential Philosophy of the Soul*. Above all, creative self-expression leads to development of one's soul. In these ways, a person can become aware of and learn to 'love' God.

Dec 24 '20 – Xmas eve, Sri Aurobindo

In spite of myself, I keep returning to the thoughts of Sri Aurobindo. He has created a vast mural-like picture of a spiritual landscape. Our terrestrial world is only a small part of the picture. Much study and reflection are required to assimilate his conceptions.

One question keeps preoccupying me; is the portrait of the spiritual landscape he describes based on his own real experiences or is it the product of his fertile imagination?—much like the imaginary visions of Dante or Milton. For me, this question is key. In any case, I certainly have not experienced the ranges of spiritual experience he describes. I have to be satisfied with my intuition that a 'supermind' exists (to use his terminology) and there is a possibility I could be influenced by it.

Dec 28 '20 – Augmenting Divinity

Silence is the great nursery wherein the soul develops. Silence is essential to hear the voice of the God within. The eyes of saints looking upward in medieval portraiture were looking in the wrong direction; the kingdom of heaven is within the self (Lk 17:20). The main objection I have to life in Mexico is the absence of silence. Noise is constant and everywhere as if Mexicans believe noise will protect them from evil spirits. They seem to shrink from silence. It is a great error on their part.

The one important intuition always appearing to me during the silence of a night is that the developed soul *augments* Divinity. This thought makes me feel that my life is worthwhile. Developing the soul means becoming conscious of as much of existence as is possible for a human being. This miniscule bit of consciousness augments God just as a horse or a cow is augmented by a blade of grass. Every *homo sapiens* should do his duty toward God – not by morality, charity, rituals or prayer, but by increasing his own consciousness of existence. A higher consciousness is the key to a spiritual, i.e. Divinity-centered life. Other behaviors have only a secondary value; often no value at all.

Sophocles at ninety years of age is said to have been asked whether he still slept with women. "Thank God I am free from that madness," he is said to have answered. With all due respect to Sophocles, I am afraid I cannot agree with the great Athenian. Sex for me is a necessary 'touch of the earth.' It helps keep me content with earthly existence.

Of course, one must adapt the sex to his physical capacities.

Dec 29 '20 – Yoga

Since it has been clear to me for a long time that my soul is a 'spiritual' entity and exists in a spiritual milieu, it should be possible for my soul to explore this milieu beyond the confines of myself with its restricted personality. I have worked out a simple 'yoga' for this exploration. Here is the description of the conditions:

i. Isolation in a dark room without interruptions. Eye patches can be used.

ii. *Silence* is essential—no external noise. Banish disturbing desires or thoughts.

iii. Assumption of a comfortable position

iv. Waiting a short interval to allow separation from the terrestrial world and the five senses.

Now, if one is spiritually prepared, one may enter into a strange spiritual dimension of being. A whole new world will open up, which can be absorbing, entrancing, enlightening. One may feel the presence of Divinity. Consciousness is freed from its earthly bonds. It may be difficult to leave this new world.

Naturally, if one does not have a spiritual predisposition that is oriented to metaphysical exploration, all this may seem to be mere fantasy. If the 'soul' is thought only to be a mental property of one's brain, then there is no reason to believe in a spiritual dimension of reality beyond the physical world. The experience of spiritual exploration will be of no interest and be felt as absurd.

Dec 31 '20 – *Fusées à la Baudelaire*
Two conditions necessary for spiritual development are leisure and total solitude. Most people do not possess either one.

Spirituality is sometimes defined as the desire to unite oneself with Divinity. However, one ought not merely to unite with Him but to bring something special to Him in the form of one's own unique soul.

One reason (but not the only one) that people have difficulty grasping the reality of Divinity is because spiritual reality is fundamentally *ineffable*. What cannot be felt by the five senses cannot be described with the usual language. (Sri Aurobindo claimed classical Sanskrit is more attuned to spiritual descriptions.)

For the first half of my ninety years of life, I was a most unspiritual person. My emphasis on spirituality in my writings probably reflects my feelings of deficiency in this area. Even beyond unspiritual, I was not a 'nice' person. I tremble to think that a final judgment about me will be based on my entire life. Repentance does not erase the past—no matter what Christianity promises.

January 2, 2021 – Dominance of Terrestrial Existence

I would be content if some infinitesimally tiny bit of my soul would augment Divinity. Sri Aurobindo seems to believe Divinity exists *veiled* in his own soul. His hubris is astounding! I feel there is no escaping the dominance of terrestrial existence while one is alive— i.e. dominated by physical life. Man born of woman cannot escape his fate. After death, the flesh and blood individual who was known as Richard Schain will not exist although his soul may enter a new dimension of existence.

Yet there is obviously something in Aurobindo's visions that powerfully attracts me. He must be the greatest metaphysical mind and most inspirational figure since Jesus of Nazareth! One must admit, however, he is garrulous and subject to too much repetitiveness, both the product of his irrepressible hubris. His concentration to unite with Divinity reminds one of the biblical Jacob wrestling all night with a stranger, who is really God in disguise (Gn 32:26). (The same comparison with Jacob might well apply to myself in these notebooks!)

Jan 4 '21 – Destiny of Humanity

SA thinks the destiny of humanity is to become spiritualized. My observations have led me to an opposite conclusion. I think the human destiny is to become 'materialized'. Science, technology, and the digital revolution are producing human beings that are strictly material. products, controlled by the laws of physical causality. The concept of metaphysical spirituality is becoming foreign to them and regarded as fantasy—which is itself regarded as an emanation of brain electrical activity.

A consequence of this mentality is that the drive of individuals toward spiritual fulfillment finds no support in society. 'Spirituality' is seen as morality, ethics, or commitment to traditional religion with their dogmas, rituals, and icons. At an intellectual level, it is reliance on the dry stick of scholarliness. I find myself totally alone in this milieu. I have constructed a mental fortress to enclose and protect myself. There are negative aspects to this condition, but it is necessary for survival of my soul.

Jan 5 '21 – Integral Yoga

Monastic life has always tempted me. But the need for female association and sexual fulfillment prevented me from embracing it. I do not think this need is mere animality on my part. I need personal *intimacy* with a member of the opposite sex to develop myself. I am a limited personality requiring stimulation and expansion. Living in the restricted bubble of a monastery would in the long run suffocate me.

The solution worked out long ago in Hindu culture is better. There are stages in life: first, student existence with a guru; then, the role of householder with spouse and family; third, a vision quest in the forest; finally, the exclusively 'spiritual' life of a homeless wanderer on the roads of India. This last phase would not be possible outside of India. This concept of stages is superior to entering monastic life without experiencing the totality of terrestrial existence. But for me, none of these solutions would be adequate. As long as I am alive, I need to experience the fulness of life in all its aspects. My personal fortress is psychological, not material.

The concept developed by Sri Aurobindo of 'Integral Yoga' comes closest to being the best. Spirituality must permeate all of one's terrestrial existence, as well as being superimposed upon it. Sadly, however, there is no sign that humanity is undergoing such a development. As a prophet, Aurobindo must be regarded as a failure. The same was true of Jesus. The gift of spirituality does not seem to be associated with the gift of prophecy. One can learn from great metaphysical minds but not worship them as divine beings; worship is reserved for Divinity alone. This is the three-thousand-year-old dogma of Judaism and why Jews reject Christology. The *Sh'ma Yisrael* is the central teaching of Judaism, "Hear O Israel, the Lord is thy God, the Lord is One" (Dt. 6:4). Henry David Thoreau said when you reach the Pearly Gates, don't talk to any of the servants; demand to see the Lord. That is an attitude with which I concur.

Nevertheless, as Schopenhauer said, Christianity is the metaphysics of the masses and I suppose one should accept that. A diluted metaphysics is better than none at all. If one looks at all the Aurobindo centers in the world, seemingly worshipping the great man and at the legends appearing about him, it may be that "Aurobindism" is going the same route as Christianity. There is, however, currently no Emperor Constantine on the horizon who might impose it on the western world.

Jan 10 '21 – Independent Philosophy
Independent philosophy as such does not exist in the United States. Philosophy has been fused with university life and university 'scholarliness' to such a degree that it is no longer recognizable as a source of wisdom or higher consciousness, never mind inspiration. Emerson commented in his nineteenth century journal that "the spirit has left the universities." The few writers outside universities with philosophical inclinations have almost always felt the need to justify themselves by turning their thoughts and erudition into money-making enterprises. Alternatively, they have turned to politics and justified their 'higher consciousness' through political advocacy. Pure philosophy as is the case of the Vedanta thinkers of India—never!

This is not true elsewhere in the western world, especially in France, which has a long tradition of notable independent philosophers. As I have said, this is not the case in America where philosophy in the universities has been extinguished by the critical analytic style of the university intelligentsia and has become a cognitive science. No one is inspired by cognitive science. A person cannot be a critical analyst of thought and a spiritually creative philosopher simultaneously. "One cannot serve both God and Mammon," said Jesus. The Harvard professor William James came closest to reconciling the two paths, although his 'system' of philosophy called 'pragmatism' has been viewed by European philosophers, somewhat contemptuously, as reflective of American utilitarianism and oriented toward material success, not philosophical insight. In James, the critical thinker got the better of the spiritual seeker.

With all this in mind, I have turned to the antique piece of wisdom *amor fati* (love your fate), popularized by Nietzsche for much the same reasons that I have turned to it. My fate is to be a total intellectual isolate in the scholarly philosophical deserts of America. I have tried to *love* this fate.

Jan 12 '21

Having just read Ernest Naville's account of the life of the French *philosophe* Maine de Biran, I am struck by how much Biran's interior development resembles mine. He began with the mentality of a scientist and gradually became an existential philosopher. The reading has provoked some new insights on my part.

Up to now, I have not quite realized that my concept of the 'metaphysical dimension of reality' is none other than God Himself. It is the same as the expressions 'the ultimate metaphysical reality',

336

the 'kingdom of heaven', and the 'kingdom of God'. My yearning to move into a metaphysical dimension or a metaphysical kingdom is only the desire to unite with God expressed obliquely. I wish to unite with Him in order to bring my own metaphysical consciousness into his existence. Otherwise, what need could He have for my infinitesimally tiny speck of material dust blown about on a small planet in the incomprehensible vastness of the universe? None, none at all.

A second insight is that the belief that Jesus can be one's 'savior', a belief that is constantly preached in Christian churches, is really a metaphysically lazy person's way of trying to relate to God. Development of a spiritual consciousness with depth and breadth is a far more meaningful way of moving toward the same end, although it requires much effort. The idea that mere 'faith' in the figure of Jesus Christ and following his dictates is somehow sufficient for one's spiritual development is based, in my opinion, on sheer spiritual *laziness*.

Jan 13 '21

Looking at the lush plant life of my Alamos garden, I feel that a Divinity is the driving force behind the great upright cacti, the giant spreading palm trees, the strikingly beautiful bougainvillea bushes, and many others too numerous to mention. Yet these are only a tiny sample of the plant life spread all over the planet Earth. Divinity must be expressing Itself in all these living things. Then there is the animal kingdom whose representatives manifest major differences in motility, instincts, and independence—unfortunately now being wiped out by mankind's expansion over the Earth's surface. Divinity must also exist in these life forms. Finally, there are we human beings who cannot compare with plant or animal life in terms of beauty, self-sufficiency, or variety. What do we have that is unique? Reason and consciousness are our special features. Reason has given birth to the sciences, which have permitted mankind to dominate or extinguish all other life on the planet. On the other hand, consciousness does not dominate anything but is the real feature of why human beings have been said by Scripture (Gn 1:27) to be formed in the image of G-d. Sadly, the special human ability to develop a higher consciousness is being lost in favor of a dominant scientific mentality. The poet Robinson Jeffers wrote that humanity as a species may be a failed experiment of God. Every individual human being ought to have these thoughts in mind when working out his relationship with his society. Individual humans have their own affair with Divinity that takes precedence over their relationship to society.

Jan 14 '21 – Defeat of Trump

Donald Trump's effort for reelection, as well as his own persona, have been destroyed by the Democratic Party and its influential media allies, both of which are dominated by an obsessive hatred of Trump and unceasing undermining of all his policies. I read somewhere that Trump came to Washington with the intent to drain the swamp; instead, he was drowned in it. The dire consequences of all this will be felt for a long time in the country.

Jan 16 '21 – Shrunken Persona

When I recall memories of my former years and read my writings of those years, I become aware of how much my 'persona' has shrunk. I am truly only a shadow of my former vigorous assertive self. Best to face this reality squarely and not deceive myself. Of course, there are reasons for this unfortunate situation:

1) My age, the obvious reason. At 90 years, I can't expect to be the man I was at 50, 60, even 80. The downward pressure of nature on one's physical powers is unavoidable. I am constantly aware of my body's decline.

2) Alienation from society. I have no meaningful intellectual or social contacts other than with my wife Melanie and, to a lesser degree, with my two sons. At one time, I claimed to be exhilarated living independently in a decaying society, but isolation has had its negative impact on me.

3) Incapacity to function in the digital age. I almost always feel frustrated trying to accomplish something online with my computer or by telephone with automated respondents and have become dependent on my wife for anything other than the simplest tasks. Thoreau's thought (or was it Emerson's?) that America cares only

for means and ignores ends has been confirmed tenfold today. Digitalization deals only with means.

4) Life in Mexico without ability to converse in Spanish. I can read Spanish, but it doesn't help me with conversation in Alamos, Sonora. Again, I rely on my wife who is fluent.

So, what is to be done? Nothing, nothing at all, except to soldier on in a metaphysically deficient society along the path I have chosen, with the hope that one day my soul will be worthy to be absorbed into the Ultimate Metaphysical Reality (aka Divinity)—whom I am sure exists.

Feb 10 '21 – A Discourse on God's Development

"It is needful for the mind to be aware of its connection to the ultimate ground of existence (God). All the rest is gratuitous." I wrote these lines eight years ago after reading Père Gratry's wordy treatise, *Philosophie. De la Connaissance de Dieu.* Now I must add to that statement that I have come to also be aware that God is not perfect and is in the process of development. He requires developed human souls for this process to continue. How I have come to this intuition is a mystery to me, but I feel convinced of its basis in truth. Perhaps all the rest I will write below is gratuitous, yet I feel compelled to enlarge on this intuitive knowledge.

Principally, God must be understood to be a *metaphysical* being, existing in a metaphysical dimension outside of time (i.e., eternity) and requiring metaphysical nourishment for his development. The metaphysical human soul is that nourishment. Consciousness is its most important 'ingredient' although there are others I have previously described elsewhere. Consciousness of what, one may ask? My answer is consciousness of the multidimensional nature of the universe; especially consciousness of an ultimate, albeit imperfect, metaphysical reality, which is its central feature. My mind must be content with these broad generalities; specific details are not possible to ascertain in its terrestrial condition.

The soul develops itself by forming a synthesis of all one's experiences—experiences in the widest sense of the term: reading, reflecting, writing, significant relationships, strivings, etc., etc. A developed soul is conscious of its own reality and its connection to God. The fuller the life of an individual, the more potential exists for forming a soul that will be ultimately absorbed into the Godhead. Does this occur before death or after? Who can know within terrestrial existence; but since God is eternal, either possibility exists.

Spiritually 'great' individuals mainly express and amplify their consciousness through art forms: painting, plastic arts, music, literature, and expressive philosophy. Their souls can contribute to God's development. Societal recognition is irrelevant; many societally-ignored great individuals that may have appeared throughout the ages would be looked upon by God with as much or more favor than the Miltons, Goethes, Rembrandts, or Emersons. Spiritual development is unrelated to societal success and is often seriously adulterated by it.

I am sure Goad does not want servile worshippers; He wants spiritually creative souls who can expand his nature. These have always been rarities in human societies. I personally do not remember encountering any in my 90 years of life and I fear they may be virtually extinct in the present era of scientism.

> *Ich weiss, dass ohne mich Gott nicht ein Nu kann leben*
> *Werd ich zu nicht, er muss von Not den Geist aufgeben.*

> [I know that without me God cannot live for one second
> if I came to naught, he must from need give up his spirit.]

> Angelus Silesius, *The Cherubinic Pilgrim*
> (17th century German mystic and Catholic priest
> earlier converted from Lutheranism)

Angelus wrote and published many such couplets of a similar nature. How he escaped the burning stake is a mystery to me.

Feb 11 '21 – Finding Favor with God

Instead of courting fame, one ought to live so as his or her soul will find favor with 'God'. I try to do so, but it is not easy. Society is immediate and can be very seductive. How to do this ought to be the central problem of every spiritual individual's life and differs for everyone just as everyone's potential for development is different.

He or she cannot rely on traditional directives or Holy Writs. And the plaudits of society are useless for seeking Divinity's approval.

Feb 13 '21 – I AM WHO I AM

If someone were to ask me if I believed in God, my initial reaction would be a dubious "I don't know." I would retreat behind a neutral agnosticism. The term 'God' (Dieu, Dios, Gott) has too many connotations of ignorant faith in foolish religious dogmas for me to profess belief. But if the same person were to ask, do I think there is an 'ultimate ground of all existence' or a 'metaphysical reality underlying everything', I would immediately answer, "Yes, of course, there must be." My instinct would be in the affirmative. An intelligent verbal expression of deity strikes a responsive chord in my soul and I can say, "Yes, I believe!" without violating my treasured intellectual conscience.

The ancient Hebrews had a more respectful way of referring to 'God', stemming from His saying, I AM WHO I AM, in response to Moses asking God for his name (Ex. 3:14). It was the tetragrammaton YHWH that was not to be pronounced (Jehovah was a later addition). Today, however, the term 'God' can without concern be used in the most crass commercial advertising, not to speak of its constant presence in admonitions from religious types. Even Jews have generally given up YHWH and unhesitatingly pronounce the common word 'God'—or its foreign equivalents—in all kinds of mundane situations.

RICHARD SCHAIN

Feb 16 '21 – Experiences Form My Soul

Significant experiences of any type expand me—relational experiences, learning, reading, reflecting, accomplishing, struggling, suffering… They form and reform my soul. Experiences that do not act upon my soul are of no value to me. Writing out and printing my thoughts is the final stage of the experiential process. For me, it is an indispensable stage. It allows me to study and assimilate the products of my own mind. This is how I justify their publication.

March 3 '21 – The Cosmic Workshop

While reading Miguel de Unamuno's *Del Sentimiento Trágico de la Vida* (*Of the Tragic Sense of Life*) for the umpteenth time, I came across a passage that for the first time awakened me to a fresh realization of the destiny of my soul. There is much in Unamuno's fertile Spanish mind that I do not follow, but this passage touched me. I reproduce my English translation below:

> We have to believe in another life, in an eternal life beyond the grave and in an individual and personal life, in a life in which everyone of us is aware of his own consciousness and feels it to be united, *without being confounded* [italics mine], with all other consciousnesses in the Supreme Consciousness, in God; we have to believe in that other life in order to be able to live in this one and endure it and give it meaning and finality. And we perhaps have to believe in that other life in order to deserve it, in order to acquire it or it may be that he neither deserves or acquires it

who does not passionately desire it beyond reason and, if necessary, against reason.

Chap. 10: Religion, Mythology of the Beyond and *Apocatastasis*

What if truly the passionate desire for the soul's survival after death were itself to enable this survival to take place in some mysterious way? Impossible and wishful thinking, a cynic might say, but the cynic might be wrong as cynics so often are. A commentary of Jesus in an inexplicable situation was "What is impossible for man is possible for God" (Lk 18:27). Expressing the same thought in non-biblical terms would be, "What is impossible in the physical dimension of existence is possible in the metaphysical one." The metaphysical insight of visionaries is usually mystical imagination for skeptics. It has always been so.

I coined a metaphor some years ago: "Each human life paints its own unique brushstroke on the pointillist canvas of eternity." Of course, one's soul is not a pigment to be applied to a cloth surface; it is a reasoning, intuitive, emotional, willing, spiritual, *consciousness-laden* existent that may find its place on the eternal 'Canvas', which is Divinity. No metaphor is really suitable to describe this cosmic drama. But an unshakable faith in the soul's immortality may add immeasurably to its metaphysical substance and thereby *enrich* Divinity. The intuition that one's soul enriches Divinity is well worth maintaining as the core of an individual's religious faith.

With this faith, Divinity (God) is necessarily viewed as continuously *self-creating* itself. Human souls are the principal tools of this divine creativity. Men, Women and God are the central features in such a metaphysical workshop. The ancient Ptolemaic cosmology placing the planet Earth at the center of the Universe might well be metaphysically correct.

The implications of such a faith are very great. Those who have it must principally look toward the development of their souls in order to play their role in the Divine Self-Creativity. Morality, accomplishments, erudition, family, professional and national commitments are all basically means to this goal. Every individual must find his or her own special path. Boccaccio's cynical triad of eating, drinking and making 'merry' (sexuality) and the more recent additions of acquisitions, games and travel should also be treated as means to spiritual development – or not as the case may be. In this way, the traditional religious injunction to "have a care for your immortal soul" acquires a new breadth and a new force.

Is all this true? My intuition tells me there is truth to it, if not exactly as I have outlined above. When it comes to spiritual matters, a fog-shrouded intuition is worth a thousand concrete facts. Heraclitus wrote that what happens to the soul after death cannot be known or even imagined. This might have been too pessimistic a thought, although it probably never occurred to him to think that a soul, whose dimensions he said, one could never completely explore, might dissipate into non-existence. But then Heraclitus did not live under the specter of Scientism.

May 2 '21 – Judgment Day

There has always been an inexplicable 'restlessness' afflicting me. It is as though I am always wanting something more in my life. Sometimes, the 'something more' is travel to places having a different culture from mine. Sometimes, it manifests itself in reading as if some special book will provide me with insight into the 'something more' I have been missing. At one time, I felt the fulfillment of erotic union would quell my restlessness, but experience has taught me that this is not the case. I have looked into the main religions of the world, including my ancestral Judaism, but have merely found social intercourse that only accentuates my restlessness. I can't worship religious symbols of human making and God is still a distant entity. The only worship I have found temporarily fulfilling is at the temple of Aphrodite.

The Spanish philosopher Miguel de Unamuno concluded his remarkable book *On the Tragic Sense of Life* with the wish that God deny his readers peace but grant them glory (*gloria*). When I first read this final statement, I was astonished that Unamuno, who had expressed such disdain for contemporary society, should have wished his readers success and fame. Later, however, I realized that *gloria* for Unamuno was a metaphysical glory, an attainment of a special status for a soul after death. Unamuno did not elaborate on how this *gloria* could be attained.

I belong to a generation nurtured on the belief that material 'scientific' progress is the key to a better life. For myself, descendent of four Jewish grandparents come to America from Czarist Russia, this belief was expressed through 'Americanization' at all costs. The religious element of Judaism was abandoned by my parents. Yiddish, the language of my grandparents, my parents' childhood, and my ancestors for countless centuries, was forbidden to be spoken in my presence, lest it interfere with my Americanization. Thus, meaningful linguistic interchange with my grandparents and even my parents was prevented. In due course, I became a physician, a medical scientist, and university full tenured professor, thereby achieving absolute success in American society.

Nevertheless, this surgical separation from the language and values of my ancestry, and success in American life, never fully quenched my restlessness. There was a worm in my heart that never gave me rest. God certainly denied me peace, but whether he has granted me glory is very much an open question. In any case, I abandoned my academic career in mid-stream and gave myself over to the life of an independent philosopher, that is, philosophy outside of the universities. It is my firm conviction that the modern location of philosophy almost exclusively within the confines of academia has led to its extinction as a vital form of human expression.

Most of my philosophical thought and writing has resolved around the concept of the human soul. The reason for this emphasis on spirituality probably has much to do with the spiritual starvation of my own soul during the first half of my life. I believe that, in general, American life with its focus on money and material acquisitions starves the soul. In my case, the starvation was especially severe since I had been cut off from any serious linguistic connection with my ancestry. Language is the vehicle for transmission of spiritual values. My parents had no consciousness of this reality.

My concentration on spiritual matters can be summarized in three propositions:

1. Souls have an existence in reality.
2. Souls survive bodily death.
3. The fate of the soul depends upon its development during life.

Two of my books are dedicated to rationally defending the first two propositions (*Souls Exist,* 2nd ed., 2013; *Toward an Existential Philosophy of the Soul*, 2014). However, I try to remember that metaphysical insight is based on intuitions, not reasons. The intuition I have at this moment that my soul exists in some manner is so strong that no reasons against it can have an effect. In whatever way it arises, it *exists* and that is the principal point.

The intuition that my soul will survive my body is not quite as strong but is still present. I hope and expect it to survive my death. This expectation must have a significance; I do not expect things to happen that are unrealistic. Hoping it will survive and expecting it to survive are very close in meaning; French and Spanish use the same word for both English terms (*espérer, esperar*). Why should I fight this intuition for the sake of a skepticism that has no place in metaphysical matters? I **expect** my soul to survive my bodily death. Unamuno believed that this expectation alone would promote the soul's survival.

The use of metaphor to apprehend metaphysical matters is a dangerous business. Metaphors are based on physical phenomena that are far removed from metaphysical ones. Nevertheless, a metaphor may help the mind to grasp a metaphysical reality that it is unaccustomed to apprehend. I offer this one: An electric heater can be compared to a living body when it is plugged into an electrical current connected by wires (nerves?) to a source of electric energy such as a generator acting as the 'soul' of the heater. Like the body, the heater generates heat, which allows it to be used for various subsidiary functions. But if the plug connecting it to the generator is pulled (death?), all these functions will cease within minutes. It is the same with the connections of the body with the soul. One may imaginatively extend the metaphor to say that the generator derives its energy from a distant source such as fossil fuels. This distant source can be likened to God.

As I have said, metaphors of metaphysical matters are only useful in accustoming one's mind to think freely outside the box of material reality. I make no claim that my metaphor really represents the body – soul – God relationships.

I can find no metaphor to support the third proposition that the fate of the soul depends upon its development during life. Only an intuition tells me that this is how it ought to be, how it must be. The human life span provides the opportunity for a soul to develop itself. John Keats wrote in a letter that this world is the vale of soul-making, a thought with which I fully concur. Just as the body returns to the dust from which it arose, so the soul must return to the Ultimate Metaphysical Reality (God or Divinity) from which it arose. When a developed soul returns to its source, it can augment it in a spiritual manner. The human soul is the spirit of an individual; thus, its development must be spiritual in nature. If someone asks me to define the term 'spiritual', I cannot, I only know it has to do with consciousness of metaphysical reality as evidenced by the unique human desire to 'know', emphasized by Aristotle at the onset of his *Metaphysics*. Beyond this, I cannot go.

A soul that augments Divinity finds the gloria of Unamuno. Whether or not its special individuality is retained is hard to say. But it seems to me that giving up individuality is a small price to pay for attaining the glory of being absorbed into Divinity.

Therefore, I believe the development of a soul involves a purpose toward which the development is aimed. If there is no purpose, then human life is truly "a tale told by an idiot, full of sound and fury, signifying nothing" (Shakespeare's Macbeth). I cannot live with such a worldview. There must be a purpose to my spiritual development. I may not know exactly what this purpose is, but a purpose there must be. I like to think it is augmenting Divinity.

The laborious speculations of Catholic eschatology about hell, purgatory, limbo, heaven, angels, and the like have little merit in my opinion. They have been rightfully discarded by most thoughtful individuals. Dante's *Divine Comedy* may be titillating to read, but has no value for spiritual development. However, the baby ought not to be thrown out with the bath water! There must be consequences for failure to develop one's soul. Perhaps undeveloped souls are discarded in some metaphysical trash heap. But there is no point in pursuing unfruitful speculation. I can only hope (expect) that on what might be labelled 'Judgment Day,' my soul will receive a positive judgment.

A supercilious Spanish critic writing an introduction to *Del Sentimiento Trágico de la Vida* has labelled Unamuno as a 'transcendental narcissist.' I imagine a similar label could be applied to myself, what with all the 'I', 'me', 'my', and other first-person singular pronouns that are prevalent throughout these notebooks. But I would take the label as praise, not denigration. Concern with one's own soul ought to be the overriding element in expression of one's consciousness. The materialist society in which I live is such a trial for one's soul that 'transcendental narcissism' is absolutely necessary to obtain *Gloria*.

I have written what I have felt and what I have thought, no more and no less. It is time for me to put an end to these entries before they deteriorate into garrulousness. Publishing these notebooks fulfills a duty first of all to myself and then to anyone who might discover and be affected by them. Be forever cursed any soulless scholar or litterateur who presumes to put a cold analytic judgment on these notebooks!

FINIS

YESHUA BEN YOSEF

Prophet and Teacher of Israel

The Jewish prophet and teacher Yeshua of Nazareth (anglicized as Jesus) is one of the most remarkable figures in the history of Judaism. He may be looked upon as desiring himself to fulfill the prophecies of Isaiah, in whose writings from centuries earlier he clearly was steeped. But not only in Isaiah, all the Hebrew Scriptures are much in evidence in the preaching of Jesus. His Jewish upbringing and the Jewish scriptural influences upon him are indisputable. Sometimes these connections are unstated, but other times are explicit. A few of the most well-known of his sayings, with their Hebrew Scriptural counterparts, are listed below, but there are many more:

> Man shall not live by bread alone but on every word
> from the mouth of God (Mt. 4:4; Dt. 8:3).

What I want is mercy and not sacrifices, for I am not come to call the righteous, but the sinners to repentance (Mt. 9:13; Ho. 6:6).

A man's enemies will be of his own household (Mt. 10:36; Mi. 7:6).

You must love the Lord thy God with all your heart, with all your soul, with all your mind and all your strength (Lk. 12:30; Dt. 6:4-5).

You must love your neighbor as yourself (Mk. 12:31; Lv. 19:18).

They may see but not perceive, listen but not understand (Lk. 8:10; Is. 6:9).

Why then is there virtually no reference to Jesus as he appears in the Gospels in the Talmudical literature and very little in Jewish religious writings? Jesus of Nazareth is arguably the most important spiritual figure in the history of western civilization, yet he is essentially a "non-person" in Jewish theological, philosophical, and devotional writings. Exceptions are the so-called Jewish 'existential' philosophers: Franz Rosenzweig, Martin Buber, and Abraham Joshua Heschel, especially Buber. Yet even these, while treating him with respect and acknowledging his origins, regard the historical Jesus as exclusive to Christianity. He is gone from the religion of Judaism. He was never in it.

There are reasons for this state of affairs that need to be brought out into full view. Jesus was without "authority," meaning he had no credentials in terms of affiliation with the contemporary Jewish sects. Moreover, he came from Galilee, an area regarded at that time as backward and provincial. "What good can come out of Galilee?" was the prevailing attitude of the Jewish establishment centered in Jerusalem. Furthermore, he bitterly attacked Pharisees, Sadducees, scribes, and lawyers leaving them in no mood to take seriously this intruder from backward Galilee. The age of prophets had apparently ended centuries before and the canon of the prophets was already fixed. A new prophet, especially from Nazareth in Galilee, did not fit into the religious purview of the leaders of official Judaism. They did not notice the profound spiritual depth of Jesus.

Then there was the question of blasphemy. Today, the idea of a close spiritual relationship of human beings with Deity is nothing unusual: Hindu Vedanta philosophy, widespread in the West, proclaims the identity of the soul of man with God. The noted Protestant theologian Paul Tillich has stated, "There is a point of identity between God and man insofar as God comes to self-consciousness in man" (*A History of Christian Thought*). Abraham Heschel, the Jewish philosopher, writing, "to become a thought of God—this is the true career of man" (*Man's Quest for God*) caused no rabbis to rend their clothes. But at that time this type of assertion was blasphemy, deserving of death according to Jewish law. Perhaps if Jesus had not become greatly popular among the Jewish masses, attracting vast followings, a fact that is often forgotten by Jews today, the high priests of Judaism might have ignored him. But since the region was already rife with rebellion against Roman authority, the High Priest Caiaphas feared Jesus' impact on the populace and supposedly said it is better for one man to die than for the whole Jewish nation to be destroyed (Jn. 11:49-51). Jewish leaders were right to be apprehensive, as was proven by the Great Rebellion of A.D. 67-70, resulting in the destruction of the Second Temple and the slaughter of thousands of Jews.

Jesus' first disciples, from humble Jewish origins in Galilee, certainly did not have his intellectual or spiritual capacities. During his lifetime, they kept asking him the meaning of his teachings requiring a more complex consciousness than they possessed. He felt he had to speak in parables in order for his metaphysical insights to be understood. After his crucifixion, he quickly became what can only be regarded by non-Christians as an object of cult worship and many supernatural legends were formed about him. He became the Lord Jesus Christ, God incarnate, instead of Jesus of Nazareth, son of Joseph. This was too much for the leaders of Judaism to accept and his followers were banned from the synagogues, even stoned on occasion. Tragically, the crucifixion of Jesus had been in vain, since after a second revolt against Rome in A.D. 132-135, the Jewish nation was completely destroyed, Jewish Jerusalem razed to the ground, and most Jews were either killed, enslaved, or forced into exile from their homeland. The Biblical lands of Judea, Perea, Samaria, and Galilee became the Roman province of Palestine.

Jesus had been a charismatic and inspirational figure among the Jews and a few Gentiles as well. He had been referred to as Teacher or Rabbi (Mk. 9:5,17). He offered a *metaphysical* teaching to the Jewish people—bringing Judaism to a new level of spiritual thought. Jesus was a great symbolist. His moral teachings are founded on the necessity not to overvalue the material element of life. He had an overpowering *God consciousness*, on the need to value the 'Kingdom of God'—the same that must have existed in Moses, the Psalmists and the Hebrew prophets before him. This consciousness reached its apogee in the unlikely figure of Yeshua ben Yosef, the carpenter's son from Nazareth. But he left no writings for posterity. Unlike Jeremiah, he did not have a dedicated secretary to write down what he said. His first disciples were not literary types and did not feel the need to record his sermons and sayings, especially since according to their Teacher, the end of their world was imminent. It was only several decades after the crucifixion, when it became clear that the End of Days was not going to occur soon, that the feeling must have arisen among certain of them that a written account of Jesus' life and preaching should be available to the followers and potential converts, now beginning to be known as Christians. Meanwhile a great transformation had occurred; Yeshua of Nazareth, the Jewish teacher, prophet and worker of 'miracles,' had become not only the Messiah, but God incarnate and the central figure of a new religion, Christianity.

It is evident that recording the words of Jesus could not have been an easy task. It was more than thirty years after his death that the accounts of his life known as the Gospels were composed. Most of his listeners had died and the memories of survivors could not have been too reliable. It was not a time of historical accuracy, as evidenced by the appearance of the numerous accounts of Jesus' life that barely resembled one another. The emphasis was on supporting burgeoning Christianity rather than on the facts of the life and sayings of Jesus. The four canonical Christian Gospels were chosen three centuries later at Church councils—largely on the recommendations of Athanasius, the orthodox Bishop of Alexandria. The apocryphal Gospel of Thomas presents a picture of Jesus as a more existential-minded religious figure.

It is virtually certain that Jesus spoke and preached in Aramaic solely to Jews, the common vernacular of the interior areas of Galilee, Perea and Judea—the Jewish heartlands in which he had grown to maturity and conducted his religious activities. He had avoided the Hellenized coasts. When a Canaanite woman begged him to cure her daughter, he responded "I am not sent but unto the lost sheep of Israel" (Mt. 15:24). Later he relented, but it is clear from his practices that his initial response reflected his basic attitude. However, the Gospels are in the *koiné* Greek, the lingua franca of the wider Mediterranean world for whose populations the

Gospels were written. Scholars do not believe that any of the real writers of the Gospels ('evangelists') were direct witnesses to Jesus' activities. Somewhere along the line the orally transmitted Aramaic of Jesus was translated by the evangelists or their associates into Greek from the stories given to them. His special style of expression that so captivated listeners probably was unrecoverable. Unless one believes that the hand of God was operative in this process, it is obvious that there is difficulty in accepting as fully reliable the accounts of the legends and prophecies attributed to Jesus. Nevertheless, a debt of gratitude is owed to the authors of the gospels, because without them, Jesus would have become just another semi-mythical founder of a religion without any knowledge about him.

As far as the early Talmudical scholars were concerned, they had little reason to pay attention to him since Jesus of Nazareth was no longer within the domain of Judaism. They must have looked upon him as an idol figure worshipped by apostate Jews who had given him over to the Gentile world. Later, when Christianity became the official religion of the Roman Empire, it would be no longer safe for Jews to concern themselves with Jesus. Intolerant Christianity had enough reasons to persecute Jews. It would have been suicidal for any Jews to publicly try to express opinions about the Lord Jesus Christ. The rest is known to history; Jews up until recent times would not dare to examine critically the status of the Christian Savior.

But today, the western world exists in an era of religious freedom. The amazing success of Christianity in becoming the world's foremost religion is spiritual evidence, if not on a forensic level, that Jesus of Nazareth had something of great significance to communicate, however uncertain may be the transmitted information about him. The Christian Greek Gospels, even through the worshipful lens of the evangelists and their later translation into popular idioms (once resisted by the Catholic Church), do reveal much of the thoughts and personality of the man Jesus and his powerful effect on people's minds. Islamic and Hindu seers and scholars have recognized the importance of his teachings. Spiritually thoughtful Jews ought not to limit their Bible study to the Hebrew scriptures, since the Greek scriptures of the 'New' Testament contain the only available records of the teachings of Jesus. A similar situation exists with the so-called 'apocryphal,' but spiritually profound Wisdom books that were left out of the Hebrew Bible (and Protestant versions that followed the Hebrew canon) because the Palestinian Jewish sages who established the canon tended to ignore writings in Greek. However, if Christianity can expropriate *in toto* the Hebrew Bible for its own religious purposes, Judaism should be entitled to do the same with selected parts of the Christian Gospels.

It should be possible for Judaism to reclaim on its own terms the memory of Yeshua ben Yosef of Nazareth, the inspired Jewish rabbi and spiritual teacher. (The movement entitled 'Messianic

362

Judaism' is essentially a Christian sect, requiring acceptance of the Christian tenets about Jesus Christ, while retaining Jewish customs.) Jesus offered a profound metaphysical and ethically advanced Judaism to the Jewish people—bringing Judaism to a new level of thought. The Christian religion bases its faith in Jesus Christ as God incarnate and divine savior. However, spiritually inclined, thoughtful individuals, especially those of Jewish origin, ought to form their own ideas of the meaning of the remarkable saga and teachings of Jesus of Nazareth. There is now no adequate justification for the Jewish Jesus to be ignored by establishment Judaism, the Jewish people or any spiritually-oriented thinkers.

The Rabbi Yeshua, who taught the following, warrants the attention of all spiritually minded individuals:

For what is a man profited if he shall gain the whole world, and lose his own soul (Mt. 16:26).

The Sabbath was made for man, not man for the Sabbath (Mk. 2:27).

For behold, the kingdom of God is *within* (εντος) you (Lk. 17:21). [not among you or in your midst]

Render therefore unto Caesar the things which be Caesar's and unto God the things which be God's (Lk. 20:25).

Thou shalt love the Lord thy God with all thy heart, and with all thy soul, and with all thy mind. This is the first and greatest commandment. And the second is like unto it. Thou shalt love thy neighbor [not the whole world] as thyself. On these two commandments hang all the law and the prophets (Mt. 22:37-40).

I and the Father, we are one (Jn. 10:30).

In the opinion of this philosopher of Jewish origins, but without religious authority, the charismatic, ground-breaking, remarkably human figure of the Jewish spiritual teacher from Nazareth ought to be reclaimed by Judaism as one of its own. He could be valued as one of the most significant figures in the history of western spiritual thought instead of worshipped as God incarnate. Beyond that, acceptance of Jesus by the Jewish world could do much to mend the split between it and the followers of Christianity, a split that has had such tragic consequences for Jews. Divergences between the two religions could be confined mainly to theologians and no longer be so important for the public at large.

The biblical quotations in this essay are mainly from the King James version. Abbreviations of the biblical books are as follows:

Dt. – Deuteronomy   Lv. – Leviticus

Ho. – Hosea   Mi. – Micah

Is. – Isaiah

Jn. – John

Lk. – Luke

Mk. – Mark

Mt. – Matthew

www.ingramcontent.com/pod-product-compliance
Lightning Source LLC
Chambersburg PA
CBHW060452090426
42735CB00011B/1970

* 9 7 8 0 5 7 8 9 2 9 3 7 8 *